SPONTANEOUSLY
Driven

GINNIE FREDERICK

ISBN 978-1-0980-3449-8 (paperback)
ISBN 978-1-0980-3450-4 (digital)

Christian Faith Publishing, Inc.
832 Park Avenue
Meadville, PA 16335
www.christianfaithpublishing.com

Printed in the United States of America

CONTENTS

CHAPTER 1
I Have an Idea

If my husband, Russ, and I had only known how exciting, fun, and blessed this trip was going to be, we would have at least done part of it a long time ago. We had never laughed so much or used words like *wow, awesome, look at that, beautiful,* and *speechless* over and over before. I always knew our country was beautiful, but God saw fit to show us mountains, rivers, bridges, tunnels, national parks, snow, bears, whales, and so many critters we never dreamed we'd see in the wild. Not to mention the hikes we took, the waterfalls we saw, the heights we climbed (at our age), the beautiful sunsets that surrounded us, the wonderful people we met, and the silly things we did that made us laugh and laugh.

It all started when we decided to take a cruise to Alaska. Many of our friends and family have been there, and they made it sound so very exciting and beautiful. They gave us all kinds of brochures and even a CD on the crystal-blue Alaskan glaciers. I was soon to retire for the second time, so Russ (my husband) started looking into travel to Alaska online. He recorded the different time schedules Princess Cruise line offers, prices, and the length of the tour. Our niece and nephew went on the 13-day plan, which included 6 days on land and 7 days on sea. Our good friends also did the 13-day trip, so we had excellent sources of information. We were also advised to get a cabin with a balcony (I could just imagine sitting out there with a cup of coffee and looking at towering mountains, covered with snow). Since this would probably be our trip of a lifetime, we decided splurging for a balcony was the way to go. Then, Russ got hold of our nephew's friend, who is a travel agent. We discussed what we thought we wanted with him, and he made the reservations. Only for the Alaska part, that is.

We knew we wanted to do the land first, because on the land excursion portion, there is rigid scheduling for luggage pick up each night as you transfer to different locations. It actually does keep you on your toes. Our friends also advised us to be sure to get a cabin (known as a stateroom on board), away from the loud rudder in the back of the ship. Sadly, they had many a restless night, which should have been a relaxing and pleasant experience. We also decided, with the help of the travel agent, to take the first dates available, which were May 13–19 on land and May 20–26 on sea, on the Coral Princess Cruise ship.

At first, we thought we would fly out to Fairbanks, Alaska, do our land and sea cruise, and fly back home. Russ discovered there were many side excursions we could take, especially while on the sea part of the trip. Our friends guided us along with the experiences they had, such as sights they had seen and some they wished they had seen. My friends at work couldn't wait to tell me of their experiences. Its funny, as soon as you mention Alaska, people have all kinds of suggestions, advice and exciting stories to tell. It's wonderful and helpful and interesting, and even people you don't know who are standing by, chime in. For instance, we heard advice, such as be sure to take two suitcases each for the cruise, one for land and one for sea; don't forget winter clothes; don't forget summer clothes; get a good camera; and take lots of pictures. One lady overheard our conversation and remarked that she was from Alaska. She advised me to be sure to take bug spray because the mosquitoes in Alaska were big enough to qualify as the state bird! Another suggestion was to take the train ride to the Yukon. All these ideas were extremely welcome and we loved, loved, loved talking about our trip.

Russ spent a lot of time online. He reserved a helicopter ride to the top of a glacier (that sounded pretty scary to me), but after we discussed it for a while, I thought, why not? After all, I've never been on a helicopter. What am I saying? I really don't like heights at all anymore. When I was a kid, I'd climb the highest tree, but now that I'm older (scratch that word, maybe wiser would be in order), my stomach flip-flops just watching the kids go on those rides at Six Flags. Russ also booked us for a hike in the rain forest and a boat ride to watch the whales. All this talk was so exciting; my head was spinning imagining all these somewhat frightening adventures.

My husband is a great fan of *National Geographic*, the *Discovery*, and *History* channels. I can't even remember any more which one of us brought it up, but the next thing you know, we were talking about the Gateway Arch, Yellowstone National Park, Yosemite, the Sequoias, the Rocky Mountains, Death Valley, and going to visit our son in Colorado. Russ really wanted to see Dodge City (imagine that—I don't think that man has missed one *Gun smoke* episode—and he still watches all the re-runs!) And I wanted to see the Golden Gate Bridge.

All of a sudden, we aren't flying out anymore, we are thinking about renting a car. Maybe even leaving a little earlier than May 17 and visiting a few places before the Alaska trip. So, why not drive across the country from our home in Marietta, Georgia to Seattle, Washington, leave the car in Seattle, and fly on to Fairbanks and then do our Alaska tour? Princess Cruise Line offered a bus back to Seattle, after the cruise, so we could pick up another car. Well, we ran that thought around for a while and it seemed that retirement excitement now became secondary to Alaska and traveling excitement.

Then, I had an idea. I began thinking—that in itself can be very dangerous!—why not just take our own car? It would probably cost a fortune to rent a car and drive across the country. Russ was surprised when I brought it up, mostly because we are the proud owners of a 1998 Ford Windstar minivan. It has its little problems, but it is paid for. We think it is going to die any day now, but we decided if and when it did, we would have to get another car anyway. I presented my case…"We have a pretty good idea what kind of car we will buy next, probably a smaller one with better gas mileage. We can do that anywhere. If she breaks down and dies on the road, we'll get our car wherever we happen to be." So that was it. We decided to "wing it." And that turned out to be the attitude of our whole adventure. Take it day by day—no worries, be happy, and wing it!

7

There was constant chatter between us now consuming our days, and we could feel the excitement grow as time came closer. We were like two little kids going to Disney for the first time.

I finally did retire in December of 2007. After raising 4 children and 2 grandchildren, this would be our first vacation without children in 39 years! We have had wonderful vacations with our children in the past, but now for the next phase in our life, we are going to fly solo! So retirement and Alaska, here we come! I must say though, all the kids couldn't have been happier for us and gave us great encouragement.

CHAPTER 2

Let the Adventure Begin

Finally, the big day for takeoff is here! Originally, we were going to leave on the 26th of April, Saturday, but we still had packing to do, so we waited until Sunday the 27th. My house was clean (love to come home to a clean house), the suitcases were all packed and sitting by the front door, ready to go. The night before, I lay in my bed, excited and full of anticipation for our big adventure into the West. I could hardly stand it and obviously didn't get much sleep, just like a kid on Christmas Eve.

We always say we are going to get up at 4:00 or 5:00 a.m., but we rarely do. We were so tired the night before and we still had a big job ahead of us—loading the car.

I have always kept a *list* that I composed for vacations in the past of what to pack. Of course, this depends on how long you will be gone and what time of the year you are going. Now, I admit, the *list* is long, so I have placed it in the back of the book, but how can you go on a road trip without one! Of course, you won't need everything on this list. Just take from it what you need, but do look at it so you don't forget anything. You might even get a chuckle or two. It really was fun to sit down and think of all the things that weren't on my original list because as soon as I thought I had it completed, I'd think of something else. Hopefully there is something in there you didn't think of too!

We tried to pack the car in an orderly and convenient fashion. We had two suitcases for each of us for the Alaska trip, two suitcases for our everyday traveling (with our daily change of clothes, plus our overnight cases; mine with makeup, jewelry, lotions, hairspray, etc.); Russ's with the camera batteries, razor, medications, etc. Just imagine, on the way back we had all that plus souvenirs and gifts we bought!

With the backseat folded down, we were able to put all the suitcases on top of the seat and floor. We had blankets, pillows, jackets, and sweaters in the middle seats; the maps in a separate bag on the floor in the middle behind us; the cooler behind my seat; the first aid kit under my seat, boots behind Russ's seat, and cameras and snacks in the middle on the floor where we could easily access them. I kept the current map and atlas with me by my feet and the movie camera close at all times. Each morning, before takeoff, I'd make sure I had the next map we would need ready to grab. I love keeping up with the cities, routes, lakes, bridges, and mountains as we go. We always said our morning travel prayer (as we like to call it) as soon as we got in the car. As we progressed on our way, it became a perfected routine the way we carried things in and out. We rarely made reservations, so if Russ was in the motel long enough, I knew he was signing us in. So I'd get all the maps and my books and cameras ready to take in and he'd come out with the luggage carrier and start putting the suitcases on it. Actually, now that I think back on it we were quite organized. It's probably not a good idea to go without making reservations, we only had a problem one time, but don't forget we were at the very beginning of the vacation season (or "off season," you might say).

At this point, I probably should say, I know there are a lot of people out there who own campers and that is a wonderful thing if you travel a good bit. But we figured the cost of a camper versus a paid off minivan; making reservations at the campsites (especially since we didn't always know where we were going to be next); versus dropping into a motel; and filling a 150-gallon tank versus a 20-gallon tank, well, we'd opt for the minivan. We did see a lot of "full" signs in front of campsites (especially in the national parks) and there were many huge mountains we traveled up, a big camper couldn't do. Now there is something to be said regarding *space* because in a minivan, taking a trip like ours, there is not room for a family. But it was perfect for the two of us.

Now, having said that, let's get back to take off. This may seem unimportant to some, but Russ and I are "hooked" on certain TV shows. We absolutely had to set up and record them before we could leave. Me, I love all those reality shows and I had to see the end of *Dancing with the Stars*, *The Bachelor*, and *American Idol*, and Russ had to tape his *Gunsmoke*, and art shows (Jerry Arnell) on the TV in his office. I certainly wasn't planning to watch TV while we were gone, and I had to know who the winners were after watching them half way through already! Anyway, it took me over a half an hour to set those shows up because I had to figure out how I could get the most important parts of the shows all on two 6-hour VHS tapes. I was recording on the upstairs and downstairs TVs. I managed to tape the last half hour of some of the shows, in order to see all the finales. I couldn't even fit *Oprah* in, but luckily she was having repeats on at that time. I always record everything anyway, because I hate commercials, this way I can fast-forward and never watch one. That works for me! I know—we're weird. *NOT!*

As we are carrying the last thing to the car, just before we close the door, the lights in the house flicker off and on. *Do you know what that means?* That means our TVs just lost all the shows we just set up! And now we have to go back in and do it all over again! And that's the real reason we didn't leave until 10:30 a.m! Nothing like starting our vacation with a little humor—Thank you God! At least it happened before we left; what if we had already locked the door? Such a catastrophe, right? We would have been so disappointed, if after all that setting up, they were blank when we got home.

Our plan now and first destination was to head up to St. Louis, Missouri, to see the Gateway Arch. We stopped to have breakfast and now we are already testing my sick sense of humor. I say we have a sick sense of humor because having been a nurse and a unit secretary (well, anyone who works in the medical field usually does have a sick sense of humor) and Russ…he just does, so we really found unusual things funny. Here is what happened: I had all my medicines in one of those huge day-of-the-week pill boxes. You know, the kind with the days of the week abbreviated on the lids. That's intimidating in itself. I always look around to see if anyone is watching. I don't know why that bothers me; I guess I can't help wondering if people think I am a druggie, or maybe even old or something. So I laid the pills on the placemat while waiting for our food. Russ and I were totally engrossed in our conversation about the route we were taking, how long we thought it would take, etc. The waitress came along and served us our breakfast. Halfway through our meal, it dawns on me I hadn't taken my pills yet. I went to grab them and they were gone. Oh, *nooo!* So I proceeded to look all over, even on the floor, and couldn't find them. I lift my plate and Russ says, "There they are, stuck to the bottom of your plate"! So here I am holding my plate up in the air trying to see them and get them loose. I got them all, but couldn't find that horse pill (fish oil capsule). How can you lose a huge gelatin capsule like that? I picked up my plate again and held it up high to look under it. Sure enough, the capsule falls and starts rolling off the table, like a meatball, but our quick-draw-McGraw waitress is coming to the table and she catches it! Right in mid-air too! I began to laugh almost uncontrollably. For someone not wanting to be noticed, I was doing a fine job.

At 11:30 a.m., we left the restaurant and drove up Route 75. By 12:30 p.m., we had already seen three accidents, sad to say, two of them involving cars towing trailers. We prayed for those people, praying that there were no injuries.

Mona (that is our cars' name) needed gas, so we made our usual pit stop. Now don't make fun, I know you big truck owners name your trucks. When I came out of the station, there was a real live cowboy, with chaps, boots, hat and all, walking toward me. *Wow!* I thought I was in the west already and I know I stared at him like I was some kind of Yokel! I wish I had grabbed my camera and asked him if I could take his picture, or at least spoke to him. I bet he would have tipped his hat at me and said "Howdy, Ma'am!" I really must get more assertive, I mean, the guy was only trying to get gas. Russ just gave me one of those strange looks, like, oh, brother!

We managed to get through Georgia, Tennessee (where we entered central time, so we gained an hour), back through Georgia and into Tennessee again (where it does a little loop). We didn't stop in Chattanooga because we already did the Chattanooga Choo Choo. My sister, nieces, and nephews live in Nashville, who I see often, so we have been there several times. I would like to have stopped in Memphis to see Graceland—maybe next time. Then we went through a little corner of Kentucky and landed in St. Louis, Illinois. I am learning geography here, which was never my strong suit, because I didn't realize St. Louis sat between Illinois and Missouri. We decided to stay on the Illinois side and drive into Missouri in the morning.

We were a little leery of where we would stay that first night, being in such a large and unfamiliar city like East St. Louis. But once we chose a motel, the man at the desk said not to worry, all the police parked their cars there because we are right next to a police academy. So we parked Mona right next to a police car. It was as though God said, "Remember, no worries, enjoy and let Me take care of things!"

By now it was 8:00 p.m., and we stopped at a fast-food place to eat. We started talking to the nicest couple from Lancaster, Pennsylvania. We mentioned that after seeing the Arch in St. Louis, we planned to go down to Branson, Missouri, and they suggested we go to see a place called Sight and Sound where they have different Christian shows. They said they thought Noah was playing and it was a huge 40 foot stage where actors performed live and it seemed like you were actually there. I really wanted to see that. Come to find out the couple was attending a seminar and he was a Baptist minister. As we were leaving, Rod (the minister) gave us a pamphlet about his church and a business card. It just warms our heart to meet such friendly people. By the way, Sight and Sound was not open when we got down to Branson, I think we were about two days early, or something like that.

The next morning, we woke to a drizzly, cold and windy day. St. Louis sure didn't need more rain because this was at the time when the Mighty Mississippi was swelling passed her capacity. We crossed over the bridge and the muddy river looked like she was bulging. The arch is right next to the Mississippi River. As soon as I spotted the arch, which is also known as Gateway Arch, I pulled out my nifty little disposable camera and started taking pictures until it grew in my lens to the 630-foot arch it is! Amazing! All that stainless steel was quite a sight to see. Little did we know this would be our first national park.

Gateway Arch

It was about 40 degrees and we were glad we had our heavy coats with us. As we approached the arch, you could see beautiful trees with red buds in bloom, benches and a park-type area with a small lake. It looked as though an "exterior" decorator had arranged it all perfectly. Once we got close to the arch, we could realize the immense size of it. We then went through a little security area and entered a huge lobby with benches all around, a giant screen movie theater, a museum, a gift shop (of course), and a big area where you could purchase tickets. From the size of it all, I figured they must have huge crowds in the summer months.

While I was browsing in the gift shop, Russ was chatting with a security guard. He told the guard about all the different places we were considering visiting and the guard said, "You need to get what is called a senior pass for national parks in our gift shop." It only cost $13 and we saved a bundle because we found out each park charges $20 to $25 per car entrance fee.

It was time to take a ride up to the top of the arch, so we followed the little crowd through the corridor until we came to some stairs. We were standing in twos and threes on the stairs in a line.

I'm assuming we will catch an elevator to the top. To the left of us were interesting pictures I was engrossed in, when all of a sudden the picture itself opened like a sliding door, and people started pouring out of that little hole (where the picture was)! What they exited was a small round "bucket" with five little seats in it. We were to climb in and be seated. That's fine, except I found myself scrunched in with three husky men (hmmm, maybe not so bad!) and one other woman and we were very up close and personal. None of the men could sit up straight and it was as though we were in a huddle. If anyone has claustrophobia, this ride is not for you! Me, I just have a fear of heights! Of course being the smart aleck I am, I had to say, "I wonder how much weight this little bucket holds?" Well, that broke the ice anyway. The door closed and it took maybe four or five minutes to reach the top. The ride really wasn't half bad either. We stood inside the very top of the arch, peering out small rectangular windows to look out over the beautiful city of St. Louis. This really was a pleasant surprise because we had no idea about the ride up. From the little windows we could view the stadium where the St. Louis Rams play, the capitol building straight out one side and on the other side we could see the Mississippi River. We enjoyed that for about ten minutes and then rode "the train"; (as they call it) back down, which only took about 2½ minutes. I have to admit, I was a little tense when we started up, but I did amazingly well.

After we returned to the lobby, they were showing a movie in their giant movie theater about Lewis and Clark, the great explorers. It was called "The Great American West." Russ wanted to see that and I thought, "Oh boy, this is going to be so boring," but that movie got my attention right off. It was very interesting and full of adventure and excitement. I wish I had bought it. After the movie, we steered over to the museum. It was enormous and also quite interesting. It had the history of the Native Americans, how they lived and what they hunted, a list of people who created the West, buffaloes, horses, teepees, bears, and much more. After we covered everything there was to see, and took some fun pictures inside the arch, we went back out and walked around the grounds. It was still very cold but the wind and rain had stopped. The trees were blooming and the red bud trees had flowers growing all over them, even on the trunk and branches, a stunning magenta color! When we left home spring had ended, and now spring is following us again.

There are several unusual facts few people are aware of about the arch. One being the people of St. Louis opposed the building of the arch in the first place. And another, that I thought was interesting, is the fact that 9 airplanes have flown under the arch and one helicopter over the years. Illegally, of course! And for some strange reason only the chopper pilot was apprehended.

We walked up to the Mississippi River and could see it swelling and overflowing onto the main street and into the little shops on the first street. We would like to have taken a river boat ride, but the water was so high the boats couldn't fit under the bridge. We settled for pictures of the boats and the Mighty Mississippi and stood in its water where it was spilling over, just so we could say we did. Traffic had to be detoured on that corner and people were taking pictures. What a sight to behold. We went to the top of the parking deck and took a few more pictures and just stood there a while to admire the mighty river a little while longer. I couldn't help think of the people who are unemployed or who have incurred damages from the flooding.

Mississippi River flooding steps

A long time ago, Russ had seen some commercials on TV about Branson, Missouri. He heard it was a community within itself, where stars of "our era," like Andy Williams, Debbie Reynolds, etc., performed. Supposedly, like a mini Las Vegas with shows and dinner clubs. We decided that would be our next stop. We gassed up again at a rest stop and took a little walk. Of all places, the restroom in this rest area was the most interesting! The sink had a place to wash your hands that really caught my attention. See...I am very easily entertained! This little soap dispenser spit out soap in your hand, then water came out and then a dryer dried your hands—all from the same spigot. How about that.

Continuing on, we went through Springfield, Missouri, and caught Route 44 into Branson, which is way down south, close to Arkansas. It was already 7:45 p.m., so we got a motel and started looking for a place to eat. We found a Golden Corral, the sign outside boasting it was the largest Golden Corral in the World. But you can't prove it by us because they were closing and we couldn't eat there, so all I could do was take a picture of it. I never heard of a restaurant closing that early, but then, we are from a good-sized town. We drove around a long time and couldn't find a restaurant open anywhere. Finally, we found a Denny's restaurant that was open 24 hours and our waitress told us there are only 2 restaurants in town open passed 8:00 p.m. Everything else was closed up tighter than a drum. I guess because we were "off-season." It really looked like an exciting town according to the brochures. Yakov was playing, but no late shows; there were showboats, the Branson Belle Showboat, but too late. There were world class performances, museums (the titanic), there were tributes to Elvis, Roy Rogers and Dale Evans, Red Skelton, and literally hundreds of appealing shows, and it looked like it would be a fun-packed place for kids, too. They had animal shows, magic shows, a toy museum, Roaring Falls (rides, water rides, go-karts, and live shows), white water, haunted adventures and many, many more. But not on our clock! We missed it all. We could have stayed another day to see the shows we were interested in, but we would have had to stick around the whole next day until showtime at 8:00 p.m. So we decided we'd move on in the morning instead.

Since we were right on the border of Arkansas, I convinced Russ to do a little loop down Route 65 into Arkansas and around into Oklahoma, then back up Route 69 (which went all the way up the border of Kansas and Missouri), into Kansas City. I wanted to be able to say I was in Arkansas and in Oklahoma. To me, if you are in a state and get out of the car and set your feet on the ground for any reason, even if it's to buy a postcard and a magnet or go potty, you can say you've been there! We drove through Berryville, Arkansas which claims to be The Home of Kentucky Fried Chicken? Go figure! We are in Arkansas, not Kentucky—*duh!* Then we went through Bentonville, which claimed they are The Home of Wal-Mart. Next we went through Miami, Oklahoma (Oklahoma is home of the Native American—Oklahoma, meaning man and *humma* meaning red). Of course, I had to call and tell Russ's sister, Ruth, who lives in Miami, Florida, that we were in Miami. Well, she didn't fall for it. But then, I had to call his other sister, Nancy and my friend Sandi and tell them we were in Miami, too. Well, Nancy didn't fall for it either, but Sandi did—ha ha!

We managed to make it to Kansas City where it was an absolute necessity for Russ to stop at Cabela's. If you are a sportsman, or even the wife of one, you know what I mean. My husband and sons are great sportsmen, so stopping there was a must. That "little loop" between Arkansas and Oklahoma cost us quite a few hours, and it was getting late, so we stopped in Kansas City and spent the night at a fairly new motel right next to the Kansas City International Raceway, which was okay since it wasn't open this time of the year. In fact, we were only two of eight people in the whole motel (which was not only brand spankin' new, but beautiful), where the rooms were $200.00 a night when the raceway was open. But since the raceway was closed we only had to pay $69.00! What a bargain! And to top off our day—God blessed us with a most stunning sunset!

After breakfast, we found the most interesting shopping center across the street that was worth driving to and checking it out. It was a very original center, named The Legends. It wasn't just a huge shopping center, and not only for shopping, but it celebrated the legendary Kansans born there, like Amelia Earhart, Wyatt Earp, and Dwight D. Eisenhower. And of course, fountains scattered throughout in order to live up to the name The City of Fountains. It had many unique shops and restaurants, and I especially liked the one with gigantic dinosaurs on the outside and in and a place for kids to hunt for dinosaur bones.

Cabela's was in the same area as The Legends, right around the corner actually. Cabela's is a 190,000-square-foot retail showroom that accommodates hunters, fishermen, and campers, and sells any related outdoor gear you can possibly imagine. They say they are the largest tourist draw in the state. Humongous animal displays are scattered throughout the store, the main one being a large mule deer exhibit which probably occupies ¼ of the store, also, an aquarium with several species of fish in the middle of the store. Even I had a great time exploring and looking at all the awesome displays. What a fascinating store, you could browse for hours, and we did just that, buying hats and shirts for the boys. All three of our sons have a great respect and passion for God's great outdoors.

Now we will get back on I-70 and pass through cities that you hear spoken of in Westerns all the time, like Junction City, Abilene, and Salina. They reminded me of Matt Dillon telling Chester, "I gotta mosey on down to Abilene and see if I can't find those varmints!" Once we got to Wakeeney, we took a detour down to Route 283 to—ta-dah!—Dodge City and Boot Hill! That's where Russ has wanted to go for a long time.

The road is ours—absolutely no one else in sight. Russ has been teasing me all along saying, "This is 'our' movie and no one else can be in it right now." We've seen several ring-necked pheasants (roosters) along the road and Russ is thrilled. What a sight, they are really beautiful and colorful birds with a white ring around their neck like a collar, a black throat (which Russ says is a fluorescent royal blue when it is in the sun) and a white head and a red face. Their chests are a bronze color, speckled with black dots, their backs and wings are white with dots and they have a beautiful grayish-white long tail made up of several feathers with horizontal black stripes. Unfortunately, they are hunted not only for the meat but also for those beautiful feathers to decorate hats. We also saw a wild turkey. I'm glad Russ knew what we were looking at because if it was just me I'd probably say, "Oh, look at the pretty birdie." No, I would have known what the turkey was. But they were the only other living thing in "our movie." It was a gorgeous day and we were traveling through it alone except for God sitting on the console between us, of course!

Dodge City wasn't a very big town, but the motels were crowded because news people and government people had come to re-dedicate the town of Greensburg, that was rebuilt after a tornado strike. But we did find a motel on Wyatt Earp Boulevard and spent the night there.

As we ate our breakfast, we met some more very nice people and we talked as we ate. They were from Washington, and after we told them we were going to Seattle, they said, "Oh, it rains there all the time, maybe three days out of the year it's clear." They were going to Florida and it was like we were going to opposite ends of the world, but they were full of information about Seattle and the mountains in Washington.

Now back to our movie. First we went to Boot Hill Museum, so we could "relive the legend" and visit Dodge City as it was. We entered the Boot Hill Museum, which starts off with a huge gift shop, (of course). We bumped into our friends from Washington and gave them a high wave and entered into Miss Kitty's Saloon. We are alone again. It's only "our movie," except for a nice young man in the saloon who took our picture in front of the bar. We are "off season" again. He said in the summer they have gunfights, can-can girls and a fun show put on by the college kids who do this for their summer job. They also have stage coach rides and chuck wagon feasts, with folks in period costumes. The museum was great fun, especially since we were alone and could do and say stupid things and get the usual silly pictures, like Russ behind the bars in the jail and sitting Indian-style in front of the teepee with the other Indians. The museum was set up with gunfighter scenes, history of Indians with clothes and jewelry they made, teepees, clothes people wore in those days, buffalo, campfires, and guns, and it was all quite informative. It had a sort of "hall of fame," with history of such colorful characters as Wild Bill Hickok, Wyatt Earp, Buffalo Bill, Bat Masterson, and even a female gunslinger whose name escapes me. As one of the pamphlets described Dodge, "Dodge City thrived in 1872–1874 with buffalo hunters, railroad workers, soldiers, and drifters who 'settled their differences' in shoot-outs, creating the need for a burial place—Boot Hill Cemetery. Some of the stones over the graves read like this: Alice Chambers (only woman buried in Boot Hill) hers was the last burial here; someone killed in a shooting spree; a buffalo hunter named McGil, shot March 1873; five buffalo hunters, bodies found frozen in a blizzard; Unknown, found hanging from a tree West of Dodge City. Then we visited Front Street, which is a row of stores; most were very old and some were refurbished. There was the Long

21

Branch Saloon, a clothing store and city drug store to name only a few. There was also a little school house with old desks and maps and an old home that was unsafe to go up the stairs, but the downstairs was decorated with those old lace curtains and pretty lamps and an old stove. They even had Marshall Dillon's sheriff's office. Across from all that sat an old train named the Cyrus Holliday locomotive #1.

As we returned to the car, I was looking at the atlas to see which route to take next. In this Atlas, at the top of the page of every state, there is always a beautiful and enticing photograph. On top of the Kansas page was a picture of Monument Rocks, but it never says the location of the photo. This urge came over me and I just had to see them. We had no idea where to find them, so we called our friend Jim, who loves the computer, and he looked them up for us. We were so excited (well, anyway, I was) when I found out they weren't very far from us at all. Jim gave us precise directions from Dodge, so we turned west again and that became the next step of our journey. What fun driving so spontaneously! We drove through Cimarron (wasn't that the name of a western TV show?) and drove to Garden City, had lunch and proceeded north toward Monument Rocks. I couldn't wait, I don't know if it was because of the excitement of another spur-of-the-moment adventure or because it was my idea and the plan was all coming together so smoothly.

At 5:30 p.m., we came to the turn which would take us to Monument Rocks, it was hard to find. It was a dirt road just like Jim said it was and it wasn't marked very well. There were no human beings in sight, and the road was very long. At last I could see some rocks in sight far away. We wondered if that could be them or did we take a wrong turn. The weather was turning very windy and cold and it looked like it might rain. There was still no one around and we were out in the middle of nowhere—but kept going, determined to find Monument Rocks. A car came toward us, *people!* And then passed us. As we came closer to the rocks, they grew larger and we pulled up to find the most uniquely shaped rocks, right here where you wouldn't expect to see anything so awesome in the middle of a huge space! Once again we were alone, and I rushed from one rock to the other as Russ snapped photos. These rocks are sedimentary deposits from an ancient inland sea, now exposed for our wonder.

The sky is gray and it's beginning to sprinkle, mixed with ice, but we continued to take pictures until we were satisfied we had enough. I stood by the rock that has a large window in the middle (known as Eye of the Needle) and I felt like the wind would suck me right through it. These tall rocks were truly something to behold, and we were so glad to have been given the opportunity to see them. It was very cold and it was kind of eerie being out there so far away in a desolated open area. I left feeling very small, like a tiny grain of sand in God's wondrous and endless creation.

The next day, we continued north to Colby, Kansas, which really is not too far from the Colorado state line. Here I will have some lab work done. We had to do this the whole trip since I am on blood thinners, but the doctors and labs were great. I met some of the neatest people and each lab was an experience in itself. We knew I would have to do this before we left and in my mind it was a small price to pay to be able to experience a once-in-a-lifetime trip such as this. So please don't let medical issues hold you back from a life-time dream. Go and do it. This is the only reason I mention the medical issues in this story. To encourage people to live your life and don't let the small stuff hold you back.

In Colby, the winds were between 40 and 50 mph. The shrubs and trees were being torn in every direction and the flag across the grounds sounded like it was going to tear to shreds. The wind was howling in the camcorder and now that I look back, it seems strange, being in Kansas, that we never considered we would be hit with a tornado. But the thought never occurred to us and we went on our merry little way. Ignorance is bliss they say. Hmmm.

Now it is beginning to snow. How exciting! We don't get to experience snow in Marietta, Georgia, except maybe once a year. Then people rush to grocery stores, get lots of water and groceries, and the whole town closes down. Not only do we have little snow equipment to care for the streets, but people don't know how to drive in it anyway. Nothing was sticking to the streets, but we decided we better get gas, more as a precaution than anything because we had half a tank. You never know what will happen in that kind of weather, it's best to be prepared. Russ went inside the station, I stayed with Mona. Russ had backed in to our parking spot so I was facing the gas pumps. I noticed a short, small framed man trying to pump gas. He literally could not let go of his car, the wind was blowing with such force. I just know he is about to be blown away. He is holding one hand on the car handle and then spreads the other arm out to reach the gas pump, then clinging to the pump takes the other hand and brings the hose to the tank; never letting go of one or the other. His pants are flapping on his legs and his hat on his jacket was everywhere but on his head. When he finished pumping and returning the hose, he was moving hand over hand on the side of his car, in order to return to the safety within it. It was quite a struggle for him. I know he feared for his life! As I said before, I have a really sick sense of humor, but I couldn't help laughing at the poor little fellow and I just roared! And I got every bit on the camcorder!

We drove on and it began to snow again, the wind blowing the snow horizontally. Ice was collecting on the windshield wipers, and the wipers would get stuck to the windshield. We had to stop and pry them loose in order to continue on. On occasion, the windshield wipers couldn't even stay on the windows from the blasts of wind. We could feel the car tremble from the force of the wind.

Through all this, I could see tumbleweeds along the fences and skipping across the road. Remember that song "Tumbling Tumble Weed?" I had to have a picture of one flying in front of the car. I didn't think I got it on camera because they were flying past so fast and I kept snapping and snapping trying to catch one on camera. Once I had a chance to look at the developed film, I had!

We are in Mountain Time now, so we gained another hour. Finally—Hello, Colorado. You could tell we were in Denver (also known as The Mile High City) as the Rockies began to surround us. The first site that catches our attention in Denver is this huge football stadium. It is called the Sports Authority Field at Mile High. Originally, it was called "Mile High Stadium." Usually football stadiums don't interest me, but when I started looking into information about this stadium, I found it fascinating. I'd like to share a little of that information with you. First, it was the home to the Denver Broncos, of course. The seating capacity was more than 80,000, but get this: it featured ingenious 9 million pound east stands that could be moved back and forth on a track of water, retracted in for football and retracted back for baseball. Three tiers of stand in a horseshoe shape, equal Mile High Stadium. It was one of the loudest stadiums because of its steel grandstands. Can you even imagine that!

There is a statue erected here of Roy Rogers' horse Trigger, which is 24 feet and 1,300 pounds. It is a fiberglass replica but Roy Rogers didn't want them to use the name Trigger, so they call it Bucky. When Mile High Stadium was knocked down, Bucky went with the Sports Authority Field and is now mounted; it measures 27 feet and weighs 1,600 pounds.

We were looking for a restroom when we came upon a welcome center, boy, I was so glad we did. This is where we found the Red Rocks of Colorado. What a surprise to find a natural marvel at the foothills of the Rockies. We had no idea these brilliantly colored rocks were here. The colors were outstanding, but of course, Russ is more concerned with the mule deer tracks in the mud. The snow suddenly stopped and the sun was trying to sneak out, like a gift all wrapped up, just for us. Thanks again, God!

The Johnson tunnel is only a few minutes up the road. The trucks in this part of the country carrying hazardous materials are supposed to drive around the tunnel via Loveland Pass. But because of the snow, the Pass is closed down leaving the tunnel the only way through for them. And the law there says when a truck carrying hazardous materials drives through the tunnel; they have to go through alone. No other traffic is allowed to be in the tunnel at the same time in case of a spill. So that means traffic is backed up for miles, but, fortunately for us, only on the east entrance for now.

The Johnson Tunnel is west-bound and the Eisenhower Tunnel on the other side is the east-bound. The Johnson Tunnel was the second of the two to be built. Construction began on it in 1975 and was not completed until 1979. I'm sure Colorado weather had a lot to do with it taking so long. Both of them are two lanes and they are amazing. The Johnson Tunnel cost $145 million dollars and required more than 800 workers. Just under 500 of those workers were employed in actual drilling operations. It was named for the Colorado legislator Edwin C. Johnson. The Eisenhower Tunnel was started in1968 and completed in 1973. It was planned to take only 3 years to complete it, but wound up taking 5 years due to unanticipated hazards and the harsh climate. It cost $117 million and at the height of construction, more than 1,140 persons were employed in three shifts, 24 hours a day six days a week. You can only imagine the obstacles they had to consider. Just a couple of examples, they had to channel a stream, the location, the wild life, possibly doing a bridge instead, making rock cuts, etc. All so very interesting.

We moved right along and the scenery: pure "eye candy," as Russ likes to say, with the white of the snow contrasted by the evergreens. It looked how I imagine Christmas. How pretty!

This is where I learn about tree lines. I noticed when I look up at those awesome mountains; the trees just seem to stop growing. Russ said, "It looks like they just stop from far away, but if you were standing among them, you could see that it is a gradual transition. The trees get smaller and scrawny until there are none, because they are unable to grow any further due to cold or lack of nutrients and water in the soil." Isn't our world interesting!

Every turn we take is prettier than the last. The snow is like a winter wonderland. We never expected to see snow on our way through Colorado. Now if we could only see a deer, or a moose, or any critter for that matter. (Never satisfied!) We are on our way to Eagle, Colorado, where our middle son lives. We deliberately planned arriving in Eagle on the weekend so as not to interrupt he and his wife's work schedule. It is hard to find words to express the beauty we see in front of us right now. Russ says, "It is like a Bob Ross painting." I am thankful, though, the snow is not sticking to the roads. And here it is May already!

We pulled into the same motel where we stayed when we came for Troy's wedding last year. It is practically across the street from where they live, so it is very convenient. We picked up our two grandsons, ages 12 and 16, who live in Gypsum, Colorado, only a few minutes from here. How they have grown, and it hasn't even been a year since we saw them last. We spent the weekend with all—cooked out, went bowling, sat around and talked, had pizza, and went to the very nice recreation center. The guys all swam and Karen and I went upstairs to the gym and walked on the treadmill. The pool was one of the neatest I'd ever seen. It had a place to swim with a net to play volley ball in one section, a slide, and a stream of water where you could hop into an inner tube and just nonchalantly drift around the pool. They had a great time. It was so good to be with them and hug them all.

It's Monday morning; Troy and Karen have to go to work. We took the boys back to Gypsum. Karen called and said she could meet us for breakfast before work, so we got to visit with her and the girls one more time. We left Colorado happy knowing we will see them again on our return trip.

Utah, here we come!

CHAPTER 3
Eye Candy

As we traveled west on Highway 70 out of Colorado, we were told to be prepared, because this section of I-70 is one of the most deserted stretches of the interstates in the United States. And prepared we were, as you could tell from our "list" (back of book). We went through Glenwood Springs and stopped at the rest area where there was a covered wagon along the Colorado River. Russ proceeded to dance a little "jig" for me as I looked out at him from the car. He was Colorado happy—Ha…that's what happens when the air gets thin. As we continued on, three short tunnels engulfed us, one at a time (always something to get our attention in Colorado). They were beautiful, as they took us right through the mountains. We are still seeing snow that blankets the tops of the mountains, as we pass through South Canyon, DeBeque, and Grand Junction, watching awesome scenery pass us by that looked like we were traveling through a picture book. Mountain ranges are all around, shaped like tiers on a wedding cake; blue skies and puffy white clouds, and the Colorado River snaking along beside us.

We stop for gas and roll into Utah. What a beautiful state Utah is! I read that the Utes used to inhabit Utah long ago. The name Ute means "land of the sun" and that is where Utah got its name. We will drive down to Moab, which is about 48 miles from the state line, and get a place to stay. We are looking at so many amazing structures and sculpted mountains, huge mountains with slick flat sides in the shapes of thick buildings. Some were in the shapes of castles, challenging our imagination. At first, I thought we were already in

Arches, because we were viewing lush terrain and exquisite forms, but Moab is 5 miles out of Arches, we aren't there yet. Things are about to get a whole lot more interesting; to our amazement. Definitely eye candy!

By 3:25 p.m., we got everything in the motel room and went and ate lunch so we could explore Arches before dark. At the entrance gate, the guard seemed pleased we had a senior pass. He said, "Wow, hold on to that. It's good for life!" As the guard greets you at the gate, he hands you a leaflet with helpful information and a map showing you where you are; the names of most of the arches and rocks; how far you have to hike to get to them and where the trail heads are, if you do decide to hike. The leaflet also tells you a little history about the park, and the do's and don'ts (not just for the preservation of the park, but for your own safety as well).

The first place we stop is the Visitor Center (which is a fairly new building), graced by many sculptures to greet us, such as a life-size big horn sheep, a ram and a ewe; two ravens and two lizards created by sculptor Matthew Palmer. Arches has the largest grouping of national stone arches in the world. It is composed of more than 3,600 square miles of incredible canyons, arches, spires, pinnacles, caves, hiking trails, and more. We learned from the orientation film that over millions of years the seas came and went. The plateau used to be sandstone 500 feet thick. It took over twenty million years for the present Arches National Park to form. Arches became a three-hundred-million-year-old bed of salt, and salt is very unstable. Over all that time the salt was squeezed into and up, to form the spires, pinnacles, and different rock formations. Take water, add ice and extreme temperatures; then mix a little underground salt movement and you get the most magical, sculpted rock scenery you can imagine. It is a delicate land that is continually changing; rocks split, arches fall and new arches form. A good example of that is in 1991 when a rock slab 60 feet long, 11 inches wide and 4 feet thick fell from the underside of Landscape Arch (a tourist got it all on video). But what is really astonishing to me is Wall Arch. I speak of this again later on in this chapter. Wall Arch collapsed some time during the night on August 4, 2008. On May 5, 2008 (only three months earlier), we stood in front of it in amazement of its beauty as we took Irreplaceable pictures. No one will ever get to have that experience again! I can't help but compare it to our own lives. Very much like those incredible rocks, we too are here one day and the next we are but a memory of irreplaceable pictures in our minds and hearts. In either case, enjoy your world God has given you and enjoy your life like the gift He meant it to be.

Wall Arch in Arches

The park consists of an 18 mile drive, we didn't get even five feet, and I can tell you our mouths were hanging open in amazement. The rocks and shapes and brilliant colors of salmon and orange to orange-red were breath-taking. My camera was going back and forth from one side of the car to the other trying to get it all on film. We had never seen anything like this in our lives. We simply could not lay the camera down.

The weather is cool and once again the sky is that beautiful radiant blue color. It is a good road, with 2 lanes and adequate directional signs. We were able to see most of the rock formations from the road, but there are also designated viewpoints or vistas. In the background framing arches are the snow-capped, 11,000 foot-high LaSal Mountains, the second in height of Utah's mountain ranges. LaSal means the "salt mountain." A Spanish Missionary named them that because he couldn't believe the mountains could be covered with snow in the heat of the summer. So he thought it had to be salt!

Almost immediately after we pass the Visitors Center, we find our first "named" area (not all of them are named). These statuesque rocks are called Three Penguins. They are three tall rocks standing close together; definitely resembling three penguins huddled close together in the Artic. With only a small stretch of your imagination, you can literally see their feet, beaks, and even the wings on the middle figure. As we move a little further up the road, we look out to see the "Moab Fault." The fault passes west of Arches, parallel to 191 and at the north end, where the fault goes east.

The next sight is called Park Avenue. The towering colorful rock wall of Park Avenue, which is a large, thin sandstone rock and stands 150–300 feet high. It stands within 2 miles of the entrance, its' name is very appropriate. It appears to be the front of a town, in my mind, like the front of a movie set, only this is bold orange rock, and I'm wondering how on earth it can stand there in all this wind (and it is very windy). I read that sometimes the center piece of Park Avenue is referred to as Whistler's Mother or Queen Victoria.

This is where we decided to stop and get out and stretch our legs, take a panoramic picture and just look and enjoy. While I was standing there, a little jack rabbit jumped in front of me and I think I scared him more than he scared me. Right away, he got his picture taken and he even posed for me, standing on his hind legs. He was adorable with those great big ears standing straight up. Seeing him was so exciting and promising, I was hoping that was a good sign, meaning we would see more "critters."

To the left of Park Avenue are the Three Gossips. The Three Gossips stand in the Courthouse Towers area and I also read that the Three Gossips are referred to as the Three Graces as well. There is no taxing the imagination here because it truly does look like three women (I say women because they look like they are shrouded in gowns and not only that, what man do you know who will admit he gossips?), and they are leaning close together as though they are whispering all kinds of juicy rumors to each other. *Yah*—I can see that!

A few feet from them are the The Organ and the Tower of Babel. These rocks were confusing to me, it was hard to tell one from the other, but what I see are more beautiful red sandstone in forms of spires (thin and tall rock), some thin and splitting, but standing tall and gallant, the one appearing to be a giant cruise ship sitting there frozen in endless time.

Sheep Rock is in the midst of all this, rightly named because it does look like a very tall sheep standing there so elegantly on a very large pedestal. On the way out of the park later on in the evening, we snapped a shot of all these tall giants, and they looked like silhouettes in the evening skies. Walking in this area one couldn't help but admire the plant life growing there, without much to hang on to for survival. I snapped some photos of the most beautiful red flowers (which later I found the name of them to be "brilliant scarlet monkey flowers") and small cactus plants called "prickly pear cactus," pinyon pine, and juniper. Considering the greenery there depends on rain, it's a wonder there is any at all in this desert land.

Next, we travel up a couple miles and go through Petrified Dunes which are fossilized leftovers of numerous shapes of sand dunes. Then, Cove of Caves, which shows sizes and different stages of arch elevation, and several caves all different sizes and depths in a row. Now we are looking at another rock that looks like a balanced rock but in the shape of a canned ham. And that is exactly what it is called—Ham Rock. Then we come to *the* Balanced Rock, balanced precisely on its pedestal. Balanced Rock is a 55 foot boulder (that is the same size as three school busses put together)! It doesn't make me feel like I would care to go and stand under it, even if it has been there doing its balancing act since before Christ. Looking at it from where I am standing, it's hard to believe it is so massive in size and is still balanced there.

As we pass the Garden of Eden, which is a jumble of spires, and fin canyons, we can look out and see forever. To the side of us stand the LaSal Mountains with snow that make them look like they are painted there. Towering above us is a huge rock in the shape of a buffalo head, complete with an eye (a small window), as the blue sky peeks through the window. If we look a little further ahead, we see an area called Elephant Butte. It is said to be the highest point inside the park, included in that butte is Parade of Elephants. Look closely and you can actually see them, like a picture carved into the side of the rock; the elephants holding each other's tails as they parade through paradise.

We decide to park and take a hike up to the North and South Windows, also known as The Spectacles. They are two separate windows in the form of eye glasses, the North Window is forty-eight by 90 feet and the South Window 50-by-155 feet—this is the eighth largest arch in the park. The hike wasn't difficult at all. It is probably only a mile to do the loop. Once you stand under the North Window Arch (looking straight out its window), you can view the Turret Arch and a beautiful scene to the right of the dry plateau. I could have stood there the rest of the day, the view was so breathtaking. The Turret Arch has its own personality, uniquely shaped. It has a little tower (which looks like a teapot spout) on one side and a rounded rock on the other side, a window in the middle that is 55 feet high and 35 feet wide, and a smaller window between the tower and the larger window. We hiked over to it so we could get a closer look. After we hiked back down the trail and looked up, we could see someone standing under the North Window where we were and he looked like a miniature toy. You don't realize how far up you were until you look up and see someone else standing there.

The sun is getting ready to set soon, so we will hang around a little while longer and get some pictures of a sunset and some beautiful creations in silhouette. While we stood there and watched the sun sink behind this magic-land, the beauty of it all filled our whole being. We could understand how small and insignificant we were in the scheme of things and yet so honored and privileged to be standing in the midst of it all, *together*.

It has been a tiring and wondrous day and tomorrow we plan to tackle the hardest thing first—a hike to Devil's Garden. Devil's Garden is probably the second most popular destination in the park and is the site of the largest number of named arches in the park. It is located at the very end of the 18-mile road.

So here it is another day. Our second day in Arches. The first thing we need to do today is stop at a grocery store and buy sandwiches and ice for our hike to Devil's Garden. We thought we were pretty smart because all the literature we read said to be sure to take water and energy bars. We were really prepared, and we even remembered suntan lotion.

If all one cared to do is drive through the park, it could be done easily in one day. Halfway to Devil's Garden, there are several varieties of spires and orange odd shaped rocks and the LaSal Mountains off in the distance. A huge pillar that looks like Jesus to me was standing there overlooking His handiwork, and rightly so. Some of the rocks are orange, topped with a lighter more salmon color, like God took time to frost those. It is mind-boggling to see so much beauty; we can hardly take it all in. My eyes are seeing and my mind is trying to convince me that it's all real. And we aren't finished yet!

A sign guides us to the parking lot just outside of Devil's Garden, where we park Mona. So Russ sticks a bottle of water in his back pocket and we are ready to hit the trail. The map said that the trail was 1.6 miles, heck; we walk more than that at the gym, no problem! Off we go onto a huge path of gravel and sand and the most beautiful scenery surrounding us. Just like when we were in the car, every single turn more beautiful than the last. We felt like we were one with nature. It was more than we could ever ask for.

Once again we have a gorgeous day, warm, but cool enough. The views are far, and the trail is good and somewhat easy. In about a half hour, we see our first arch and I believe it was Partition Arch. After a few more steps on a path lined with a wooden fence, we were standing in front of Landscape Arch. It is a huge Arch and spans 290.1 feet long, almost the length of a football field (some sources I read later says it is 306 feet long from base to base), sitting between two vertical block sandstones. The arch itself is six feet thick. Therefore, it claims the title of the longest arch in the park, but not in the world. And as I mentioned previously, in 1991, a massive slab fell from its underside, resulting in the fence that is there now to prevent people from standing under it. In the orientation film, we saw the video of it falling that a tourist had taken. Imagine, standing there at that very moment and you just so happen to catch that on your camera. Amazing!

Here, I understand, is where most people turn around and go back. Smart! However, we decide to continue on. It seems more like we are in God's Garden instead of Devil's Garden. Beauty everywhere, we couldn't help but keep going, even though I was very short of breath. We just took our time, and my patient husband was always understanding. Slowly we trudged on, determined to "see it all." Even more than that—wanting each other to see it all and share it together. Another corner and many ohhhs and ahhhs and wows would come out of our mouths; but only because we couldn't even come up with a better expression or words to describe it any more.

We bumped into some teens climbing all around and up and down and took pictures for them with their camera, as they posed and smiled. The path is not so easy anymore and not so wide either, and getting steeper. It is more like a narrow trail, no gravel, just sand. Lots of rocks to climb and canyons to squeeze through and we are still going up. Sometimes we wondered how this could only be 1.6 miles. Some of the trails were squeezed around the rocks and you had to balance yourself as you braced your body against the sides of the rocks in order to pass through. We have our cameras and took so many great pictures of our trail. We sat down in the shade to take a little break and we noticed we are down to a half bottle of water. We decided not to drink anymore right now, but save the other half for on the way back.

Our goal is to hike to the next arch called Double O Arch. It is the next major arch in Devil's Garden with the grand prize Dark Angel at the very end. The panoramic view is fantastic as we come upon Wall Arch. I mentioned this arch earlier in this chapter. Wall Arch is 71 feet wide and 33½ feet high and ranked 12th in size among the parks' 2,000 arches. We bumped into our little teen friends again, and they were climbing all over Wall Arch. They gave me their camera to get more pictures for them while sitting under the arch. Little did we know that would be the arch to collapse only 3 months later, on August 5th. How sad, I wonder if those kids know. It was the first collapse of a major arch since sections of Landscape Arch fell in 1991.

Every shade spot we find, we want to take a break, as we are hot, tired, and thirsty. But we continue climbing, walking, hopping from rock to rock and we're still not there. The trail is very difficult now, uneven, and steeper. As the trail gains height and enters a maze of narrow, sandy floored ravines between sheer fins and ridges, we are beginning to wonder if we should go on, even Russ is getting short of breath, but we attribute it to the altitude.

We find ourselves coming to the edge of a cliff and a 15-foot solid rock wall to climb *up*! Okay, don't forget I am afraid of heights! I thought about it a long time and didn't think I could do it. My fear was, if I fell I'd keep rolling, and off the ledge I go (we have climbed up about 3 ½ miles now). Russ went up (that long-legged guy) and coaxed me to try. I have a terrible feeling in the pit of my stomach, in other words, I am scared to death. But after several minutes, I gave it a try with an "I can't believe I am doing this attitude." I got up a couple of feet with my toes wedged in a little crack, moving them sideways inch by inch, my hands spread wide on the flat wall like suction cups. Russ was already up, leaning down, with his hand held out to me, but there was no way I was going to take my hand off that rock in order to grab his big hand. My knees began to quiver and I was starting to hyperventilate. I was frozen. I could not move, not sideways, not down and definitely not up, I am just froze there and shaking. My dear husband spoke very softly and calmly trying to convince me that I could do it. He is still holding his hand out to me, but my feet just would not go and my hands were glued to the side of the mountain. My whole body begins to tremble and all I know is I wanted down. But down was a ledge and I didn't want to go over it! Not today! Finally, Russ climbed down and tried the rescue from the rear. "Just let go, Ginn. I'm right here," he said. I was probably about 5 feet up and the ledge was probably about 6 feet wide beneath me, but in my mind, it was right behind me and certainly didn't seem that wide either. Russ said, "It's okay, Ginn, take little baby steps to the left [which slanted downward], and we will work our way back down." He kept talking and coaxing softly and convincingly, which for him is very difficult as he is a very loud person. But he knew this was serious. I finally got that left foot to move a tiny bit and then the right until I got maybe two feet from the ground where Russ could grab me tight and help me down. I was shaking so much I just sat down on the ground with my back up against the rigid rock wall and couldn't move.

After Russ felt comfortable that I was okay, we agreed he should go ahead toward Double O Arch, although we were both disappointed we couldn't do it together. We had to have our pictures of Double O. So with our camcorder around his neck and my little disposable camera in his pocket, he climbed back up and began his hike toward Double O. Within a few feet, he found a woman sitting on the rock up there. He sat and talked with her for a minute only to discover she was afraid to go any further and was taking a break, soon to go back down. Well, at least she got further than me. Russ kept going for what seemed like hours; as for me, I couldn't budge. I sat in the same spot for at least an hour before I could get enough courage to even stand up. I had told Russ to go on and get pictures for me, and I would start the hike down and he could catch up with me. But here I am, finally getting enough courage to stand up. Now, I am leaning with my back up against the mountain wall, afraid to take a step any further. I am only just becoming aware of my surroundings. I noticed a small tree right next to me. So I slowly extended my arm and grabbed hold of the little trunk like a security blanket, as if that little thing would hold me if I were to slide. I couldn't make myself start the trail down alone, even though I managed to hike up just fine. I believe this was one of the scariest times in my life. I didn't think Russ would ever get back and I was starting to get a little worried.

Several hikers passed me, some asking me if I was all right or if they could help me. As they went up, they made it look so easy. I began to think…come on you can do this, just step back a couple steps and leap up and keep going. I turned and looked at the slab of rock for a long time. Why was I so scared, I can do this. Everyone else just took a fast walk up; maybe it wasn't as hard as I thought. I watched hiker after hiker run up it. I wondered what was wrong with me. I tried to convince myself, you can do this, go ahead, then I wondered what I'd do if I did get up there. Where would I go from there…Russ was far ahead. Even the little teens we kept bumping into came along and offered to help me up the mountain. I came to my senses, and thought, no, I can't do it, I can't even let go of this little tree (come to think about it, when I was talking to all those people passing me by, I must have looked pretty dumb standing there holding on to that little tree), it was such a tiny little thing! I stood there for some time longer simply trying to get enough nerve to let go. I thought—Atta girl—1 finger, 2 fingers. Oh yes, I am standing here, both hands free—now go ahead and take a couple steps away, you're okay. The path is solid, and you'll be going away from the edge. I walked out a couple feet down the path and had to go over some big rocks. Even though I came over them on the way up just fine, gosh, they seemed to be so much bigger now. And all this from a person who as a girl was the biggest tomboy. Not afraid of anything. (And now you'll think I'm lying when I tell you I could out-run and out-jump any boy on my street)! I figured I better sit down and wait for Russ. I couldn't wait until he came back to take my hand and tell me of his adventures. Thirsty doesn't happen for me often because I don't care for water, but thirsty was happening for me now.

At last, a familiar figure is coming over the ridge on top of the mountain. Thank God, it was Russ and he was safe. I was so glad to see him. He looked worn out. We took our last sip of water and he proceeded to tell me of his "solo hike." He said he was glad I didn't go any further because I would have never made it over some of those ridges. After we got home and looked at our film, we realized he forgot to turn the camcorder off while he was hiking over those rocks to Double O. So I was able to see the terrain he had to hike, as the camera swung back and forth from his neck, pointing down at his feet and filming the ledge on both sides of him. I felt like I was there with him as I watched the tape; my stomach doing flip flops again, and I could see how dangerous it was. If you can imagine the back of a whale, the way it is rounded and long, that is the shape of the rocks he had to walk on. The terrain ahead of him was filled with cracks and crevices that he had to jump to get over to the next rock, and with no water. He had quite a challenge on his hands. I could see he was walking right on the edge. Now I feel a little better about it; I'm glad I didn't go any further too.

At one point, Russ said he was sitting on the side of a rock to take pictures. He said he felt like his toenails were like claws digging into the stone, and his stomach was churning. I don't know how he stood back up and filmed more, he got such wonderful shots. I wouldn't have been able to keep my balance to do that. If you lose your balance up there, it is a long way down. The trail was very challenging to say the least.

While he was still on top of the world he saw a large black arch, and we're not aware of a name for it, so he named it, Black Arch. We did see a lot of arches with no names. At last, after many more ridges and canyons, as the trail continued straight up, there it was—Double O Arch. Double O arch consists of a larger arch on top of a smaller arch, almost like a figure 8. The largest arch soars gracefully over 100 feet above your head if you are standing under it. Russ got good pictures of it and he could see the ultimate and last feature of the Devil's Garden, called Dark Angel. It is a tall, dark rock pinnacle, only 0.4 miles from the Double O Arch. There was a very narrow ledge to climb around to get to Dark Angel; we were quite satisfied with the picture he took from right where he was (0.4 miles). As Russ turned to come back down, he dropped my little disposable camera, it rolled about 15 feet straight down, so as soon as he saw someone else coming up the trail, he called to them to bring it on up with them. But it was so good to have him back down.

Of course, by now we are out of water, how stupid are we? We even bought a little back pack and didn't bring it with us. We obviously misunderstood the length and time this trail would take to get to Double O. After we got down we realized Landscape Arch was 1.6 miles, but it was 4.2 miles up, up, up to Double O. Four miles is one thing, hiking on even terrain, but quite another when you are going up 4 miles! I don't know how we did that or what we were thinking, I just know that now we are very tired, hot and hungry, and boy do I have to pee! We realize it has been 4 hours and we still had to hike down, so we will take it easy and stop in shade more often in short intervals. We didn't take in to account that a mile here, with the rugged trails is more like two. We may be dehydrated, but we are happy and excited and loving all those feelings and sights we are carrying in our hearts and minds. As we descend, the rocks are so beautiful. They are orange with salmon stripes going horizontally through them and next to them are towers big as silos that are orange with salmon lids. As soon as we came to the end of the trail we all but ran to the pit bathroom, and then got to our little Mona who cooled us with her lovely air conditioner. We opened our cooler and had our sandwich and lots of cool, clear water. So much for being prepared!

Rested and ready for more, we continue on and find Skyline Arch. Another beauty. And then hundreds of tall spires, caves, and domes, all free-standing and riddled with salmon colored trim around the top. Now we are approaching Sand Dune Arch. Again it is exactly like its' name. You start out on a small path of gravel and sand. Then there is a narrow split in two large rocks that form a canyon, which you climb through. It was up hill, but once you pass that entrance, you are in a great canyon with very thick red silky sand. I can only imagine this must be what it's like to walk on a beach on Mars. One other couple was in the canyon besides us. Their two small boys had their shoes off, running and jumping in the soft sand, and we could hear their shouts of glee echoing in the canyon. Hidden a few feet ahead sat the Sand Dune Arch. It was a pleasant surprise indeed because it was so different from the other arches sitting out in the open. It is so beautiful and serene in there, like we found it accidentally all on our own, and only one other family did too. I didn't want to leave the cool air and this safe secluded space. The path we went in was a little harder to get out because it was downhill and slippery. I think this Arch was my favorite.

Right outside of Sand Dune Arch was another arch called Broken Arch. It looked like it came up and connected itself in the middle and someone soldered it together. Again the park is framed by those sky high LaSal Mountains that dominate the view. The peaks are a bright white the way the sun is shining on them and the bottoms are a beautiful dark blue-gray from the shade.

Fiery Furnace, next on our route, is a maze of narrow canyons and tall red sandstone fins. I read that this maze is so confusing and so easy to get lost in; you must hike it with a guide or get a permit to do it with a group. This section lights up when the sun hits it in the evening. People sit there with their big zoom cameras in the evening or early morning hours, waiting for the sun to shine on them just right so they can get pictures of them. We are driving back to the entrance now through the Salt Valley Overlook. The view is endless and filled with orange rocks and piles of almost white smaller rocks sprinkled with greenery throughout.

We have come to the end of our adventure in Arches, so to bid us farewell stands the symbol of the park, Delicate Arch. It is like the grand finale. It stands 65 feet high and the opening is 35 feet wide. In the old days, cowboys called it the Schoolmarm's Bloomers. It is a fascinating Arch, the one Arch I knew from pictures of it on calendars. What an awesome sight to see in person. No climbing is allowed on any of the "named" Arches.

I couldn't help but wonder if people were injured or even killed in Arches National Park, because some of the hikes are so dangerous. So when I got home, I researched it and found that in 1941, someone fell off the top of Wall Arch, while getting a friend to snap their picture. They fell 30 feet and suffered serious injuries. And soon after we left, on July 2, 2008, while hiking the trail to Delicate Arch, a 35-year-old French woman collapsed. A bystander performed CPR for a half an hour but was unable to revive her. Heat perhaps? But, all in all, when heeding safety precautions, the park in general is very safe.

We will leave this magical land now, go through the Klondike Mountains on Route 191 and pick up Route 6 north to Salt Lake City. But not before we stop at the gift shop and I pick up my usual post cards, magnet, and this time, an Arches T-shirt. This has been an awesome two days. The wonders of Arches National Park will live on in our hearts forever, and I feel so blessed to have been able to look on only a very small part of what our God gets to look at every day. The Greatest Sculptor of all!

CHAPTER 4

Tabernacles, Needles, and the Princess

As our adventure unfolds, we are surrounded by incredible light-brown mountains that appear to be frosted with chocolate icing. Our little Mona is very small as she takes us between them as they tower over us on both sides. Soon mountains riveted with snow are in front of us again. The elevation is 7,700 feet as we pass Soldier Summit on our way to Provo, and then Salt Lake City, Utah, where I would love to see the Mormon Tabernacle. Friends have told me not to miss it. I suggested it to Russ but it is raining and he didn't want to stop. As we went on, I must have looked like I was pouting because after about half an hour up the road, with the sun now shining, we are sitting in work traffic. I present my case (in a small sweet voice)…"for as long as we will have to sit in this traffic, we could be visiting the tabernacle, honey." (Pretty good huh?—Well, when would I ever be in Salt Lake City again?—*Never!*) Suggestion accepted! Ha! Russ turns Mona around (he didn't even sigh at me; I bet he's thinking the same thing as I am). Besides, he's a pretty sweet guy; he knew I wanted to see it.

Oh, how beautiful as we approach the temple with its pointed towers and finial spires sprouting up and over the trees. We found a parking spot immediately—right in the middle of downtown Salt Lake City, and walked up to the temple grounds. Right away two young ladies greeted us and offered to take us on a tour of the grounds. The temple sits on 35 acres called "Temple Square." The temple, according to their literature, is recognized by Latter Day Saints throughout the world. Seldom are tours accepted in the temple because the temple is considered sacred.

The first thing that catches our attention is the elaborate and beautifully manicured grounds. Not to mention the flowers and flower baskets in a variety of brilliant colors. There is also a sparkling fountain and you can see that spring is in full bloom—still—for us.

The Tabernacle is the home of the Mormon Tabernacle choir, which has 360 unpaid volunteers. The choir's first radio broadcast was in 1929. The public is invited to their rehearsals, but we are a day early—I would have loved to have heard them sing.

The two tour guides are very sweet and informative. Next we are guided to the Conference Center directly across the street, which is a dome-shaped building with a waterfall falling straight down against the marble wall, in the front. The Center features a huge 21,000 seat auditorium that could house two 747s within it. Looking up toward the sky, there is an intricate glass dome. This huge space also houses the largest organ in America. The organ is massive; it has been enlarged or renovated five times and has grown from its original 2,000 pipes to its present size of 11,623 pipes. The organ is hand carved from Utah timber. Our guides tell us some of the pews and pillars are original and the acoustics are extremely acute. We were sitting way in the back (about 170 feet away from the pulpit), and a woman at the pulpit tore a piece of paper, slowly, to demonstrate how sound carries throughout the huge building. It sounded so perfectly crisp. They say you could hear a pin drop as well, the acoustics are so sensitive.

Next we are guided back across the street to the North Visitor Center, all the time the girls explaining their beliefs. The North Visitor Center is graced with an awe-inspiring, eleven-foot marble statue of Christ with His arms open and welcoming you to Him. This statue is named the "Christus" and sits in the center of a huge round gallery. All the way around the gallery are incredibly huge paintings that measure about 10 feet in length. They portray Jesus's life and ministry, and when you stand in front of them, you become entranced in each story they have to tell.

Looking around the grounds, behind us stands The Assembly Hall, which is also a spired gray and white, granite building, where weekly concerts are performed. Also there is a museum, a South Visitor Center, Joseph Smith Memorial Building and the Family History Library, which houses the largest genealogical collection of its kind in the world. Anyone is welcome to go in and use the collection free of charge. We would have loved to do that but our half hour tour has now stretched into an hour. At the end of the tour, we were asked to see a short film and fill out a card. It was a very nice presentation; we were glad we took the time to visit this beautiful place.

We began our trek toward Boise, Idaho, and from a distance; we caught a glimpse of the "Great Salt Lake" (from Route I-15), only 34 miles from Idaho's border. This is where we switched over to I-84. It's starting to get late and I could see we were in for a beautiful sunset. Soon the mountains in the distance were framed with colors of pink, orange, red, and then golden-lined clouds. The mountains were silhouetted in front with a beautiful purple and gray. There is nothing more breathtaking than a sunset, oh, how I love them. So, of course, I am putting my little disposable camera to work. "The dawn and sunset SHOUT for joy!" (Ps. 6:8). It surely does seem as if our Creator is shouting out His Glory. We decided to end our day in Burley, Idaho, where we stayed the night.

In the morning, we continue to cross the south end of Idaho, still on our course to Boise. Here, Idaho is pretty flat, but you can see the mountains far away. It's a beautiful fresh morning. In the distance, we can see a snow-capped mountain range surrounding us. The weather couldn't be more beautiful and we are traveling in short sleeves and no coats. Naturally, we have to go to Cabela's in Boise. I would think there was something seriously wrong with my husband if we didn't stop at Cabela's. Russ picked up a few more hats for the kids and I just had to pick up a post card that had a recipe on it for Idaho baked potato soup. *Yum!*

Welcome to Oregon! Mona needed gas so we stopped as we always do. Russ got out to pump the gas and all of a sudden this young man is running toward him—*fast!* I believe Russ thought he was going to be attacked because I saw his eyes get big and he took a stance that told me he was in defense mode. He said loudly to the fast approaching boy, "What are you doing?" because the boy was trying to take the hose for the gas from him. I thought for a minute I was going to witness a tug of war, or worse, but the boy immediately expounded "I am going to pump your gas, sir!" His eyes were as big as Russ's, wondering why Russ wouldn't let go of the hose, I'm sure. Russ said, as he is tugging the hose back toward him, "No, no, that's fine, I got it." To which the boy explains (as he is tugging the hose back toward him) that the law in Oregon states "the customers are not allowed to pump their own gas in order to prevent fires." So hearing this, which seemed like a sensible statement, Russ seemed okay with surrendering the hose to the boy (who was very relieved). So Russ released the hose and settled himself down in surrender mode. That was very strange.

We continue on I-84 toward Baker City, Oregon. Our flat lands are getting hilly and I believe the little river following us is the Snake River. Our mountains, full of snow, are coming to meet us once again. Soon there is patchy snow on the ground and I filmed the great scenery as I suddenly realized how many flying critters decided to hitch a ride on our windshield. *Yuk!* We must get in the habit of keeping all the windows clean for as much as I video through it. We also noticed there are strange looking metal fences about 20 yards out, all along the highways, in a bent, leaning fashion. Being from Georgia, I wondered what they were there for. At first I thought they were to keep animals from jumping on to the highway, but Russ said maybe they were to keep the snow drifts from building up so fast.

What an amazing country we live in, it is so picturesque, and we feel so blessed to be given this opportunity to experience driving each mile. We are continuing up I-84 across the Northeast corner of beautiful Oregon. The streets wind through huge mountains, literally cut in half in order to lay the road. Our tour through Oregon was short, but what an incredible panorama this state has to offer.

Now, a beautiful bridge carries us into the mountainous state of Washington. As we cross into Washington, the mountains are larger and there are warning signs for truckers going down them. Apparently their speed depends on how much weight they are carrying. The mountains form silhouettes in front of yet another beautiful sunset, but this time it is a pale yellow with gray clouds in the horizon. Russ said he hasn't used the gas pedal for the last five miles. We are simply coasting down this mountain. It doesn't seem possible a whole day of traveling has gone by. What a wonderful feeling of relaxation and wonder inside; there are no words—I just take a deep breath—and feel at peace with the world.

Beginning another wonderful day, the state of Washington is taking us through a valley. I believe it is Mount Stuart in the distance, glaring white from the sun on the snow and a blue glow in the middle. What a ride, as we move on and find Mt. Stuart dead away. Pine trees by the millions stand stately everywhere to escort us through. It seems every corner we turn brings us a new and exciting view. As we pass a lake, there are parts of it still frozen. I couldn't envision a more beautiful winter scene if I tried. If I were an artist I would have to take out my canvas and easel and paint a picture.

We pass through a little construction, which makes us feel right at home, after all, what's traveling without construction? It just wouldn't seem American somehow. As we pass the construction, Russ picks up speed and every time I ask him to slow down he says "I am." *Not!* This went on the whole trip on these mountain roads as Mona drove us through our "movie." We've also noticed a lot of trucks carrying hay. Which I'm sure is not unusual for the locals, but for us it is. Especially since any hay I've seen transported is in big bales, but this is piled on the truck almost scientifically, in cubes that resemble cement blocks. So every time we see a truck with hay we yell *hey!* You know, like if we were saying hey to someone in the south, in two syllables. He-ey! After being on the road only about 12 days, we are already picking up little quirks that aren't funny to anyone at all except us. And they get funnier every time we say them like when Russ says "going up" every time we start up a mountain, loud, like an elevator operator. Silly, but we are having a great time. Like kids, laughing and giggling all the way, mostly about stupid and insignificant little things.

Remember our friends we bumped into at breakfast, from Washington? They commented that it rains all the time in Seattle, except a very few days out of the year. Well, it's not raining. In fact it is so bright we can see the reflection of the mountains and trees in the lakes, resembling huge mirrors. Speaking of the lakes, they seem very high, like they could overflow.

I have been in touch with the lab, to find out where the closest one is in Seattle so I can get my blood drawn, again. I found a number in the phone book in the motel and got in touch with one of the nicest people I have ever talked to, named Phyllis. She was actually in Seattle and gave us great directions. We have met some of the nicest and most accommodating people our whole trip. She went more than out of her way to help me find a lab number to labs I would need to seek out as we traveled. We set up our GPS for the first time and it took us right to it. That was the neatest thing. Okay, we are seniors with a new toy. Sometimes the GPS would start to talk to us and scare the heck out of us. It's like having another person in the car with you that you forget is there. This type of electronics is all new to us. I did manage to set it up though. The first thing you do is choose a person that will give directions and guide you, whether it be a male or female, foreign or not, etc. I chose a woman, and I chose English of course, but I didn't realize it was a British voice, so her language was fun and made us giggle when she told us to get on the "motor-way" in a very British accent. Sometimes I have to stop and think what my Mom would have thought of such inventions. I mean she didn't even get to see a computer, not to mention iPods and cell phones. It is amazing how far technology has progressed over the years.

As we emerge from a tunnel into Seattle, we see Safeco field where you could catch a Seattle Mariners baseball game and right after that is the Qwest field, where Russ said the Seattle Seahawks play football. We stop at a train track, and a cute little bus/train goes by on the tracks! I guess it is equivalent to our Marta in Atlanta, or is that their monorail? After we find the lab, I only had to wait a few minutes, the technician drew my blood and we found ourselves deep in conversation. She was a sweetheart. What is this with Seattle, where everyone is so kind? I love this city already. She was an older woman and I was explaining my adventures to her and how God has been taking care of us. My goodness, she took my hands in hers and said how happy she was to meet me. For someone I had never met before, she made me feel so cared for and she sent me on my way with her blessing. Angels come in all forms, don't they? I happily, almost skipped out of the building and we went on to find a bank to take care of some business, since we were going to be gone so long. Russ parked me and Mona in front of a Bank America. As I looked around I noticed everyone was Asian. But when Russ came out of the bank, we rounded the corner and came to a very pretty arch (a man-made arch this time), with Asian writing on it. Come to find out we were in a heavily populated area where the Asian population is eleventh in size in Seattle and surrounding areas. I wasn't aware that Seattle hosts one of the nation's best established Asian populations composed of the seventh largest in Japanese, eighth largest Vietnamese, ninth largest Korean, and eleventh largest Chinese and Filipino. Also the state's Governor is a Chinese American.

Seattle Southside, where we were, likes to be called the "Emerald City." It makes me think of the Wizard of Oz. The modern day Seattle was built on top of "Old Seattle." Seattle also proudly boasts they have more coffee and espresso shops than any city in America.

There is a jumble of overhead wires everywhere, and I was thinking of trolley cars but these were buses and they were all running on those electric wires. That was interesting to see, I bet they save a lot of gas that way and it was nice to be behind one of them and not smell those awful fumes. The only thing is, it looked pretty cluttered, but then I guess that is a small price to pay. Its 4:00 p.m. now, so we decided to find a place for the night, and a place to eat and then tackle the Space Needle in the morning.

We found an inn close to the airport that would transport us to the airport with their motel bus. The bonus was we could house Mona there while we were in Alaska, as long as we return to the same inn on the way back through. Plus they will pick us up from the airport and bring us back to the motel on our return trip, and it wasn't that expensive either. It would have cost us more to put Mona in a Park and Pay, and we would have had to find our own transportation to and from the airport. What a great deal! Are things going right for us or what? After we got all that settled, we found a place to eat at a restaurant called Roasters, and the food was out of this world!

For some reason, we are unusually tired tonight and we are having trouble staying awake. We will "hit the sack" early and plan to have a "laundry day" in the morning before we go to the Space Needle. The only drawback for going to bed early is you get up early. So in the morning, we went to the continental breakfast for a change. The dining area in the motel was huge compared to most motels we stayed in, and full of people, chattering and gathering their luggage. It was fun to look around the room and watch the faces of the people sitting there, and you could hear the excitement in their busy voices and feel the electric and anticipation in the air. My guess is they were waiting to be taken to the airport for some exciting cruise, not to Alaska though, because from what I understand, we are taking the first cruise of the year.

It was quite a trip from our room, in this huge motel, to the laundry room in the older and adjoining building. But that is a good thing, we will get our exercise! After the second load was through washing, I threw them in the dryer and while I was doing that a nice young man came in and put a load in the washer and left the room. I say he was nice because he was very polite and held the door for me—good manners. In the meantime, I went back to the room since it would be a while until our clothes dried. As I returned to the laundry room a woman was in there and had taken all the young man's wet clothes out of the washer and she was throwing them on the counter. She was a little pushy for such a small room and I was standing there in my little corner folding our clothes. She took over the only 2 washers and as she left I could see what was going to happen next. So I took my remaining clothes out of the only working dryer and put the boys' clothes in it. It had a few remaining minutes on it, so (probably out of spite) I put a couple more quarters in the dryer and left, smirking all the way back to our room.

We went to the grocery store to pick up some of my medicine, post cards (of course) and some fruit. From there, on to the Space Needle! How exciting, although I was a little nervous about going up 520 feet in the air. We found our way back downtown and I never saw such a busy place. I guess because it is Saturday, but people are walking everywhere. Everyone focused, like they were on a mission. Of course, we got caught up in traffic and every other street was a one-way street. Hello, Atlanta! We finally asked directions as we were stopped at a red light, and these two very kind young ladies in the car next to us pointed us on our way. We could see the Space Needle from where we were, but it seemed that every street we would get on was going in the wrong direction and we kept going in circles (or should I say squares)?

The Needle Seattle, Washington

Parking in downtown Seattle was fairly simple and we didn't have very far to walk on this beautiful sun shiny day (yup, I'm rubbing it in). There were all kinds of interesting things to see on the way to the needle. As we got closer, there was sort of a park with a small roller coaster, a few rides for the kiddies and loud music on a huge screen with groups singing songs we had never heard of. And the closer we got to the Space Needle, the more my stomach was doing flip-flops again, because I guess I imagined some kind of scary ride to the top! We stepped into what looked like an elevator at the bottom of the needle with glass windows and up we went and it only took 41 seconds to exit onto the panoramic O deck. It was a very gentle and quick ride, actually. The O deck has an unobstructed 360-degree view. As we walk out to the deck, I am stretching my arm way out in front of me toward the railing because we are so high up. I have that insecure feeling of, *whoops*, one more step and over you go in the pit of my stomach. So I grab on to the railing for dear life. Way down below, we can see they are having a tugboat race. It was fun to watch and listen to them toot (which again reminds me of a little story I used to read to the kids—"Tubby the Tugboat"—except Tubby was red). It is extremely windy and cold up here, but we walk all the way around to see the spectacular 360-degree view of Seattle. We take pictures and then go inside and sit at a small table for two with a nice warm cup of coffee (it felt good warming my hands around it) and look out the glass windows while we warm up. Also, in the distance were the beautiful Cascade Mountains, ferry boats going back and forth on the river and a cruise ship awaiting its passengers.

There are many gift shops, small coffee shops, eateries and of course, souvenir shops. There is also a revolving restaurant above this level called Sky City. When I got home, I researched the Space Needle online and found "Discover the Needle" from which I discovered some "Fun Facts." Here are just a few of the facts I thought were very informative and interesting.

The structure:

- At the top of the Space Needle (605 feet), there is an aircraft warning beacon.
- The bottom of the foundation is 30 feet below ground.
- There are 848 steps from the bottom of the basement to the top of the observation deck.
- During the construction of the Space Needle, it took 467 cement trucks less than 12 hours to fill the foundation hole (30 feet deep and 120 feet across); this was the largest continuous concrete pour ever attempted in the West.
- The Space Needle is fastened to its foundation with 72 bolts, each 30 feet in length.

- The Space Needle sways approximately one inch for every 10 mph of wind. It was built to withstand a wind velocity of 200 mph, doubling the 1962 building code requirements. When winds around the Needle reach high speeds, 35 mph or higher, the elevators are designed to reduce their traveling speed to 5 mph for safety reasons. During the 1963 Inaugural Day storm, wind gusts reached 90 mph and the top house was closed for an hour and a half.
- On a hot day, the Needle expands about one inch.
- There are 25 lightning rods (24 actual rods plus the tower) on the roof of the Needle to withstand lightning strikes.
- The diameter of the halo is 138 feet.
- The entire Space Needle saucer does not rotate, only a 14-foot ring next to the windows rotates on the Sky City restaurant level.
- The restaurant turntable revolves on a track and wheel system that weighs roughly 125 tons. All it takes to make the turntable revolve is a 1½ horsepower motor.

The elevators:

- Each elevator carries 25 people.
- Each elevator has seven cables total, even though one cable is strong enough to hold the entire weight of the elevator. The cables are changed annually.

These are only a few of the facts, there are so many more, but I thought these were the most interesting.

After a fun-filled day and we had returned to our motel, we hear on the news there was a bomb threat on one of the ferries and all the visitors were being held for a search. It is very hard to understand why such things happen, but it is always a wakeup call and snaps you right back to reality. But no one was hurt, so the best thing to do is thank God for that and keep on keepin' on. And that is exactly what we will do.

Tomorrow we will be leaving for Alaska, our beautiful 49th state. Now we must get our suitcases organized and together (the one for land and the one for sea). We had to kind of re-organize and get some of the things out of our everyday suit cases. So we put our tennis shoes in the Alaska bag for "land" and decided to wear our hiking boots so they wouldn't be so heavy in the suit cases. Actually, it got a little confusing, I was starting to get my suitcases all mixed up, this one is land—no, this is the one that needs to go on the ship without us. At last, all was organized, including our carry-on luggage and heavy jackets over our arms.

At 9:30 a.m., we were having a little continental breakfast when a young man began to walk toward me with a wide grin on his face. He said, "Aren't you the lady I met in the laundry room?" I said "Oh, yes, how are you?" He said, "Did you put my laundry in the dryer for me?" I honestly can't believe he remembered me from that very short encounter. By now I am grinning too and acknowledged that yes, I did. He grabbed me and gave me a big bear hug and said, "That is the nicest thing anyone ever did for me!" Well, you can imagine the look on my face when he grabbed me like that but, *awww!* That made me so happy. How sweet of him to say so, and in a way how sad that doing laundry is the nicest thing anyone ever did for him.

My day is already soaring as we boarded the motel bus and started on our way to the Seattle Tacoma International Airport. This is a huge airport with the humming sounds of people busily going here and there. My husband has one of those suitcases with the long handle on it, the kind that has wheels and you can pull it behind you, which is his carry on, and he is desperately trying to balance my carry-on on top of it, and I can't help but giggle. We see others with their little piece of luggage, one on top of the other, and it fits so nice as they just quickly walk through the airport, and the luggage follows all nice and neat. But here goes Russ and the top piece falls off. He picks it up and puts it back on top and it falls off again. So he wraps the strap around the handle but it kind of slides off anyway around to the underside. Now he is walking with my little carry-on upside down, on the underside of his. He eventually sets it back up there and in a few minutes it falls off again. By now I am grinning from ear to ear. This is becoming some kind of a slap-stick comedy as I begin to giggle because his face is so serious. Then we stop a minute for me to go to the restroom and he stops and leans against the wall to wait for me, all cool, macho, and nonchalant, when suddenly the whole thing falls over backward onto the floor with a loud *clunk*. I laughed so hard I almost didn't make it to the bathroom because there was a line and I know those ladies were wondering what on earth I was laughing at.

We walked for what seemed like forever until we got to gate N-8, and as soon as we arrived, we were told that our gate was changed to gate D-3, exactly where we came from. So, we turn around, go back on the tram up an escalator, over and down another escalator to D (as in David) 3. Meanwhile, Russ has figured out that if he hooks the handles of the small bag over the bag with the wheels a little tighter, it doesn't fall off, but it goes sideways instead. He is a hoot to watch. But then we get on our last escalator and the little suitcase fell sideways again and I thought he was going down! And I would have gone with him. He never did really figure out how to make that little suitcase stay put!

Have you ever noticed how people walk in the airport? They're eyes are focused straight ahead like someone with a neck brace on, never turning to look on either side, and leaning a little forward in motion. They don't seem to notice there are other people around as the back wheel of their luggage rolls over your foot. They don't seem to notice that when they are in line, it is a single lane maybe two feet wide, that the two of us are not going to fit in that same spot. They obviously don't see me, because their suitcase is about to buckle my knees from under me any minute and I am going to fall down if they keep pushing and I know I won't be able to get up if I do. It would not be a pretty sight having to pick me up off the floor!

I always have to go through a separate line, since I have a pace-maker. This is quite an ordeal, not to mention embarrassing. I usu-ally walk up to someone (a person with a starched shirt, hopefully a name tag and looks like an employee) who is standing aside from the others. I explain that I have to go through another line and try to hand them my little ID card, that they never look at, that states I have a pacemaker. Finally, they raise their arm in the air and point in another direction across the room and say, "See that man over there with the long-sleeved white shirt? Go over there and he'll take care of you." Well, there is usually a separate line for people like me and those in wheelchairs, but there are a million guys in long-sleeved white shirts "over there" so as I move along to each aisle I have to ask "is this the aisle where…is this the aisle where…is this the aisle where…" In the meantime, everyone is giving me the evil eye, like I'm trying to butt in front of them or something! "Excuse me! Excuse me! Excuse me!" Finally I find someone to help me. But in the meantime, I can see my poor husband way across the room juggling my shoes, his shoes, my purse, my carry-on (still hanging off the side of his carry-on), both of our coats, and my purse! Here I stand, I am finally in the correct line, but have to wait for a female security person to check me out and make sure I'm not carrying a bomb, or that I am a terrorist. I know…it's a small price to pay for our country, and I am more than willing to do it, just don't make me stand here all alone. I am a very self-conscious person (even at my age); it feels like everyone is staring at me, as I stand in this large singled-out area, alone. I begin to look all around calmly with my arms folded over my chest and stare at the ceiling as though there is something up there to see. I find myself tapping my foot and sort of rolling my eyes when the female guard shows up. I think she must have been on a lunch break or something. While she is feeling me up with the back of her hand, everyone is staring and looking at you like they are thinking, uh-huh, you got caught, didn't you? The guards really are very nice, once they get to you. After that she escorts me to a pair of foot prints painted on the floor. Sometimes they use a wand rather than the backs of their hands, and I now understand that you can request to be put in a private room, which sounds even scarier to me. Now I am standing on the painted feet with both arms out like a telephone pole and everyone is gawking at me. No, it is not my imagination! Then I have to sit on a chair so she can look at the bottom of my now dirty socks.

After my little escapade, I look across the room and I see my poor frazzled husband, whose heart is probably more out of sync than mine, looking all around the room for me (he has his paranoid look on his face now, probably thinking I have been kidnapped or locked away somewhere). This process does take a while. He really gets nervous in airports, I think it's because there are so many things to think about and so many rules to follow. Get your ticket ready, have your passport or ID ready, make sure your luggage isn't too heavy, find the right place and airlines to check in, find the right gate (only to be told you have to go to yet a different gate which may be three football fields away), don't forget the luggage when you stop for the restroom, get something to eat, hurry, hurry, and for heaven's sake get that suitcase to stay on top of the other one! Don't get lost and heaven forbid we might be late and miss our flight. And so I guess now I have figured out why people are looking so zoned, we are all just trying to find our destination while all these things are flying through our heads! But I must add, I have been in other airports, and if one person has to go through the handicap line, they will let the whole family stay together, which is very nice.

So we can relax now and go get a snack before we board. The flight is supposed to be 3 hours and 10 minutes long, but after we are in the air 3 hours, the pilot announces that we will arrive in Fairbanks, Alaska, in another hour! I didn't get that, so I asked the flight attendant, "Did the pilot just say we will reach our destination in another hour?" He said, "Oh, yes, there is a time difference." Okay now, I really don't get that. Did they not know that when we boarded? How can you lose or gain an hour in the air? I get it on the ground, but in the air?

All in all, the flight was beautiful, and the clouds were puffy and awesome and I took a couple pictures from my window of the plane that came out great. I was sitting next to the window, Russ in the middle and a very nice young man near the aisle. His name was Luke. Name change here, just in case, because I can't see his name listed on the team roster as I write this. We started talking with "Luke" and come to find out he was accepted to be a defensive back for the "Fairbanks Grizzly's." It didn't take more than that for Russ to get into a conversation with him, bringing back memories of Russ's old football days, when he was a quarterback in high school. To quote him, "the days before there were face masks and mouth pieces." I thought Russ was very encouraging to this new, young rookie. Luke seemed very interested in Russ's stories. He mentioned this was the first time he had ever flown or been to Alaska, so I offered him my seat so he could sit by the window. The man sitting behind us heard us talking about Alaska. He said he was from Alaska and began to narrate the scenery below; it was very helpful and informative. Talk about a person being in the right place at the right time!

CHAPTER 5

On Land and Not by Sea

Fairbanks International Airport in Alaska is close to downtown Fairbanks. It was very shiny and clean in appearance, and as I looked around, while we're waiting for our luggage, I noticed a sand box with toys in it for children to play. What a great idea. Everything was on a slower pace than in Seattle and it was good to see the consideration for children. My young'uns would have had a great time while we were waiting. It wasn't long, though, before Russ was gathering our 4 pieces of luggage, and we were greeted by a very personable young lady from Princess Cruises. She guided us to where we would board a bus to our lodge and even called them for us. We had arrived a day early in Fairbanks, so we could do a little sightseeing on our own for a day. Russ had also made arrangements for a rental car. The young man from the bus picked up our luggage and loaded it on the bus like they didn't weigh anything at all. So now we are on our way to Pikes Waterfront Lodge! We are both happy and excited to finally be in Alaska.

Fairbanks is also known as Alaska's "Golden Heart City." It is located in Alaska's interior north where those beautiful aurora lights or northern lights can be seen in the winter months. Before the construction of the Alaska Highway, which was built in 8 months' time as a World War II supply route. Fairbanks was a bustling mining town then. The time here is 4 hours behind Eastern Standard Time and is called AST (Alaska Standard Time).

How beautiful! Everything we've seen up until now has been outstanding to say the least, and it just keeps getting better. Pikes Waterfront Lodge is one of the privately owned lodges used by

Princess Cruises, located on the Chena River. The rivers and streams in Alaska serve as both transportation and recreational areas linking cities and rural communities. We have a room with a balcony and we can watch people go up and down the river from here. It is 68 degrees and probably wouldn't feel so cold except that it is very windy. Since it is late we went over to the Pike's Landing Restaurant for dinner. Just a short walk and you are there and guess what; it is Mother's Day, so they are having a wonderful buffet. If you mention what you want to eat to the waiter; it was put on the table, and was delicious. There is a deck outside where you can eat if you prefer, overlooking the river. There are a lot of people out there in that cold weather, but it doesn't seem to be bothering them a bit. However, they look very cold with their red noses and cheeks, and not one with a coat or sweater, behaving as though it was barbecue weather in the south. A boat ramp is right here in between the restaurant and the lodge and Russ stopped to chat with a fellow that was getting ready to take his boat in the river.

The lobby in the lodge is decorated in a "Cabela" fashion with all sorts of animals decorating the walls and cabinets. Right in the center of the lobby is a huge jade rock on display worth $110,000 that was found in British Columbia. There is a gift shop right here too, where I met the nicest women working in there. It was very cozy, and as I browsed, I mentioned I was from Marietta. The lady with the blonde hair and the "to die for" figure was so surprised and said her sister was a doctor at the very hospital I just retired from. I just got a new meaning to "It's a small world," and you aren't going to believe this, but three months after I got home, I had a garage sale, and a woman came to it and said she worked at the hospital I retired from. I asked what department she worked in and she said mother-baby. I asked her if she knew that same doctor and believe it or not, she was a sister-in-law too. It surely is a "small world!"

We had lots of time left, so we decided to go down in the beautiful lobby and play some cards before we went to bed. There were round tables set up all around, near where the continental breakfast was being served that morning. A lot of people were sitting there watching TV, talking and just people watching. A woman approached us and began to talk to us like she was a long lost friend. I never saw anyone talk that much, and I've talked with a lot of people. By the time she left, we not only knew everything she did in her whole life but also her occupation, marital status, and the fact her husband didn't know how to handle his daughter. It's a good thing she was in his life to keep him in line. I'm being facetious now! After she left, Russ and I just looked at each other, flabbergasted and wondered what that was about. I'm sure she need someone, anyone, to talk to.

The native Alaskans say the sun doesn't set until 9:45 p.m., and I hate that we won't be able to see the Aurora. Now that is something I'd love to see but they say it's just too light in the summer months. Maybe we'll see it at the museum. We went to our beautiful room and Russ called a rental car agency to get a car for tomorrow so we can do a little sight-seeing and get acquainted with Fairbanks.

I couldn't resist, when I woke up at 10:45 p.m., the sun was still glowing across the Chena River outside of our bedroom window. Of course, I got a great picture of it on the camcorder and Russ never woke up. Sneaky, huh?

In the morning, a young woman named Aaron from Budget Rental Car Services picked us up in front of the lodge. A small world indeed, when we find out she is from Reading, PA, where Russ was born and raised. A great conversation flew around me as they shared experiences and places they hadn't thought of in a long time. I had to smile as I listened in on the conversation. Aaron said her husband was home on leave from the army and would be returning back to Iraq for the second time in the next few days. Another awakening while on vacation, back to reality, and I find myself saying a little prayer for all our men and women in the armed services. Here we are enjoying America while these brave men and women are out there keeping it safe for us to do so. We have two sons who served in the marines and I am very proud of that. They weren't in Iraq, but if that happened to be the time when they were in the marines, they would have been proud to protect our country. Most of the service men I have ever met feel the same way. I have a shirt I wear a lot that my sweet daughter-in-law gave me that reads on the front, "I may look harmless but I raised two marines." God bless them all.

The following morning we took our rental car and went to a huge store called Fred Meyers, where we bought hats and shirts and had subs for lunch. We ended up on Johansen Expressway where we found the greatest Wal-Mart. Russ was so impressed with a huge gun display, which we've never seen in a Wal-Mart before. We got some better binoculars and of course, my magnets (since I am collecting one from every state) and shirts that were half the price I paid in the gift shop. Next time its Wal-Mart first. From there, we went to the University of Alaska Museum.

We can see the contemporary structure of the university from far away. Within the University of Alaska is the "Museum of the North." It is an eye-catching snow white building, which wraps around in points and ridges and fits right in with the Alaskan culture. There are exhibits of native arts, geology, plants, birds, mammal specimens, and the geography and history of the region. I wonder if we found the right display for the aurora because it was small like a TV and I guess I expected something large and spectacular, but we didn't find that. One of the most interesting things to me, as we were walking into the museum, we saw a few cars in the parking lot that had plugs hanging out from under the front of the hoods. They were parked in front of what appeared to be a parking meter. But it wasn't. We discovered that in the winter, the Alaskans plug their cars up to these electrical meters to keep their engines warm; otherwise, they would freeze in their subzero temperatures in the winter months. Now, that is amazing. I never thought about what people do in such freezing temperatures before, and I guess I never really realized how bitterly cold Alaska can be.

Today we return our rental car to Aaron after filling it with gas, of course. It is finally our big day, our first day of our long-awaited "Princess" adventure. We chose Princess because everyone we had talked to so far had gone on their cruises through Princess Cruise Lines and what better source is there than "word of mouth?"

People are beginning to arrive at the lodge; these will be the people we travel with for two weeks. The Princess crew has also arrived and suddenly the little lobby appears as busy as an airport. The crew is manning a small desk in the front of the lobby in order to answer all questions and help with tickets, tags for suitcases and handing out the itinerary. Busy, but very organized, all questions being answered. We were given green tags to attach to the luggage for the land portion of the trip labeled "Travel with me" and pink tags for the luggage that will go on the ship ahead of us labeled "Join me on board ship." I wonder who thinks of all these wonderful ideas to organize. Now we are really getting excited. Tomorrow morning we are to be in the lobby 15 minutes early for an 8:30 a.m. date to go and pan for gold! Who knows what we will find! After that we will be taking a riverboat ride on an authentic sternwheeler called, "Discovery." What fun!

We are up and at 'em early, so we can have a quick continental breakfast and meet in the lobby for our bus. Our bus driver's name is Rob and oddly enough he is carrying a stuffed animal with him whom he calls "Binky." He says he stands with Binky or sits him in the windshield of the bus, so his riders can find him easily. I thought that was an excellent idea. The bus is huge, with Princess printed on the side in giant letters, and it is comfortable too. Everyone piles in for our next adventure, chattering with anticipation of striking it rich! It's an informative ride, Rob is so knowledgeable about Alaska, and seems to be able to answer any questions asked of him, making our ride seem short in time.

We arrived at the "El Dorado Gold Mine" where a little train is sitting there with open cars. It is a replica of the Tanana Valley Railroad and reminds me of the one we would always go on at the zoo with the kids. Such sweet memories. We stop for a couple of demonstrations. One gold miner with a pick-axe and a head lamp discussing how they looked for gold and the other demonstrating how they hauled the gold out of the mines the hard way. We enter a permafrost tunnel that is lined with prehistoric bones up to 30,000 years old and the conductor plays some old tunes on his fiddle. Then we meet two more colorful characters, Dexter and Yukon Yonda, who give us an entertaining demonstration on how to pan for gold in a sluice box with freezing water. As they lead us inside a covered area and hand us a "poke" of gold (a small bag), a pan and a bench next to a sluice with warm water (how nice), we pan for our gold with their assistance, if we need it. It was a little harder to do than I thought it would be, but I found a few chips of what I thought was gold. There were none in Russ's, so he asked Yonda if he was doing this right. She brought him another "poke" and he found some gold in that one.

After that we were led into a huge gift shop called the "Cook Shack" with counters set up in the center, where people weigh your gold in front of you. I could hear people saying theirs was $3.00 and $2.50, etc. I was disappointed because I was thinking ours was going to be worth something, but not anymore. When we got to the counter ours weighed in at a whopping $25.00! *We're rich!* So again, in front of you, they either put your gold in a little vial for you or in a necklace (remember the necklaces with the four leaf clovers in them in the '50s—like that). I had more than enough to go in the necklace with some left over, so Russ not only bought me the necklace and chain, but also earrings to match, in order to use the rest of the gold. Come to find out we got more gold than anyone on that bus. We then were offered complimentary fresh-baked cookies and coffee or hot chocolate and of course, I got my magnet and postcard in the huge gift shop.

With about one and a half hours left before our riverboat ride, we got lunch at Pike's restaurant again. Where you ate was pretty much dictated to you, because the choices nearby were very limited. Generally, the lodge restaurants were very expensive.

The Princess bus arrives once again for our "authentic stern-wheeler riverboat" named Discovery. I don't know how I missed it in our itinerary, but it turned out to be a surprise when our driver pulled in at the Trans-Alaska Pipeline. This is an 800-mile long crude oil pipeline that cost 8 billion dollars to construct in the 1970s. Alaska's economy has had quite a boost from the pipeline for more than three decades. It travels all the way from the Alaskan North Slope to the port of Valdez on Prince William Sound. It took 21,000 people from around the country to construct this marvel, and 31 of them were killed doing it. The pipeline crosses an active fault line, three mountain ranges and hundreds of rivers and creeks. The pipeline system is designed to withstand 8.5 on the Richter scale (maximum) and lateral movement of two feet. Much of the pipeline is buried and special ventilators that look like coils inside, called pigs, are used to keep the permafrost frozen and the line stable. Otherwise, underground, the heat of the oil would melt the ground and sink the pipe. The word *permafrost* confused me so I researched it to find that permafrost is soil at or below the freezing point of water (32 degrees F) and sometimes as low as 10 degrees F, as on the North Slope. It tolerates a considerable amount of thawing. Where we are standing the pipe sits on a cement piling, in the shape of a sled. It is not bolted because the pipe needs to contract and expand. There are also two poles on a post close to the pipeline that look like something out of a space movie. The post goes 70 feet down to keep it cool so the pipe doesn't melt the permafrost. As I said, this was a surprise tour, and one of our shortest, but one of the most interesting.

The Trans-Alaskan Pipeline

As we board back on the bus, I get the feeling people are staring at me and I get the feeling they are talking about me, too. Remember those feelings from our high schooldays? Finally, after getting half-way down the aisle on the bus, I asked one of the ladies, "Is there something wrong?" She said, "Oh, we are just talking about your beautiful gold necklace and earrings." Which of course, I am wearing! Wow, all that over $25.00! Whoo hoo!

We are welcomed aboard for a 3-and-a-half-hour ride down the Chena River. There are about 900 people boarding the Discovery III riverboat, which is owned by Capt. Jim and Mary Binkley. This is not new to them, the narrator explains, as the riverboat business has been passed down through the Binkley family for a hundred years. A bush pilot greets us and shows us how they take off and land on pontoons on the river. We are told that the people in that area do not put up fences because they use their backyards as runways in the winter months. Imagine a plane going by in your backyard.

The Tanana River is beautiful and we can see old buildings on shore as we pull up to Susan Butcher's Trail Breaker Kennels. She was a four-time winner of the Trail Sled Dog Race in Alaska. As you probably know, Susan lost the battle to leukemia in 2006. However, her husband and children show off her Iditarod champion sled dogs, some adorable pups and give an actual demonstration of them in action as they pull a 4-wheeler. All the dogs were so excited, jumping and barking and wanting to take off, and that they did. They pulled that 4-wheeler all over and around and back. You could see all the other dogs in the kennel, barking and rooting for their buddies as they ran around them. It is reported that Mushers take excellent care of their dogs and treat them as part of the family.

The riverboat has four viewing decks, the top deck is open and the three lower decks are enclosed in glass, heated and set up with 19 viewing monitors, so no matter where you sit you have a good seat. I can't remember having to look at the monitor even once, the view was so open. All of a sudden we see a little beaver swimming along the river; just love it. Next we come up to a demonstration off shore of a woman cleaning salmon and a drying shack next to her, where they dry the salmon and feed it to the dogs. There are also birch trees on shore with their beautiful white bark. The riverboat is moving slowly at about 13 miles an hour and to our right there are a few reindeer, behind a gate, running around. We come upon the Chena Village, which resembles the original Chena Athabasca Indian Village of the early 1900s.

We disembark and it seems to be getting colder, we are all bundled up and ready for that though. We have a short walk through the woods where we spend an hour visiting. Reindeer and their adorable little calves are standing behind a big fence and, of course, we are getting all kinds of great pictures. Then there is a demonstration of beadwork and animal skin-sewing by Dixie Alexander who is a natural Athabasca Indian. She actually resides in the Chena Village in the summer months. Her artistic bead work is fantastic as is the coat one of the girl's is modeling. These people are very proud of their heritage and you can tell that when they talk; by their proud and bubbly nature. The coat being demonstrated was made of timber wolf furs sturdily sewn with carefully chosen beads, which used to be made of seeds and the buttons are crafted from moose and caribou. There is wolverine fur around the hood next to her face, which she said has natural oil in its fur to keep the head warm. The speaker also said that if a woman would walk into another village, the women there would know what village she was from, simply by the way the coat was designed.

We were all sitting on long benches to watch the demonstrations. There was a gentleman sitting in front of us with a hat on, when I noticed there was one of those giant mosquitoes sitting on his hair, around the bottom of his hat by his neck. My impulse was to whack it one, good thing I stopped to think, because if it was Russ I would have automatically done it. But I kept an eagle eye on it just in case it got on skin, then I probably would have nudged him to tell him. The Alaskans say Alaska is infamous for the size and quantity of their mosquitoes and they kiddingly refer to them as their unofficial "state bird." They say many a vacation has been turned into a nightmare because of them. They have all kinds of secrets to avoid them such as DEET, which blocks out the carbon dioxide detector in the mosquito, which they are attracted to from your skin. They also suggest you get a bug jacket?? and/or wear light-colored clothes? It sounds to me like you need a butterfly net and a bulletproof vest. I was wondering what a mosquito is doing in this cold weather, anyway. I can only imagine how big they must be in the summer.

The village consisted of huts (one covered with evergreen branches and one with furs), cabins, a cache for storing food above the ground with pelts of wolf and coyote hanging in the front, a canoe made of birch bark, a smoke house (the odor was not pleasant there), and more salmon drying racks. In the center of it all was a large gated area with more of Susan Butcher's dog team and some of them jumped up on big boxes to be petted. Upon exiting the Village at the water's edge was a fish wheel that can catch up to 1,000 fish in a day, in the summer months. It was relaxing to hear the wheel as it turned, hitting the water in a continuous splashing sound, like waves.

It was time to board the Riverboat once again and it has gotten very cold and breezy. We are treated to a snack of salmon, cheese and crackers. I am not a salmon fan, but it honestly was very good. There is a little eatery on board also, called "Captain Jim's Galley," where you can order regular beef hot dogs or reindeer chili dogs, Alaskan reindeer chili and, of course, a little gift shop. As we disembark from our fun riverboat we end up at the Steamboat Landing Gift Shop, which claims to be the largest family owned gift shop in Alaska.

After the bus carries us back to the lodge, we decided we'd had enough food in Pike Landing's restaurant, so we took the shuttle, and ate at a restaurant in town. Not to say Pike's didn't have great food, but we just needed to get away from fine dining. We decided to get to bed early, so we'd be rested up for our train ride to Denali in the morning. We had to have our luggage out in the hall by 8:00 p.m. In the back of my mind, I always wondered how they could keep up with all that luggage, but they did a fantastic job. We never had a problem and I certainly didn't hear of anyone else having one either.

Rise and shine for another beautiful day. We got up early so we could get to the continental breakfast again and it was *gone*! Much to our surprise there is a large buffet breakfast and there was a charge, of course. We were all surprised and confused and I'm sure everyone felt the same way we did—*disappointed!* There were a lot of us grumbling over that one. Their excuse was because it was the first day of the season! What? I wasn't sure what "season" they meant. A celebration of charging the customers season; it somehow doesn't make sense to me.

Well, naturally we weren't going to let something like that spoil our new day. We were all taken to the Princess train by bus. It was a glass covered train surrounding the sides and roof so we could see everything on the way in to Denali. This is one of the special side trips we signed up for.

While we were waiting for everyone to board, there was a train loaded with truck trailers a couple tracks over from us. It was so interesting to watch them being unloaded by a tractor with long robot arms that literally lifted them off the train. We were sitting with some women from Taiwan who seemed as interested as we were and started asking us questions about it. Russ, having worked for a trucking line for so many years, narrated the whole procedure as it unfolded in front of us. Amazing the small things you see unexpectedly that you've never seen before and the wonder that goes with it. We watched the hostlers come in their tractors and hook up to the trailers and take them to another location in the yard away from the track. Strange, how we came all the way to Alaska to experience something that happens back home every day! Oh, how I love it!

Our train began to roll about 15 mph to start with, and again like a kid, I was all excited. Inside the car we could hear the click clack of the wheels. We could see the University of Alaska in the distance. They were serving breakfast in the dining car if you cared to dine there. While Russ dozed for a little while, our guide, Fallon, who was great, very knowledgeable, sweet and an outstanding speaker, kept us abreast of what we were looking at, and a little history to go with it.

When Russ woke up, he had a cup of coffee and I had a cup of hot chocolate. Finally, far in the distance we could see some "critters." We could see moose (meese? mice?-Ha-don't you think it should be mooses?), far out in the distance and some small Dall sheep up on the mountain side, that looked like tiny white dots. Thank goodness I had binoculars and Russ had a zoom on the camcorder or we wouldn't have been able to see them at all. They guarantee sighting of reindeer, yeah, well, they're behind a fence! Our speed is anywhere between 35 and 55 mph as the multi-shades of green pass us by. How relaxing this is. Also there are black spruce, birch, and pine trees dotted throughout the scenery.

We stop to watch another train pass next to us and it seems dangerously close, I thought I might have to brace myself for a collision, but I'm sure the conductor knows what he is doing. None of the people on the train passing us seemed worried as they were all making funny faces at us and waving with great big silly smiles. Funny! I bet their conductor put them up to it. Ha!

As we continue on, we are seeing some fabulous snow-capped mountains in this strikingly rich land. Approaching Denali there are stop signs for cars to stop for our train, no gates, and sometimes there are as many as two cars waiting there for us to pass. Fallon says three cars are considered a traffic jam in Alaska. We cross over the Tanana River and the Continental Divide. All the water to the right of us is flowing north.

We are taken to the Denali Princess Wilderness Lodge; the lodge is huge and made of logs that are reddish in color, almost Georgia clay color. There are many large groupings or sections of buildings, sections divided around the grounds perfectly placed, with restaurants all around (it was about $29.00 for a salmon dinner at the King Salmon Restaurant and $30.00 for a steak), a dinner theater, several gift shops, a large and beautifully designed lobby, and statues of different critters like moose, placed along the paths and streets. When we got to our room our luggage was there waiting for us. That is so amazing! Princess is so organized, that's for sure. Of course, the gift shop was first, for my usual post cards and magnet. Our day ended with a very expensive pizza, as we were surrounded by a winter wonderland that God had landscaped perfectly by His hand.

We had asked the desk to call us early, but no call. It's a good thing I wake up early because we had to be in the lobby between 6:15 a.m. and 6:20 a.m. to meet our bus. Our trip today would take us on the "Tundra Teklanika Tour." In other words, a big yellow bus was going to take us on a tour of Denali National Park. We could hardly wait because we knew we would surely see some critters now. We had just enough time to eat at the dinner theater where breakfast is served in a home-type situation where we pass the food on the table to one another. We ate, but I hate to say the food was cold. Other people we ate with from our group also stated theirs was cold as well. Our breakfast there was $24.00 and I did get a chance to try reindeer sausage for the first time. Tasted good to me, I couldn't tell the difference.

As we boarded the bus and found a seat, there was a boxed lunch sitting on our seats for us which I thought was a nice gesture. It only took a few minutes from the lodge to reach Denali National Park. We were actually scheduled for the 8-hour tour, but there was too much snow so we could only do a 5-hour tour. We were really disappointed because we would have gone deeper into the park, otherwise. Our bus is a light yellow and white with very squeaky windows, but we are allowed to keep the windows down on the top half so we can lean out and take pictures.

Denali National Park is larger than the state of Massachusetts spreading across 6 million acres of beautiful, wild country with only one 2-lane road to get you there, which after the first 15 miles turns into a narrow winding gravel road. The first 15 miles, up to the Savage River, is paved, and the only road visitors can go it alone, unless you take a shuttle or a tour bus to continue on the whole 91 miles to the Kantishna Mining community. The park's first concern is for the wild animals. This is their home and we are the guests here. We need to respect that and not the other way around. We are told that in the winter months the park rangers do patrols in dog sleds. The weather here can change rapidly at any given moment, so we all dressed in layers, to be on the safe side.

The very first thing we see on the side of the road is a cute fluffy little bunny with great big feet. I was corrected immediately, it is not a rabbit it is a snow-shoed hare. The hare is brown on his back with white tipped ears, some white on his face and white chest and feet. Our guide says he is completely white in the winter snow and is now gradually turning brown with a very little white. But it was adorable and Russ got a great shot of it on the camcorder, which has become our new best friend (the camcorder, that is). We saw many more hares and both male and female willow ptarmigans (the p is silent.) These are beautiful birds with red around its eyes, a beautiful bronze neck and shoulders and the rest is white with some of the bronze kissing the rest of his body. About the size of a chicken he is an amazing creation. They were putting on quite a show for the females, it is mating season.

There is such beauty and grace surrounding us with snow still covering most of the mountains. The very highest point of the mountains is called the alpine, 10,000 feet or more in elevation (only warm-blooded animals live here); the tundra is a vast open and treeless plain with an artic or sub-artic climate and a layer of permanently frozen soil several inches below the surface. It is steep and rugged. The taiga forest is covered with dense vegetation, trees and underbrush at a lower elevation. Our guide informs us that in the fall, in a very short period of time (about two weeks), everything dramatically turns the beautiful colors of orange, red, and yellow.

Any time someone sees a critter, the bus driver stops so everyone can get pictures and get a good look. We see several more hares, and suddenly someone spots some caribou in the distance. The difference between a caribou and a reindeer, Russ says, is the reindeer is the same animal only in captivity, and the caribou just lives in the wild. Our guide was informative and stopped frequently both for sites of animals and potty breaks. The landscape is awesome and the huge mountains look like castles in the sky. Our guide says there are people up on those monstrous mountains climbing, because this is the season for it. He says about 1,000 people try to climb Mt. McKinley every year, but only half succeed. Life-saving rescues are not unusual in Denali. Sometimes back-packers are missing and dog teams are sent to look for them. On June 15th and 16th of 2008, not only dog teams, but 3 aircraft failed to find 2 such hikers. In July 2008, a 51-year-old man from Illinois collapsed and died while attempting to climb the Summit. CPR was administered for 45 minutes to no avail. And the list goes on of those who dare to challenge the dangerous and mysterious mountains of Alaska.

Another interesting fact found in the Visitor's Guide says dinosaur tracks, just recently discovered in 2005, show for the first time that prehistoric creatures did live there once. Since then, many more fossil discoveries have been found throughout the park.

The Grizzlies in Denali National Park

Suddenly, our guide stops the bus and says he sees something moving in the brush toward us. He wasn't sure what, and then he said he thought it might be a wolf, no, it's a grizzly and her cubs! Talk about excited, everyone on the bus was scrambling to get their pictures. Mom prisses herself right in front of our bus with her two cubs close behind and walks to the left side of the bus where we are sitting. Our guide says the cubs have probably been with their mom for about a year now. There is a man parked on the side of the road ahead of us with his camper and he is squatting next to it taking pictures, with his back to the grizzly. I scream, "There is a man in the road and he doesn't see the bears." The momma bear moves along slowly because she knows the road is hers and the two little cubs follow. The man realizes the bears are there now and he is only a few feet away. I thought he'd back up slowly and get in his camper, but he didn't, he continued to film the bears. How stupid is that? I saw the momma bear turn around and look at her cubs as if to say "Are you afraid, because if you are, I am going to take care of this brazen human." But the cubs were playful and so cute bouncing around and didn't seem to care one bit about all the strangers gawking at them.

Everyone is hanging out the window trying to get their picture and we got quite a few good shots of the backs of people's heads, as well as some good shots of the grizzlies. I would have never known they were grizzlies. I would have thought they were brown bears. The difference is in the shape of their noses. Heck, who's going to take time to look at the shape of the nose, not me! Everyone on the bus is so excited as the bears continue on and finally into the brush. We never expected to see a grizzly. They are looking for food. *What a great tour!*

We stopped again and had our lunches on the bus. The lunches were good, but what amazed me the most was how our guide painstakingly collected all plastic in one bag and the rest of the trash in the other bag, as we all got off the bus to potty and stretch our legs. I became convinced how much the tour guides respected the beautiful and natural wilderness around us and how very careful the park is that the animals didn't pick trash up from visitors' litter that could harm them.

Our guide was from North Carolina. He came up here on vacation to the park one time and fell in love with Alaska. He now comes up every summer and drives the tour buses and feels Alaska truly is the last frontier. I have noticed that a lot of people that work at the lodges and the national parks do the very same thing. What a great idea for the teens too that work in the restaurants and shops. They get to visit the parks, and see sights they may never get to see otherwise.

Refreshed and with full tummies, we resume our tour. Our next stop was an owl's nest high in the trees, our guide knew right where it was and stopped for us to look and photograph it. He said the nest would probably only be there about a month.

We are entranced with the mountains reflecting in the Tamika River. Next, the Sanctuary River is snaking through the pine trees and brush, with ice and snow still on the edges with only a very thin ribbon of water that had finally melted the snow in the center. The Alaskan range behind all this is glaring white and extends as far as 600 miles. We got some heavenly pictures, what else can you call them, because it did feel like that's where we were—*heaven!*

Totally Alaska taken in Denali National Park

On the return trip, we continued to see more hares and more ptarmigans, but after seeing the grizzly bears, it seemed that everything else was minor now, even though it was beautiful and unusual. Off in the distance, we could see more caribou and then way far out we came upon our grizzly family once again. You could hardly make them out but they looked like they were rummaging or eating something. Russ got a zoom picture of them on the hillside with the camcorder. We love this camcorder.

Our last sighting of the tour was a huge moose in the shallow water, surrounded by ice and snow. What a sight that was, they are so big. The tour was great even if we only did the 5 hours and all the excitement of the day wore us out. So we decided to take a nap. After all, we did get up early… ZZZZZZZZZZZ

Back at the lodge, it is so peaceful and the birds are chirping against the rivers bubbling sounds. There is a branch in front of me with sweet tiny pink flowers to prove spring is here, yet in contrast, winter still lurks with chunks of ice on the sides of the river. It is said that the Alaskans bet on what they call the "break-up;" the first split of the ice. They bet money on the date and even the time and whoever gets the closest wins the pot.

For dinner, we went back to the pizza place and we are still bumping into the friendliest people including our friends from Taiwan. Russ claimed the attention of the whole restaurant, because the main question everyone asked was "What did you all do today? Did you see anything?" (Not everyone was on the same bus.) The grizzly bear tale seemed to be the most interesting of all. Luggage had to be set out by 8:00 a.m., so we got that ready, played a game of cards, and nestled in to dream of Mt. McKinley Wilderness Lodge.

We got our luggage out early and went over to the main lobby to eat at the little snack bar with all kinds of fattening things. We had a little extra time so we took a little sight-seeing ride on the tram around the grounds and visited the Rapids Restaurant on the Nenana River. They had a huge selection of food and it made me wish we had eaten there. Check out from the lodge is 11:00 a.m., and then our coach will be here to pick us up at 1:00 p.m.

At 1:30 p.m., we boarded the coach to Mt. McKinley Princess Wilderness Lodge for a two-hour ride. We are all full of anticipation and somewhat anxious because our guide says Mt. McKinley and all the mountains surrounding it don't show themselves very often. He said, maybe only 6 days out of the year are you able to see all of them at one time because of the clouds hiding them. Our guide tells us a story about an old man, a miner, from the old days who built himself a little shack in an area close to Mt. McKinley. As the story goes, this old man had a tendency to drink too much. One day several months later, he woke up, went outside, and lo and behold there stood Mt. McKinley! He was so in shock that God had put a mountain there in the middle of the night, he stopped drinking because he had never seen it before! *It's a miracle!*

Finally, Russ gets to see another moose and what a beautiful sight. They are such huge graceful animals. And the scenery is stunning, dominating our brains with mountains laced in white snow everywhere we look. We never knew there were so many mountains in America. Mt. McKinley is the tallest mountain in North America, standing a massive 20,320 feet or four miles high, and growing about an inch a year, plus it is surrounded by six million acres. Hallelujah, we could see it, and couldn't wait to get out of the coach and run as close to the mountain as we were allowed, so we could photograph it before it went away. We disembarked right in front of the lodge and ran through a huge lobby that we never even stopped to look at. We rushed to the back where there was a gigantic deck to accommodate all the tourists, to either stand at the railing or sit in one of their comfortable chairs. The striking view in front of us could hardly be taken in as the sparkling white mountain was framed in the most gorgeous blue sky. Russ couldn't stop filming, to the point that I had to remind him that it was an inanimate object, and wasn't going anywhere. I think we were afraid it would though because we were told so many times we'd be lucky if we could see it. But this is not luck in my book; it was purely a gift from God. So far, we have seen so much captivating scenery and magic wilderness, our hearts were literally singing. We began to get chilled, so right behind the deck was an area you could sit inside, surrounded with windows in order to take it all in a little longer.

Mt. Mckinley Alaska

I don't know how long we stood there, but after some time, and taking pictures with my little disposable camera; first with us in front of the mountain, then pictures of the mountain at an angle, pictures of it from inside, and pictures of the mountains around it. But when we finally turned around, almost surprised, we realized we were standing in a beautiful lobby at Mt. McKinley Princess Wilderness Lodge. Russ began talking to the security guard and once again we were told how fortunate we were, since the people who arrived there yesterday didn't get to see the mountain because it was shrouded in clouds. How awful to come all the way to Alaska and not be able to see the "Great One," as some Alaskans call it. Not only could we see Mt. McKinley, but all the mountains on each side of it, which is even rarer.

Our little Princess guide letter tells us that in the months of March and April combined, there was approximately 125 inches of snowfall here. The weather changes so fast and so often that the front desk agents will add you to an "alert list" and call you if the mountain is "out." That's why it is important to always read the information Princess leaves for you so you become an informed guest. It also gives information on any extra excursions, restaurants, paths to walk, etc.

We walked over to our assigned room to see if our luggage had arrived as scheduled and good ole faithful Princess saw to it, it was. It would be an hour before the restaurant would open so of course, gift shop here I come! With a little time to spare, we went back to look at the mountain, just to make sure we weren't dreaming, and take even more pictures!

We ate at the "20,320" Alaskan Grill and they sat us next to a window so we could view the mountain the whole time we ate! We considered taking one of the excursions but it was getting late, so we decided to pass on it this time. Russ did get on the computer at the lodge to find out how our little football friend on the plane was doing (Luke). His name (and his brother's name) was there on the team's roster, as he just got signed as a team member of the Fairbanks Grizzlies football team. Hooray for him!

We ended our exciting day relaxing in the glass closed portion of the lobby, coffee in hand, just sitting and staring at the sky high mountain that sits there in its glory like no other. It doesn't get any better than this!

When we woke the next morning the mountain was hiding, much to our disappointment, but it just proves what everyone had said, that it is not visible every day. Our luggage was out by 8:00 a.m. for Princess to load up again for another trip on the bus. We did play in the snow a little while, throwing snow balls at each other and just feeling glad to be alive. We feel so blessed. Thanks God!

Boarding onto another bus we are in route to Anchorage where we will spend the night at the Hotel Captain Cook. But first we stop at the Alaska Native Heritage Center. We visited the Hall of Cultures to understand the different Alaskan natives, such as languages, geographic proximity, symbols, masks, hunting tools, drums, bows, animals, clothing, and artwork.

We saw a movie in the theater then we were escorted to the "Gathering Place" where young men showed us some of the games they played and then some elders and young people sang in costume, one gentleman had his adorable young child about 3 years old on stage with him, and he sang along with them and played a little drum.

We returned to the bus, our guide once again extremely informative and cute as a button. Her name was Freedom, and that was really a coincidence because Russ had his America shirt on that said "Freedom" at the bottom. She said he was wearing her shirt. As we traveled on toward Anchorage, we passed a shack that had the name of Wal-Mike. That was really funny; it looked like a flea market with all kinds of goods piled in front of the store.

Hotel Captain Cook was our destination in downtown Anchorage. Another privately owned hotel. This is considered Anchorage's only true luxury hotel close to the Cook Inlet. Cook Inlet stretches 180 miles from the Gulf of Alaska with the Chugach Mountains behind, which are the northern most mountain range of the Pacific Coast Ranges. Its position along the gulf ensures more snowfall in the Chugiak than anywhere else in the world, with an average of 600 inches. There really wasn't much time for us to explore Anchorage, we only had the rest of the day to spend there.

Anchorage is Alaska's largest city and probably best known for the "Good Friday Quake" of 1964. The earthquake measured an unusually large 9.2 on the Richter scale making it the strongest North American quake in recorded history.

We arrived at the hotel around 4:00 p.m. and immediately walked around the lobby and gift shop where I went to buy another camera. The cashier was extremely rude, so I wished her a good day and left without the camera. It was cold outside but not too cold to try to find a place to eat. We walked for several blocks trying to find something that didn't cost an arm and a leg, but that was impossible except for one small place that had sandwiches and looked like a dump. So we wound up at a restaurant called Brewery House. We wound up paying $61.00 for our meal without any dessert or extras, but that meal was out of this world!

After dinner, we decided to walk it off and walked to a little park right off the ocean where children were playing and giggling and swinging, while the parents kept a watchful eye. In the far distance, we could see an enormous freighter passing by very slowly. In between the park and the ocean was pure emptiness extending hundreds of feet because the tide was out. I would have thought it was dirty sand, but it was called "silt," or mud flats, like a quicksand almost. People are warned not to go near it because you would be stuck there for a very long time. There are warnings not to get in the water any time of the year because of the mud. When the tide comes in there, it may come as high as 25 to 30 feet high! That is a really high tide. Behind the park and right at the edge of the mud was a trail to walk that went for 11 miles. Instead we took a walk around a few of the streets in the neighborhood. It looked like a rather poor neighborhood from the shape of the homes and the up-keep.

Once we got back to the hotel and found the elevators, a man was there already holding the door open, so I proceeded to step in. He said, "Oh, no, ma'am, this elevator is reserved," and with that, several suited men and a woman (that looked like spies or something) hurriedly stepped into the elevator and closed it almost in my face. I just stood there in shock; I was beginning to think I was in a

007 movie! Who reserves an elevator anyway? Okay, I get it, probably politicians, government, or military people of some kind.

I understand that some places in Alaska don't have air-conditioning, but you would think a "luxury" hotel would have. It was so hot we had our window open which made for a very noisy and restless night. At about 5:00 a.m., a very loud alarm went off and sounded for about 5 minutes. I looked out the window and there were a bunch of black cars and people running into them and some guy entering the building with a flash light. I guess he was trying to stop the alarm, which was screeching with great intensity and then the cars quickly pulled off. I'm assuming it was the people we saw getting on the elevator earlier. We *are* in a 007 movie! Weird!

The next morning, we had to have our suitcases ready again by 8:00 a.m. but since Princess didn't own this hotel; we couldn't leave them in the hall but left them in our room instead for pick up. For lack of a restaurant elsewhere, we ate breakfast in the hotel which was very good and I have to be honest and say that I did ask people at the desk if they knew anything about the commotion last night. But they denied knowing anything about it. Hmmm.

On the bus on the way to the train station, we saw scenery full of stunning snow-covered mountains and rivers that continue nonstop for the whole half-hour ride. Not to mention the graceful swans and their babies swimming in one of the lakes. It's amazing, no matter how ugly a baby may be, they are still so cute.

All aboard for a ride on the Alaska railroad for a ride across the wild country. The train is an outstanding yellow and black in color. The Alaska Railroad is the last full-service railroad in the United States, meaning it carries both freight and passengers through major ports and towns in Alaska. The railroad is now owned by the state of Alaska and offers tours of Alaska that pass through the best scenery of all. I don't know how there can be a best when all around us is nothing but *the* best.

It will be another half hour and we will be in Whittier to board the Coral Princess Cruise Ship. We are ready to stay put for the next seven days and just enjoy the ship. We are really getting excited to do the cruise as treasures are still unfolding in front of us, fabulous mountains, Dall sheep, waterfalls from the snow run-off and the lulling sound of the train as it curves around mountains and the river. It was interesting to see the front end of the train as we took the curves. We also passed through the area where the earthquake hit in 1964 (on Good Friday), where you could still see evidence of several landslides and the snow had to be cleared from both sides of the track. The railroad suffered $27 million in damages in just 5½ minutes in that quake. But believe it or not, within one week, the rails were repaired, and the train was back on track (no pun intended!)

At last in the distance, we could see the ship and I got butterflies in my stomach. This is the part of the Alaskan adventure that I was looking forward to the most. We have so many excursions planned plus the cruise itself, and this is what we had been dreaming of for so long, and now it is sitting right in front of us.

CHAPTER 6

On Sea and Some by Land, See

It is May 19th and a beautiful sunny day in Whittier at 49 degrees, windy and cold. But it could have been a snow storm for all I cared, seeing that beautiful huge ship sitting there in front of us. It has been a long, exciting and busy week, but we are ready to get on that cruise ship. This has been our dream, and to our delight, we will nestle into our haven for seven whole days, for an adventure we can't even begin to imagine. The ship is sitting there with the railroad and hundreds of fishing boats on one side and huge snow-topped mountains on the other side. We are thinking, if this is any indication of what the rest of the trip will look like, it will truly be our memory of a lifetime. There are rows and rows of boats, and the thing we notice, having lived in Florida for so long, is that the cabins of the boats are all closed in. Indicating how cold it is up here on the water, versus the open boats in Florida where it is so hot.

Whittier is approximately 65 miles south of Anchorage, lying at the base of the Chugach Mountains bordering Passage Canal. Whittier was established as a World War II secret supply port for cargo and troops of the Alaska Command until 1960. It is a unique but small town with only approximately 290 residents relying largely on the fishing industry, the port, and increasingly on tourism. We'll only be spending a couple hours here, mostly getting on to the ship and getting settled, which doesn't leave much time to explore this beautiful town.

As we are getting ready to board, we face a long covered white tunnel that people are walking through to get to the ship. We don't care if it's 5 hours, we would have stood there until tomorrow if that's what it took. It took about 45 minutes to get inside. Once we did we had to fill out a little form declaring we did not have the flu and that we were not presently sick. There has been a worldwide increase of mild gastrointestinal illness, and Princess is doing everything they can to be sure no one gets ill on board. Finally, we are one of the last to go to a counter and show our tickets which took probably all of two minutes. Then passports and security, where this time, I had no trouble at all just walking around the security check and we were fine. Actually, it all went pretty well considering there are 2,000 or more people boarding the ship.

This is not our first cruise, we have been to the Bahamas before, for three days (the first time I retired), but still, the excitement was almost the same as the first time. Well, it is the first time for Alaska. As soon as we step on the ship, there is a photographer who kind of swoops us over to the side and takes our "welcome on board" picture. Of course, after being outside, I look like some kind of wild woman. We got to the lobby, which to me is like a theater all decorated with beautiful bright, colorful lights everywhere. All the smiling employees are standing in the lobby and in the halls, greeting and guiding the guests to their rooms. Cheerful music abounds and the air around us is jovial with eager to help employees, some trying to offer us a drink in glasses that light up. After we are guided to the elevator, some that talk to you and tell you what floor you are on, we find our room.

Our room or stateroom is huge compared to the one we were in when we went to the Bahamas. We had to climb over each other to get in the bed and could barely move our luggage on that cruise. That's the difference in the costs though. But this room is wonderful; with a queen-size bed, a huge closet, a small refrigerator (if you take a drink from it such as a soda or water, your stateroom steward will simply add it to your charges and then replace it with another) and a balcony where we could see the blue, blue ocean and the mountains full of snow. The balcony is such a treat. We would stand out there in cold weather; looking here and then there feeling suspended in time for a little while, enjoying that moment.

One of the neatest things about cruising is the convenience of the little card the cruise line gives you that looks like a credit card. You never have to use cash, or deal with change, because you simply hand over your little "credit card" for anything you purchase on board and at the end of the cruise, an itemized statement is delivered to your stateroom. Oh, and there is a little safe in the room to put your wallet or valuables in as well.

The ship will not be departing until 9:30 p.m., which means none of the gift shops or casino will open until we are out to sea. All the more time to walk around and explore the ship, the different floors, pools, and decks, and it seems like we are still the only ones in our movie once again. I don't know if everyone else is still in their rooms or what, but they sure aren't out on the deck. We went on a little stroll and took pictures of all the restaurants, cafes, lounges, the casino, pools, the beautiful staircase in the lobby all lit up like Hollywood and we stopped to listen to the piano player as we walked in and out of the main lobby. It was strange to see a swimming pool on the top deck surrounded by snowy mountains; it is very cold, but gorgeous! We found some lounge chairs facing the mountains and just sat there alone for a little while and it was such a serene, memorable time.

We went up to the all-you-can-eat-anytime-"trough," and ate until our hearts were content, or should I say stomachs? What a selection of food, oh, my goodness, I was in hog (great choice of words) heaven, well, heck, who is going to diet on a cruise?

By the time we get back to our room, our "join me on board" luggage is sitting right there in the middle of the floor. Princess, you are good! The ship started in motion at 9:30 p.m. as scheduled, and we walked on toward the lounge to see the 10:00 p.m. *Welcome Aboard Showtime* starring comedian Hal Spear. He was very funny and the dancers were excellent entertainers. What a great way to get started on our fun-filled week. Later we went back to our balcony. There were mountains as far as we could see and at 11:30 at night, a beautiful sunset. I couldn't get over that, 11:30 at night and a sunset. *Wow!*

Sunrise is at 4:55 a.m. and I am right there on that balcony to see that too. There are pieces of ice in the water and we are in the south end of College Fjord (a fjord is a narrow inlet in the coastal sea with steep sides often formed by glacier action) where it is about 46 degrees. *Brrrr!* We will cruise on up Prince William Sound. Our announcer says the name of the Sound was changed from Sandwich Sound to Prince William Sound in honor of King William's third son. Prince William would later become King William IV and nick-named "Silly Billy" because, our announcer adds, he was not a particularly effective king.

I am out on the balcony again bundled up in a heavy coat with a hood and gloves and my camcorder. I don't plan on missing a thing even if I do feel like an icicle. We took a walk out on the deck and it had sprinkled a little. Back to our balcony and you could see a lot of people out on their balconies as well. An announcement came over the loud speaker and the captain said some sea lions had been spotted. It is a huge colony of them, barking and splashing into the water. It is a very small piece of beach in front of the mountains. There is also a little sea otter between us and the sea lions. Wow! Nature at its best! The captain slowed the ship down so we could all get a good look, they really do have the passengers in mind, and I can see that the crew's true goal is to make it a pleasant and exciting trip for us.

A huge fin in the water passes me by and I scream for Russ to come see. It had to be an orca whale because no dolphin or humpback whales have fins that big. Since I was so excited, our neighbor in the room next to us came running out on their balcony too, but it was too late. She said, "Yell again if you see anything else," in a loud high-pitched voice that sounded like Edith Bunker, because by now I am the only one stupid enough to stand out on the balcony in this freezing weather. It is quite hazy and the outlines of the mountains look like a whisper of a painting.

We ate breakfast in the Province Room with a group of fun and interesting people from Australia. It was nice to sit and chat with them as we ate and shared similarities and experiences. We will spend the day at sea today and just relax and enjoy. There are all kinds of activities going on (fruit and vegetable carving, art auctions, and wine tasting but tonight we will attend the production show and then see the comedian/magician later). When we returned to our room, we immediately went out on the balcony and spotted two or three whales. We could see them blow from their spouts in the distance, cruise in and out of the water and then dove and showed us their massive tails. It is 41 degrees out here! And the scenery is stunning. We feel compelled to stand here and embrace awesome Alaska.

Princess provides a channel that informs us at all times, where we are, how long it will take to get to the next destination, weather conditions, and overhead they announce it if they see anything, like the sea lions, whales, etc., and where to look to see them. So they keep us well informed.

Someone is yelling in an excited voice, you know the sound, and I realize they are yelling, "There is a bear out there!" It was really hard to see, but we could pick it up on the zoom on the camcorder, and we could tell it was moving; otherwise, it would have been hard to tell it was anything other than a big black spot. But, it was in fact, a bear way far away. We remained on the balcony. The excitement calmed down and we saw another whale in the distance. We were sure this time because it spouted, came up two or three times and then did his beautiful tail thing. This country is full of endless wonders!

Today we will enter Glacier Bay around 10:15 a.m. There are many activities going on today, such as games, line dancing, cards, presentations by the park rangers, music, and an afternoon tea. Of course, one could always go to the gym, or play golf, and for those with young'uns, late night babysitting is offered if desired.

Glacier Bay has dozens of glaciers. Our "Princess Patter" (a daily newsletter) tells us that the ship will get as close as a quarter of a mile to the glaciers. Our hope is to see a glacier "calving," which is what happens when a large piece of ice cracks off the face of the glacier. That is a new word for me; I can't imagine why they call it that unless they are equating it with giving birth. But the captain takes the ship into the bay and does a U-turn, practically in slow motion, so that if calving does occur, we all get a chance to see it. All at once, people around us are screaming "look over there!" and it happens for us. Russ just barely got it on tape. I know sometimes it is a big slice of ice, but this time it wasn't that big, big enough to make a good splash though. I almost missed it, but at least we got to see it and there is the most heavenly color of blue behind the ice when it falls. Just like that, it's over! Awesome! We stayed in Glacier Bay until 8:00 p.m.

I didn't realize Glacier Bay was a national park and there is much more of it than we will see today, 3.3 million acres to be more accurate. The only way you can reach it is by boat or plane. Two hundred years ago, there was no bay. It was covered by ice. But by 1916, the glaciers had retreated 65 miles. Our "Official Map and Guide" states there is no such rapid retreat as this anywhere. But now it is calm and serene and the water is still and glassy.

After dinner, we will once again attend the production show and then see the comedy show time. The shows are all so entertaining and it is well worth trying to see them all. When we return to our room, our bed is turned down, as always, with a chocolate on our pillow. Only in your dreams! Ahhh!

Our ship docked in Skagway at 5:15 a.m. where once again it is about 48 degrees. We will stay in Skagway until 8:15 tonight. Skagway sits atop and marks the northernmost point of the Inside Passage. The name Skagway comes from an Indian name "Skagua," which means "the place where the north wind blows." This little town averages approximately 30 inches of rain per year and 39 inches of snow. There are approximately 16 to 18 hours of daylight during the summer months. If you really want to explore this cute little town with a population of less than 1,000, it would probably be on foot, taking a walk down Broadway with its false-front buildings. But this day, we are scheduled to take a trip on the White Pass and Yukon Route Railroad.

Oh boy, another train ride, only this time we will be zigging and zagging up some of the most rugged terrain in Alaska. We will climb nearly 3,000 feet over 20 miles of mountain. One can only imagine the manpower and determination it must have taken to cut through these treacherous mountains, ledges, and steep grades with weather sometimes plummeting to 60 below.

All aboard! The train is just a few feet from where our ship is docked. We found our seats and waited patiently for everyone to board. Our next adventure was about to begin as our train rolled to our favorite musical click-clack sound once again. We are starting out at sea level which is elevation 0. This is where it all began for the hopeful gold seekers as they struggled toward the Klondike gold-fields. The scenery is breathtaking already as we climb up higher and higher. The turns around the mountains are so sharp; we can see the engine in front of us like a long yellow and green caterpillar. It feels like we are on the edge of a cliff, maybe because we are, since the rail sits on a 10-foot-wide rail bed. But the track is very safe and maintained on a daily basis.

When this track was built, it was a $10 million project and it took tens of thousands of men to conquer this part of Alaskan wilderness, 35 of these men losing their lives. Our "All Aboard Magazine" also states it took only 24 months to construct. From Skagway to the Summit was solid granite, and they didn't use dynamite in those days. Instead, they used black powder for blasting. The mountains were so steep some of the men had to be suspended by ropes to prevent them from falling off while cutting the grade. Just imagine how they must have built the tunnels and the bridges. In the winter months in the past, they used what was called a "rotary snowplow," with 10 huge blades that looked like a giant fan on the front of the train. In reality, the plow was pushed by two helper engines and could move up to 12 feet of snow in order to clear the track.

To the right of us is the Tongass National Forest. After a couple miles, our narrator tells us of the cemetery to our right called the Gold Rush Cemetery, mostly for bandits and people who died in shootouts. After we'd traveled up 5.8 miles, we cross the Skagway River doing a U-turn over a beautiful bridge. This point is called Denver where a red caboose, fixed up like a cabin, is parked here and can be rented through the US Forest Service by hikers. As we come out of our turn, we can look down on Skagway, and see the River down below with whirlpools; this area is called Rocky Point. We have climbed to an elevation of 637 feet. What a dramatic scene with the mountains and glaciers in the background.

Our tour guide announces we are approaching an area where a blasting accident buried two railroad workers under a 100-ton granite rock. She reports that the rock was so big and heavy it could not be moved, so it became the men's grave. A black cross marks their resting place, and the area is called Black Cross Rock.

Bridal Veil Falls is our next scenic wonder, cascading down 6,000 feet. The first waterfall we've seen since our adventure began. Striking! We have traveled uphill 11.5 miles now. At 16 miles up, we go over a bridge and then through a tunnel known as Tunnel Mountain, on a curve no less, which made it great to get a picture of the train, tunnel, and bridge all in one shot. It was like someone had turned the lights out. After passing through the tunnel, we were right on the very edge of the mountain, when someone yelled "Bear"! Everyone ran to that side of the train, and I looked right into that bear's eyes. He had such a determined look with his paws on the edge and pulling his giant body up the hill, like there was no stopping him. He didn't seem to care that the train was there at all. Russ tried to get him on the camcorder but couldn't get to him fast enough. That black bear was determined all right because the conductor said the train behind us was yelling "bear on the tracks"! Wow, it all happened so fast. Now that's what I call seeing a "critter"! I hate that I got to see him and Russ didn't. The comradeship on these tours is very interesting. When a fellow-traveler spots a critter or any exciting occurrence, they want to experience that moment with everyone else! It's priceless!

Now at 17.5 miles, we are passing through Dead Horse Gulch where 3,000 pack animals were killed from being overloaded and neglected during the gold rush. At 18.6 miles, we are passing Steel Bridge built in 1901, now reconstructed and being used since 1969. It is threatening to see the bridge broken and aged so high up in the mountains, at one time carrying tons of train across the deadly canyon. We go through another tunnel, and the snow next to the track is about 5 feet high, the tunnel is 675 feet long and as we emerge we arrive at the US/Canadian border. This is White Pass Summit and we are 2,865 feet up. Here we will stop and on the double track, transfer our engines to the front of the train and head back down. It is a glorious sight to see our American flag waving there in the cold air next to the Canadian flag. A large pillar standing in front of the flags marks the division of the two countries.

The trip back was uneventful, but beautiful, and we just sit back, relax, and enjoy. Once again we are filled with anticipation for the second half of this amazing day, because this is the day we go on the helicopter and walk on a glacier. I am scared to death to even think about it. After all, much of Alaska's beautiful features are hidden and largely inaccessible—one way to tackle that is go up in a helicopter!

We only have enough time to grab lunch and then rush to catch our bus to the helicopter pad. We both are dressed very warm because we expect it to be freezing on the glacier. I have an undershirt, T-shirt, V-necked sweater, a hoody, and a heavy coat. Also long johns, jeans, and waterproof jogging pants underneath those, plus two pair of socks and my hiking boots. Russ the same, so we are rarin' to go. We can hardly walk but rarin' to go just the same.

After a scenic, but somewhat short bus ride, we arrived at the helicopter pads and were escorted into a large room with several cabinets, all the doors hanging open, full of equipment. Then we are handed "glacier boots" and a life jacket. We are told to put the boots on over our hiking boots, which were kind of like the shoes boys where to play football with cleats. Oh my gosh, I can't even bend over with all these clothes on, not alone tie boots. Now what? Finally, one of the very nice girls came over and tied my boots and Russ had to help me put on the vest. I really could not move. My heart is beating out of my chest! I have never been in a helicopter before, and I can't believe I am doing this. *Why* am I doing this?

Standing outside now, we watch the helicopters land, each on their individual pads. There are six pads all together, at which one bright red helicopter after the other land. It is so perfect, each one slowly hovering over the pad and gracefully sitting down, ever so gently. It looked easy! I can do this, I know I can. I just wish they'd hurry and let us on before I turn around, and go back inside. Tourists are all around and one can feel the excitement. Some are sitting on a bench singing in a foreign language, Swedish, I think. It brought such a happy and up-beat feeling to all of us.

People pile out of the helicopters and we are given numbers, so we could proceed in the proper order. One woman was seated in the front with the pilot and Russ went in the back first next to the window; because he had the camcorder. Then me in the middle and another woman on the other side of me. I was concerned about stepping up to get in with all these clothes on. But it was easy enough. We are handed head sets and told to put them on so if we have any questions we could talk directly to the pilot, and we could hear everyone else's questions as well. We were instructed what to do in case we should need to use those life jackets, after all, we are flying over a lot of water. Then we are in the air before we know it. I'm so glad the pilot kept talking; it kept my mind off the fact that *I am sitting in a helicopter!* I am absolutely amazed at how smooth and easy it was to get up and into the air. Wow, it is wonderful and I'm loving it! We are flying over mountain peaks full of snow; mountains we have had to look up at this whole trip, we are now able to look down and over. Gorgeous waterfalls, lakes, ice and sparkling landscape everywhere. We are flying over a body of water, and I am peering into it to see something dark, like the shadow of a whale. My mind is reeling with thoughts of delight and amazement. This is everything and more than I could imagine it would be. It reminded me of my dreams as a child when I could soar above our world, smiling and happy and just enjoying the splendor of it all.

But now, negative thoughts are creeping into my mind! This is so great, but what happens when I have to walk on all that ice on the glacier, and what if I slip and start rolling, I just know I'm going to fall. I have all these clothes on and definitely won't be able to get up. And what if I keep rolling and roll slap off the mountain to who knows where. I just know this is all a bad idea. I don't know why I ever thought I'd want to do this, what on earth was I thinking. Even though all this overwhelming scenery is passing me by, I think I am going into a complete and total panic.

Approaching the landing pads, there are now signs of life. There are people walking about with colorful jackets and hats. We will land on the glacier in a minute and I am now beside myself. I'm really scared. Someone runs over and opens the door to let us out. There is a little bar to step on to get out of the helicopter. My little short legs can hardly reach it to get out and they feel really weak and shaky. I land in the snow, and amazingly my boots don't slip and so far I am doing fine. Trying to console myself I am thinking, one step at a time. It is a large flat area right here, and our spiked boots grip the ice and snow. We are led over to a group of kids…These are our guides. They hand each one of us a ski pole and say, "Follow me!" I'm wondering how on earth they expected me to do that. Russ was doing fine, and I lagged behind, because all those crevices (cracks in the ice) scared the heck out of me. Some of the crevices are small, but some are quite wide; I'm thinking, one foot in front of the other, go slow and keep moving forward! People were walking along like there was nothing to it. I didn't want to get anywhere near any of those big cracks, so I was trying to go around most of them. I was afraid they'd crack open and I'd fall in.

Once I caught up to everyone, they were peering into a huge crevice that must have been 70 feet long, about 5 feet wide and probably 80 feet deep. And they were standing on the very edge of it! Now that is just plain crazy! I yelled for Russ to step back. He just nonchalantly, but at the same time excitedly said, "Come over here and see this. It's beautiful!" I got a little closer, but not much, and from where I was standing I could see a little of the most captivating color of ice blue I have ever seen. I think I will name it "Glacier Blue." Man cannot create that indescribable color. The guide spoke of life there and the environment, and we came upon a tiny little stream where the water was trickling by, and we were asked to stoop down and take a little sip, because this was the purest water you could drink. Are they out of their minds?! I know good and well if I try to bend down with all these clothes on and try to scoop up that water, I'd topple over like "Ralphie" in *A Christmas Story* and *never* get up. I'd probably keep rolling and never stop, just like a snowball. And that was my biggest fear, falling and rolling and keeping on going! But Russ is almost as paranoid as me, only for different reasons. He said there was no way he was going to drink any of that "pure" water. Because he feared there might be some bacteria in it from the dinosaur days, and he might catch some disease no one would know how to cure in modern day time. Now, who on earth would think of that?

Top of the Glacier in Alaska Heavenly blue

After walking around for about 30 minutes, I was finally beginning to relax a little and enjoy Alaska in its purest form. It was already time to turn back and get in our helicopter. In a way, I wanted to kind of just stand there a little longer, not walk, just stand there and enjoy this once-in-a life-time beauty. But I was also glad to get back in the helicopter, which I never thought I would say, and off the ice. Not to say I didn't appreciate the exquisite and unique beauty of every single inch and every single minute.

The flight back was as breathtaking as on the way out. We landed ever so softly and went back inside to take off our boots and life jackets, and then return to the security of the ship.

It has been a very busy and exhausting day. We ate and laid down and never saw daylight again until the next morning. We would have to get up early again because tomorrow we are to hike in the rain-forest and go on our whale sighting boat. But, we went to bed with thankful hearts that the Good Lord allowed us to see another small part of His world, and slept knowing we shared it together.

When we woke in the morning, we were already in Juneau. It is much warmer here at 55 degrees. It is Friday, May 23. Our "Princess Patter" tells us that Juneau is the capital of Alaska, and the largest city, in size, in the world with 30,000 people living there. Juneau is the home to 38 major glaciers.

I noticed there are all types of interesting activities going on onboard today, such as ping pong play, dancing, honeymooners celebration, and ceramics at sea, just to mention a few, but we will be heading out on a hike and adventure into one of Alaska's rainforests. Yes, there are rainforests in Alaska! And then off to board a boat for guaranteed whale sightings. Yippee, I can't wait!

Our bus was a little late. But with this kind of scenery to look at, who cares? Once we boarded our bus with our next guide, named Jamie, you could hear the murmuring and excited voices all around us like when something very exciting is about to happen. Jamie was so informative and intelligent, and when she talked, she lit up with passion for what she does. You could sense her love for nature and for her beloved state, Alaska. There wasn't one question the tourists asked her that she couldn't answer and she did so with much enthusiasm. Our group discussed many topics with her, such as: people who wish to live there and build homes, the cost, and stumbling blocks of living there. She informed us of the weather, politics, taxes, and our surroundings. We felt very fortunate to have her as our guide.

We parked our bus in a large parking lot, disembarked and were divided into smaller groups, our group totaling 15 people; ranging from about 22 years of age to maybe somewhere in their '80s. We were led straight to the forest, while others to the glacier, and some to other areas of the forest. We had to cross a wide street, and as we approached the pathway, I saw a large black bear walk across the other end of the street near the glacier. Wow! Like a child I'm screaming," There's a big bear, look out, look out!" As quick as it appeared, it disappeared into the forest. Everyone looked, but kept on going, so I figured it wasn't anything to get upset about.

This is so exciting; Russ has his camera ready as we move along toward a small pond to our right, with a little duck showing off by dipping in and out of the water. Jamie is explaining the history of the area, which used to be covered by a massive glacier. It has carved out a beautiful pathway, with greenery, yellows, and every shade of green imaginable; lichen and moss hanging or clinging to the trees, branches, and even the huge rocks (some boulders) left behind. It's so hard to imagine how it used to be and it is always changing, even now…It rains here almost every day, and it is damp but it is not raining right now.

We come to a babbling brook and cross over it on a wooden bridge, and within a few steps, lo and behold, there is our black bear. Oh, my gosh, how does our brain work anyway? I never gave it a thought that we would bump into her again, even after seeing the bear cross the road before we entered the forest. Well, maybe this isn't the same bear, because this bear has two little adorable cubs in tow. *Uh-oh!* This is a time to be especially cautious; there is nothing more dangerous than a mama bear with her cubs, especially if she thinks they are in any way threatened. This time we are on foot and not in the safety of a big tour bus, like when we saw the grizzlies in Denali. Oooh, she is beautiful. She is huge; one of her cubs is black (leaner and taller), one is cinnamon in color (smaller and fluffier) and *so* cuddly, cute, and huggable. Of course our guide stopped us in our tracks. She said, "Remain quiet and still. It seems we are safe at this distance for the moment." The bear was just minding her own business, knowing very well these humans were there admiring her little family, all of us gaping with our mouths hanging open and trying to catch it all on camera. Slowly Mama started to mosey toward us, her head still down, and eating the rich underbrush with her cubs frolicking close behind, content and happy to do the same. But she is moseying just a little too close and I think she decided this is long enough for our visit, so our guide tells us to get back to the bridge. We stood there only for a few seconds more, when the bear seemed uneasy, looked up at us, and started to move our way, and the guide forgot about "quiet and still" and yelled "everyone back to the bus, but don't run!" Yikes! I'm grabbing Russ by the arm, and in a raspy whisper said, "Come on, honey, let's go!" because he'd stay and film if I didn't say something. Like I said, tourists do stupid things and I knew I couldn't out-run some of the people in that group! I think Russ felt like he could, so I'm glad I kept tugging on his arm!

The excitement of this experience has been staggering as we proceed to the Mendenhall Glacier. I mean, here we are standing right in front of it, trying to embrace the crisp air, the pristine lake it has formed in front of it, and the ice floating within it. What a dramatic change in scenery…from rain forest to glacier! If you were to fly up and over it, you would see Mendenhall Towers—rock sentinels that rise 4,000 feet out of the glacier—and ice spires and deep crevices. This is only one of the 38 glaciers flowing from the Juneau Icefield. The glacier is 1½ miles wide and 150 feet high at its face. According to some of the literature I picked up, you can take a raft boat tour from here through stretches of moderate rapids.

We moved on to another walk way that was part of the forest, and at the foot of the glacier, as Jamie explains, this is one of the bears' favorite feeding places, because there is a stream off the glacier that is full of salmon. Salmon will run in a couple more weeks. What a mesmerizing place to be, but all good things must come to an end; in this case, more good things are to come. So we board our bus, running a little late because of the time we took to watch the bears.

At this point, we are ready to board a cute little boat which will accommodate our same little group. It seems the captain is a little out of sorts with Jamie, because we are causing him to get behind his schedule as well. It looks like this boat is designed for close-up whale watching, with large windows that open all around the boat. We are all packed in the boat perfectly, and the captain gives another lesson on the safety jackets. It seems there is another boat that works with him like a "search boat," that calls him when they spot a whale and then he sets out in that direction. Our hopes are soaring, but Russ reminds me that this is a "guaranteed whale sighting" event. There are some orcas in these protected waters, but we will probably see mostly humpbacks. This is so exciting, to be able to actually see in "person," the largest living thing on earth…the *whale!*

The Wave Juneau, Alaska

On the mountains to our right, sits a beautiful eagle and another soon joins it, landing with such elegance, just like all the pictures I've seen on calendars. Again, the scenery is like Russ's "eye candy" with snow topped mountains and forest all around. We went a little further and Jamie said to go ahead and open the windows if we'd like, which were about shoulder height, but you could stand on the seat if you wanted. Suddenly, there it was! Water spouting in the air and a large back fin, rolling in the water and up again, down in again and then most exciting of all, here comes this beautiful tail with an unforgettable wave! *Incredible!* Jamie explains the length of this beautiful huge monster is probably about 40 feet, and what we were observing was only 1/3 of the whale. She said they don't usually stay on top of the water very long, because their skin is very sensitive to the sun. Imagine that. They are an endangered species, and well protected, so our boat was not allowed to go any closer than 100 feet. And believe me the park rangers were on top of that too; in fact, we could see a tower over on the land where rangers watched. Our captain could have his license taken away if he didn't observe the rules.

We were privileged to sight three or four more beautiful, graceful humpbacks, each entertaining us with a dramatic wave, when the captain had us all sit back down and went full speed ahead for a while. The atmosphere was comfortable in our little boat with the sounds of the waves bouncing off the sides, our small group spellbound over all we had just witnessed. We had been together all day and comfortably began talking and sharing our stories, as Jamie chimed in with her great knowledge. We soon came upon a large red buoy that our captain and Jamie fondly called "The Can." The closer we got, we realized it was loaded with sea lions. It was big and had just enough of a rim on it for them to lie around it. The sea lions were huge and there were 4 or 5 of them all crammed up there. They must have been the big grand-daddies, because as soon as the captain cut the engines and drifted closer, many other sea lions that seemed quite smaller popped up out of the water all around the buoy. They were calling to each other and making all kinds of noises and putting a grand show on for us. Even Jamie seemed amazed. We think they expected us to feed them but of course, we didn't. They flitted under the boat, swam on their back, called to the "elders" on "the can," and squeals of delight and laughter came from our boat, where we had all walked out to the front. The sea lions (not seals) seemed to enjoy hearing us, as one little guy even tried to jump into the boat. We sat and watched them for a good while, but time came for us to move on. On our way back in to the harbor, we spotted a couple more whales and stopped to watch until they waved. I couldn't help but wonder, after this *big* and successful experience, and this land of endless discoveries, how anyone could ever doubt a Higher Power. Even Jamie said, "There must be something about this group, because I've never had such a fun and fulfilled day." Russ and I just looked at each other in that familiar and knowing way and did a high-five. She doesn't know that God planned our whole vacation that way. There has not been a day yet, since we started this phenomenal journey, that God didn't make it exceptional! On top of all that, once we dock, there are eagles flying all over the place, one swooping and almost hitting the back of Russ's head, so close, but so quick I couldn't get a picture with my camera. This whole adventure is just plain captivating and we will never forget it. Many other eagles gave us opportunities for pictures, landing in the trees and curiously watching all the people pass by.

Before we went back to the ship, Jamie dropped a few of us off in town so we could shop around a little. Russ's sister had asked him to pick up a mug from the "Red Dog Saloon." We walked a couple blocks over and came upon this old drinking establishment claiming to be the oldest man-made tourist attraction in Juneau. We walked into this loud and colorful Saloon, with ragtime music and jovial occupants, through big swinging doors. We pick up Nancy's mug after a quick sweep of the place, noticing there are many bear, moose and deer mounts on the walls, wagon wheels, and lanterns and memorabilia all around. But the cutest thing I heard was, "In the old days, a man used to meet the tour boat at the docks with a mule that wore a sign saying, follow my ass to the Red Dog Saloon."

We wearily walked back to the ship. At 5:00 p.m., we were drifting out to sea already. The ship wasn't the only thing drifting, as Russ drifted off in a deep sleep, and me, I donned myself with our trusty movie camera and took off to make a tour of the ship on camera for my sister, who will probably never be able to make a cruise like this.

This is so much fun. I am filming the ship from top to bottom. Cruise ships are like gigantic hotels floating on the sea, and the buzzing of activities are endless—from an afternoon tea to trivia, singles get-together, and music everywhere. There are several pianos throughout, and everyone waves when they see my camera on them. Small bands wave from the bar and restaurant. An orchestra of violins on the main floor are playing beautiful music, it would be a challenge to get bored here, with computer rooms, the casino, ice cream parlor, and there is even a Jewish Sabbath Eve service going on in the wedding chapel. I have reached the food court and the chefs are doing a little dance for me. So much happiness on board, everyone reaches out to you for a smile.

We have two shows to go to tonight: one is a comedian, they are always the best; and one a hypnotist! We have enjoyed every single show we've been to. After that, it will be pretty late so we will hit the sack and be ready in the morning for a visit to Ketchikan.

We docked in Ketchikan at 9:40 a.m. As soon as we disem-barked, there were horse-drawn trolleys at the curb waiting to take tours around the city. Russ and I decided we would go it on foot, visit the cute little shops and maybe get our souvenirs. We will be here most of the day. Our Princess Patter says Ketchikan is known by many names, but from what I've read in other literature, their favorite title is "First City," because it is the first major city people visit that are traveling from south to north. Tourism plays a large role in Ketchikan's economy, but they are mostly famous as the "Salmon Capital of the World." We visited many cheerful and bustling shops, and loaded down with gifts, such as hats, T-shirts, jewelry, etc. The Princess left booklets for us in our rooms the night before loaded with coupons. I bought all the girls necklaces that are a grayish black, the Alaskans say they are Alaskan black diamonds. The price of those will assure you that is not true! But they are beautiful just the same. We skipped lunch *for once*, because tonight is our formal dinner night in the main dining room.

After a successful, fun, and relaxing day in Ketchikan, we read-ied ourselves for the formal dinner and sat at a table with three other couples. It was fun to meet more people, talk and get to know each other and eat lobster (which were very small), but the key words here are "all you want." Of course, Russ had to have a second help-ing. Afterward, we went to see the production show "Dance." It fea-tured the Coral Princess Dancers who put on a great performance as always. Tonight on board, there is a late night dance party, a peer factor game show, live music everywhere and a champagne waterfall. We watched as the waiters made a tower of champagne glasses (full of champagne) ever so tenderly placing glasses one on top of the other. As the tower got higher and higher, the crowd let out their oohs and ahhhs. This certainly is a fun-filled place to be, to say the least.

When we return to our room, we find a little monkey hanging from a hangar with two little red eyes made of chocolate candy. Our steward had made it from towels like our swan, and it was *so* cuddly cute. Of course, we had to take lots of pictures of him and then went out on the deck to see the most unforgettable sunset. It was colors of orange, pink, and pale yellow streaking through it. It glowed on the water in a deep orange and the reflection made my heart sing. A perfect kiss good night to send us off to another night of bliss.

We wake up to our last day at sea this beautiful Sunday morning. It is 59 degrees today, crisp and refreshing. Such a relaxing time and after working all these years, we're not having one bit of trouble sitting around, enjoying the comfortable surroundings with our carefree attitudes...truthfully, just being plain lazy! Today we will get our suitcases ready for pickup by 10:00 p.m. There are activities such as culinary and carving demonstrations, an art auction, and a movie if you like. We had a leisurely breakfast and watched dolphins play and frolic almost right next to us, much to our amusement.

We are cruising through the straits of Georgia on the inside passage of Canada, and we leave waters calm like glass to a heavy current. The captain says this is in our favor, since whales love to hang out in this type of current. Russ guesses the current is running about 16 knots. Since we are from Florida, he was comparing it to the Gulf Stream which usually runs at 6 knots. There are small whirlpools caused by the current from all sides bumping into each other from one strait to the other, where the two intersect. Far ahead we can see a lighthouse wedged in by two small cabins and mountains crowned with glistening snow. And then mountains where they have been cutting down trees for lumber (clear cutting). As we go on, we see a flock of geese flying overhead in a giant *V* formation, honking as they go. The arrow was pointing back from where we came like an arrow saying, "No, you are going the wrong way, go back, go back!" Talk about interesting and beautiful all together.

Throughout the cruise, I found some interesting facts in our "log of the cruise." One of them being the information that pilots from different areas would board ship, pilot the ship through that particular area, then disembark. For instance, when we began the cruise, we had the South West Alaska Pilots on board who then disembarked in College Fjord. In Glacier Bay, the South East Alaska pilots embarked and also a team of park rangers, who informed us overhead on the intercom system of wildlife in that area. It was like that the whole cruise, but these are just a few of the events that happen on the ship, that we aren't aware of. Other interesting facts, according to the "log of the cruise" passed out to us, are the gross registered tonnage of the ship is 91,627 tons and the overall length is 964.3 feet. The maximum passenger capacity is 2,368, fuel capacity 1,938 tons (heavy fuel oil) and 1,786 tons (marine oil), and fresh water capacity 2,199 tons. Cruising speed is 21.5 knots, generally. I mean, Russ and I sat in awe sometimes just thinking of the weight these mammoth vessels carry. Not to mention, the food, the people, the safety boats, swimming pools, laundry and linens, and when we were on our balcony—just the plexiglass itself wrapped around it; it looked very thick and heavy! Also the Bridge is manned 24 hours a day (thank God!) by 2 officers working 4 hours on, and 8 hours off in a 3-watch system. That is all a wonder in itself amidst all the natural wonder around us. I think we are in heaven.

Today we will also fill out the passenger questionnaire and let Princess know how well we felt we were treated, fed, and literally taken care of. Our steward was great; I could tell from day one how conscientious he was. When we first boarded the ship, our luggage hit the wall as we walked in the room and made a black scrape mark. I figured I'd take care of it after we came back from lunch, and when we returned, the mark was gone…just like that. He was very attentive and friendly whenever we saw him and made the cutest animals for us, including a swan and a monkey. I know they do this on most of the cruises, but I think it has a lot to do with the steward how often they do it. He also left chocolate candy in the shape of a heart on our pillows. I definitely had to get his last name. That had to be done by 3:00 p.m., with prizes to be won for completing them.

It is May 26th, Monday (Memorial Day), we are up very early, so I don my wonderful red, white, and blue, and we go to our last breakfast at sea. We will disembark here in Vancouver, British Columbia, Canada at 8:20 a.m. We bid farewell to Coral Princess, but we will not be touring Vancouver, Canada's third largest city, because we will catch our bus right away.

The line waiting to go out is moving pretty fast at first, then we come to some big double doors that once entered was like a waiting station for the buses that would transport us to Seattle. The woman manning the doors said someone made a mistake and let the wrong group go first. So we waited…and waited…and waited…An hour and a half has gone by and our feet are starting to hurt. It's not so bad when you're walking but to stand still like that for that length of time is rough. Well, I guess nothing is perfect. It seems they were short a bus driver here, because we boarded the bus, and waited… and waited…and waited again. At last, a big loud woman appeared and manned the bus. She said she was new at this and apologized for the wait. Off we go, and so glad, but the big woman went the wrong way. We are now sitting in front of a huge chain linked fence with a chain and lock around it and she can't go backward or forward. Suddenly, an elderly gentleman with a uniform came over and spoke with her, unlocked the gate after much grumbling and off we went.

Shortly after we got on the road, the "rookie" said she was starving because she had been called in for this run and hadn't eaten. She pulled into a little store and we all got a small snack after a warning not to take too long. All I know is I needed a potty! The driver ate her candy bar and drank her coke as we traveled up the road, while she was driving. I was wondering if that was allowed, not to mention dangerous, but she had a great personality which somehow made it easy to go along with whatever she needed to do.

When we got to the Canada/USA border, our "rookie" driver said everyone would have to get off the bus and pass through the nearly empty "United States Port of Entry" building. We were to have our passport out and hold it in front of us; we had to carry everything with us we had on the bus, our carry-on luggage, cameras, pocket books, etc., so the agent could inspect the bus. The bigger luggage that was stored in the luggage carrier underneath the bus could stay there, but we were told if we left anything on the bus itself, there would be a fine of $10.00. As each one of us passed the agents, we were asked if we had any seeds, plants, fruits, or vegetables with us. With a big smile I might add. I was wondering what kind of farce this was, but our bus driver said not to make any smart comments or complaints or they could hold us and give us a hard time. I told Russ to keep quiet. I bet his tongue was bleeding! Meanwhile, here comes a truck, and it goes passed without an inspection of any kind. Just waved on through, and I'm wondering what kind of nuclear weapons or illegal drugs he was carrying over the border, while we were being pulled off the bus and being checked for fruits and seeds.

Our big "rookie" really felt bad about the whole ordeal, but we made it to the airport without incident, thank you, God! As we walk in the airport in Seattle and find the area where we were told to pick up our luggage, we spotted ours right away, our beautiful bright-colored luggage, next to the Princess representative. In the back of our minds, we fear our luggage will be lost as probably most people do. We were so happy to see it. Russ got a cart, we got out our card to call the driver at the motel and just as Russ was dialing I noticed the bus from the motel pull right up almost in front of us. This was too good to be true, everything was going so smoothly. We flagged him down; it was good to see Michael's familiar face. The first thing we did was get Mona (so glad to see her too), and then we went to eat.

After catching up with our laundry and chatting with an adorable girl in the laundry room, who was there taking her final tests the next day to be a flight attendant. We brought all our luggage up to the room and re-organized so we would be ready for our next destination…Mount Rainier National Park.

CHAPTER 7

Three Volcanoes and a Lake of Sapphires

We didn't start out until 11:00 a.m. today. I've noticed Russ likes to sleep in a little later these days, and I'm thinking it is because check-out time is 11. I thought maybe he just wanted to get his moneys' worth. No getting early starts here, unless he absolutely has to. So we went straight to the grocery store and got a few snacks to go with us and by then my prescription was ready and our pharmacist from Marietta had left a hello message for us. That was very touching for me. She is so sweet.

After I got my blood drawn, *again*...I guess I should mention here—the only reason I bring up my health issues is because it is important to know that you can do these things, and do it with health issues. Plus we are up there in years as well. It's okay to leave the comfort of your home, travel, and enjoy God's world even if you have medical issues. Just take it at your own pace. I admit this is a huge undertaking, this wonderful adventure of ours, but even a week, or a few days to any one of these beautiful destinations, is a blessing. So go for it and enjoy it if you can, while you can. I wish we could have done it sooner.

So anyway, with that being said—we drove straight out Highway 5 toward Mt. Rainer, down roads lined with beautiful stately fir trees. We stop a lot to film the waterfalls, the absolutely gorgeous scenery and of course, snow. Such a beautiful state Washington is. We are driving next to the White River which is bubbly, fast, and furious. As we stop to take pictures, the sounds are so relaxing; the river is thunderous and white. There is a lot of water from the snow melting, causing water falls where they wouldn't normally be in the summer. The mountains have been blasted right through for these winding roads.

As we get closer to Mount Rainier, we see deer on the side of the road, critters, at last, and they cautiously look at us and then run off. We can see the mountain in the distance; it's like a roller coaster…up…snow piled 10 feet on each side…coats on…turn the heater on…turn the heater down…take coats off…roll up sleeves…turn on the air. But we are having trouble finding a place to stay. We enter a place called Crystal Village, a small tourist village that isn't even open for business yet. But there is a couple working, getting ready for business, so we stopped and asked for directions from these very friendly people, who directed us to a place called the Paradise Inn. The woman said there was a lodge called Paradise Inn, not far from here; it was being remodeled for the past two years but was now open. It is about an hour and a half away. So off we go enjoying striking scenery all the way, and we can see Mt. Rainier from many different turns and angles as we go round and round the curves. It looks like the mountain is shrouded all around by clouds. Oh, I hope it will be visible by the time we get there. We can see signs of little rock slides on the side of the road, and the higher we get the higher the snow is again. Because of the time of year, the park itself actually is not open, so we are privileged to see snow drifts most people won't see during the regular tourist season. I suppose that wouldn't matter to people who see snow all the time, but being from Georgia, it is a dramatic change in scenery for us. It makes us feel like we are trodding in places where others won't get to go. It is still *our* movie, and we are alone in it once again. Clean, solitary, and refreshing, our spirits are soaring high. We notice there are places where a car can pull over and put chains on their tires, which also puts a little feeling of danger in our minds, we're certainly not used to this and I don't think we expected this type of weather. It just never occurred to us that there would be this much snow in May and June.

While most areas in the US measure snowfall in inches, Mt. Rainier measures in feet. The visitor's guide states that in 1972 they got more than 93 feet, a world record. I know in the summer months this whole area is covered in wild flowers, but what we see is a sheet of white everywhere. Simply a haven.

At this point, it doesn't even matter how far we have to go, as waterfalls are everywhere and the further we go the bigger and more forceful they become, some with snow on top and the waterfall running out from underneath it. We are driving from Highway 5 to Route 706, toward Chinook Pass which isn't even open in the winter months. A tunnel unfolds before us and it spits us out into a wonderland of elegance. We just had to get out of the car and play in the snow a little while, in short-sleeved shirts no less.

We venture on and see another waterfall cascading down three tiers and yellow flowers all over the place painted into all the right spots. Around the bend, there are still more waterfalls, most certainly from snow melt, and another and another even bigger. Off to the side, simply placed, there is an elegant little stone bridge making it all picture perfect. Suddenly, a grouse decides to cross the street in front of our car. It's a good thing we were able to go only 5 to 10 miles an hour right now because he was in no hurry. He nonchalantly *stroooolled* across that road in front of us as if to say, take my picture, I'm beautiful! Of course, we did, 'cause he was. We were going through some very thick clouds at the time, and it's a good thing or he would have been road kill. Russ said he was "posturing and drumming" to attract a female, who must have been around there somewhere. His tail was fanned out like a turkey, what an amazing sight.

Another twist and turn in the road and we find ourselves face-to-face with Mt. Rainier, clad in clouds, and finally reached a large parking lot, to view this striking mountain. There are many entrances to Mt. Rainier. We entered the park through the Nisqually entrance, which is said to be the most popular. As we gazed up, Mt. Rainier is still hidden and we're both disappointed. Mt. Rainier is Washington's highest elevation of 14,411 feet. It is only three hours out of Seattle, a dormant volcano with dozens of glaciers on its surface. So big is Mt. Rainier it also creates its own weather. It stands three miles above sea level and is totally covered with more than 35 miles of snow and glacial ice all year.

It is quiet and serene here, and there are only a couple other cars and two hikers who just descended the mountain. We asked the hikers how it was on the mountain. They said, "There is some serious snow up there." They were with another couple who were still on their way down, but they said they could hear the crevices splitting and cracking and felt it was too dangerous to keep going. They said a group of hikers went up yesterday and someone fell in one of those crevices but was rescued safely. See! I had a good reason to be afraid of those crevices on the glacier in Alaska.

We were so engrossed in the couples' conversation that we weren't thinking of our disappointment anymore. The couple finished packing all their gear into their jeep and drove off. As we turned around to look at our mountain again, much to my surprise, I began to cry. God had blown the clouds away and revealed His Majesty to us once again. There she was in *full* view, Mt. Rainier! It was like God was whispering in my ear—"Oh, Ginnie, why do you doubt Me so?" We sat there…for a long time, basking in His gift.

An adorable little bird was running around me…close. He wasn't afraid of me and not one bit worried where he was or where he was going to stay. He was small and dark gray with a little white dot on his tail, pecking, pecking, pecking.

Once we came to our senses, we figured we'd better get over to the lodge and get our luggage in. Russ parked me and Mona in front of the Paradise Inn, while he went to get us registered. I was organizing our cameras and maps when I looked up and I thought I saw a dog coming out of the snow toward me. As he came closer in my view, I realized this was not a dog, it was a *fox*! He was bouncing along in my direction, in a happy-go-lucky fashion and suddenly he spotted me already out of the car, movie camera in hand, and filming him. He went toward the drivers' side of the car so I stepped away from my door to keep him on camera. He stopped in his tracks, turned and he looked right in my eyes, just like a sweet little puppy dog coming to his master for a treat. As he walked closer and closer toward me, too close for comfort, I realized what I was doing, and I got scared (this is a wild animal after all) and I jumped into the car. He continued on passed the car on my side now and walked along the sidewalk in front of the lodge. As soon as he got a little passed the car, walking in the other direction with his back to me, I got brave again, got out of the car, and started to film him once more. He was a handsome little guy with a coat of white and gray for the winter, black paws and just a little tint of a reddish color to his fur in the sunlight. As soon as he got to the end of the lodge, some girl must have spotted him from inside and came charging out of the door and tried to coax him to her. She was much braver than I. He turned around, looked at her, and sat right down on the sidewalk again, just like a dog! He finally got bored with us, since no one was offering him food, I'm sure, gave us a big yawn, showing off all of his sharp teeth and nonchalantly walked away. Darn, I wish Russ could have seen that.

My fox Mt. Ranier

The lobby of the inn was enormous with big bulky tables and chairs, a huge fire place, and someone was playing a piano. There were no TVs, and it looked like families were enjoying the fire and playing games, and many people were curled up in the big cedar furniture, reading. The inn was originally built in 1917 and recently remodeled. The dining room was to the left; it was also huge with only a few customers scattered about. We approached the dining room to be seated and were told it closed at 8:00 p.m. My goodness it's only 2 minutes after! How rude! We decided the heck with them remembering we had diet bars, a can of chocolate slim fast, bananas and chips in the car. *Yum!* We took off to the car and drove back by the mountain and had a picnic and just enjoyed the dominating view. This immense mountain can be seen as far as Seattle and Portland. We enjoyed the sunset and the clouds began to fill in the valley next to it like a blanket of cotton. If you didn't know it was a valley below it would appear as though one could just step out and keep walking on. Light colors of orange and pink surround the mountain with bright white reflections from the clouds behind. Then colors of deeper oranges, pinks, and grays reflected themselves across the snow.

All of a sudden, this young man came out of nowhere and asked Russ to take a picture of him in front of the mountain and the sunset. It seemed like we took a million, because he wanted the picture to appear as though he was balancing the sun on the tip of his finger, by holding his finger in just the right spot for Russ to snap the picture until he got it right. Then he returned the favor and took a picture of us too.

We returned to our room, which by the way, was very highly priced. Just so you know lodges and inns are like that, because if you wanted a bath or shower, you had to request that special, at an additional cost of $29.00! Never heard of that one before; I wonder if they charged extra for the toilet too. No, maybe not, just the toilet paper! The bathroom was in the old building (which apparently was not remodeled), since it looked very old. I couldn't even raise my arms in front of the sink to curl my hair that next morning because it was so small. The shower curtain was an accordion-type folding metal and plastic door. The floors creaked and you could hear the people next door go to the bathroom and carry on conversations. Nothing private here. Of course, there is no TV, no hair dryer, and absolutely no telephone. I do have to say the beds were very comfortable, however.

Much to our surprise, breakfast was buffet style. We were disappointed in this inn, which boasts to be included in the most prestigious Historic Hotels of America register and one of the two

National Historic Landmark Inns, according to the flyer we saw in a restaurant.

We loaded up the car and took a return trip to Mt. Rainier to view it one last time, but part of it was covered in clouds. On the way out of the park, we got more pictures at the foot of Mt. Rainier and there was our cute little fox, with his mate. She had a creamy-colored coat and they were digging for food at the edge of the road by the curb in the snow. To see them there made it another perfect ending to a perfect experience.

So, on the road again to begin our adventure to Mt. St. Helens, this was one of my picks to see. We pass many more astounding water-falls from the snow melt and a little deer grazing on the green grass that was beginning to pop out by the road. The road is winding here and there and giant redwoods gracefully line the road standing so straight and tall, reaching for the sky. This is such a beautiful and rich land.

We made it down to a little town named Morton which was about halfway between Mt. Rainier and Mt. St. Helens. We asked some locals which way would be the best way to go to Mt. St. Helens, and they suggested we take the east entrance. Talk about hanging on to your seat, I was clinging on like I was on a roller coaster. The weather is cold and the turns in the road are sharp and unceasing, interrupted only by a sprinkle of rain here and there. The solid tall redwoods make me feel a little safer because they protect us from the very edge of the mountain. There must have been a storm here the night before because there are trees down and debris all over and a little further on; rock and debris on the road show evidence of a small land slide.

It seems like we have been on the road an awful long time, the streets are certainly not as clean as they were in the beginning. The turns in the road are sharper than before and it feels like we are running out of road. We are seventeen miles into the park, there are two entrances and we had chosen the closest one. The snow on the road is about a foot deep now, and there are tire tracks, as though someone before us tried to get through also. And then it came to an end, covered completely with snow and we had no other choice but to turn around and go back. Thank God Russ turned around, somewhere deep in my gut I was afraid he was going to try and wing it. It took an hour to get to this point. Seventeen miles may not seem far on the expressway, but when all you do is make sharp curves and travel roads snaking around mountains, of course, you are traveling at a limited speed and it takes forever. An enjoyable forever most of the time though. There were no signs or anything stating the road was closed; it seems the local people we talked to earlier should have known that this road is closed in the winter. Turning the car around in that spot was so scary because we couldn't tell if we were on the road or not. My stomach flip-flopped; I was so fearful we were going off the edge of the mountain.

Trying to get to Mt. St. Helen

We went all the way back down the mountain and just as we get to an intersection, here sits a little café, right out of nowhere. It was like a little country store and all the good ole boys were gathered, smoking and shooting the bull, if you know what I mean. We asked them if they knew of another way to get up the mountain. They were eager to share their knowledge with us about their mountain and assured us the west side was open, so we had a hamburger while we were there and decided to give it another try, determined to see Mt. St. Helens.

Traveling down Interstate 5 onto US 12 East, we are next to Riffe Lake, which has a reservoir on the Cowlitz River (which we crossed over several times.) It is pretty and still, and we decided to stretch our legs and get pictures of it. It stretches out 13 miles, and I read it is a great place for trout fishing.

The land is greener than ever as spring is approaching here too, and there are miles of yellow flowers scattered in contrast to the bright green. But as we climb higher, the land becomes dimmer and what few trees there are, are surrounded with desolate land and dirt. The weather is colder as we climb on and we are driving in clouds, which makes it difficult to see, so we are going at a very slow pace. To the side of the road, it is obvious now that disaster struck here. The soil is becoming darker and there are dark broken dead trees in ponds and black rocks in piles. A deer looks up at us almost in sadness it seems, as it stands in the middle of sparse greens and muck. There are small fir trees scattered here and there, that are fairly new as the land tries to replenish itself.

Still going up, the ground is black and barren from burning and the contrast of the snow against it is staggering. I read once that a burnt area will resist fires for at least 50 years. The higher we go, the more snow there is and the more ash, fog and mist, too. It is eerie as we look up at the snow-scattered dark mountains around us, with only sprigs growing out of the soil. And yet in all this, around the next curve is another beautiful waterfall. It's been a long and rather sad drive, and the cold is in our bones, but not from the cold weather as much as from the desolation and destruction that occurred here.

We have Mona practically crawling now in this inclement weather, and I am a little nervous. There are signs along the way noting that new trees have been planted in this particular area…some in 1987, and 1991, etc…a dead mountain trying to come back to life. The clouds are so heavy and thick, we feel like we are going to drive right off the mountain. We go over many more bridges and see many more waterfalls and the snow drifts are getting higher too.

Finally, after a very lengthy and emotionally exhausting drive, we are at the top and find a parking lot. There is no one here but us… again. Come to think of it, we didn't pass one car on the way up nor did one pass us going the other way. The wind is howling and we find the door to the visitor center. Just as Russ put his hand on the door, it flew open. We jumped back awkwardly and five rangers, three men and two women, were barging out like there was a fire or something awful inside. They startled the heck out of us. As our surprised faces looked into their eyes, they said "Oh, we are closed!" Our mouths fell open; we couldn't believe it. I was thinking, *You're fired, get out of my movie!* We asked, "Why?" They smiled and said, "It is 6 o'clock." Oh no! But they said, "We are sorry but you are welcome to look around out here if you like," and I swear the lady ranger said there was a bathroom around back if we needed to use it. They locked up and got in their cars and were gone and that was that. Here we are standing on top of Mt. St. Helens all alone, we can hardly see 5 feet in front of us, and the wind is about to blow us away. I don't know how they got out of there so fast. I think they were ghosts and really never existed at all. One minute we saw them and the next they had disappeared without a trace! Suddenly the parking lot was completely empty except for poor cold Mona! *Where were all their cars anyway?*

We looked around us only to see singed and dark tree stumps, jagged from the explosion. Some of the tree stumps were sticking out of the snow broken and at an angle, and some had snapped right off from the bottom. We were standing on the sidewalk that wound itself around the visitor's center. Since the ranger said there were bathrooms in the back, we decided to go around and look for them. We paused and I took a picture of Russ in front of the black rubble and fog and you could only see a few feet behind him.

The horrendous eruption of Mt. St. Helens occurred on May 18, 1980, 39 years ago this month. The force of the explosion blew 1,300 feet of the mountain top completely off, leaving a crater one mile wide, 200 feet deep and spread ash eastward across our country. The height of Mt. St. Helens use to be 9,677 feet and it is now 8,365 feet. I didn't realize that it all started because of an earthquake of 5.1 in magnitude, which caused the mountain to release the gases trapped inside and triggering this massive explosion. According to the Cowlitz County Tourism Bureau publication, named "Awesome," "the blast carried winds up to 670 mph, temperatures of 800 degrees Fahrenheit, and flattened 230 square miles of forest. Both animals and fish were obliterated, 57 people were killed and the largest land slide occurred in recorded history."

Within the crater is a lava dome imitating a larger volcano, but it is smaller and spews steam. But Awesome states this small dome is growing, and if it continues to grow at its current pace, it will replace all the material lost in the 1980 eruption.

We are freezing now and continue on around the back of the visitor's center in search of the bathrooms. Russ stops to peer out at the dramatic landscape in front of him while I wander a little ahead of him (very brave of me…just a couple yards), when all of a sudden something runs in front of me, which appears to be a quick shadow. I screamed to Russ and said, "There is something out there and if you keep looking, maybe you'll see it since it's heading in this direction." Sure enough, the shadow passed around a dead tree a few feet out and Russ identified our newest critter as a coyote. Once the little guy realized we were there, he took off and disappeared into the fog. We notice there is a large raven following us; I guess he thought we would feed him. His presence added to the eeriness of this place; he was but a black silhouette against the fog and the dark background. He remained perched on a dead, burnt branch, watching us, still and quiet, and I shot the perfect outline of him.

We got to the back of the building and we could not find a bathroom in sight. I must have been delusional or something, but I swear that ranger said there were bathrooms in the back We gave up and decided to end this movie for the day; in which we are the sole characters. It's late, dark and darn right scary up here. Russ did stop for a minute in the front of the building to take a picture of the pictures posted on the wall of the "before and after" of Mt. St Helens.

I can't wait to get to the car. It is so windy I can't even keep the hood of my coat on my head; and it's so foggy we can't see Mona from here. The snow drifts are about 20 feet high where they had pushed the snow off the parking area, and in the bottom of the drifts, there are dead roots and broken trees hanging from underneath. It's too bad we couldn't go inside the visitor center, but being alone and experiencing what we did was an adventure. I'll bet very few people got to experience what we did. Oh, it would have been nice if the rangers were available to give us more information, and at first we thought it was terrible that they would allow us to be alone up here, but after we experienced this evening alone, we think they actually did us a favor. As a final note, Russ picked up a stick and wrote our names in the snow drift. "Russ and Ginnie"...*Awww!* We will always and forever embrace this memory.

The descent from Mt. St. Helens was as frightening as the trip up, except at least this time we knew where we were going. Sort of! Once we got down to about 2,000 feet, we saw a critter right in the middle of the road, (again, a good thing we were going so slow in the fog). It was so foggy. Russ said, "Is that a horse?" and I replied, "It almost looks like a llama," a llama? As we got a little closer, Russ realized it was an elk and what a great viewing, but by then the animal was skittish and took off before I could take a "shot" of him.

I realize we left on our journey very early in the spring, so we did see so much snow and wintry weather. If we had left a couple weeks later, we would have had a totally different experience, but I'm really glad we got to see the snow, plus we didn't have to deal with massive crowds because not many people venture out in these conditions. But Russ and I were alone, something we hadn't been for years, and it was so special for us.

At last, we are at the bottom of the mountain and say goodbye to Mt. St. Helens Volcanic National Monument. Absolutely thrilling, all the way out, with the waterfalls and deer and stunning landscape.

We finally got back to Highway 5, where we decided to eat at a Burger King. Right next to it was a nice motel. I can't help but compare it to Paradise Inn because it had a refrigerator, microwave, shower/tub, large bathroom, and large bedroom with two queen-size beds, TV, hair dryer, two luggage racks, and a telephone. It runs circles around the inn, not to mention the cost which was about a third of what the inn cost. We settle in after a wonderful but harrowing day. *Cut!* Tomorrow we will continue on Highway 5 toward Crater Lake, Oregon, the next adventure in our movie!

It is Thursday, May 29, 2008. Call me ignorant if you want, but I didn't know anything about Crater Lake. I had never heard of it and tried to question Russ about it. It seems he didn't know much more than I did except he did know it is a volcano, but not much more than that. He just knew he wanted to see it. So we headed south on Highway 5, went through Vancouver, Oregon, Intersection of Routes 5 and 84, where we ate at a place called Sheri's. It turned out to be a very good choice. Sometimes being spontaneous pays off! While we were there, I decided to go over to a friendly looking group of people who were kidding around with the waitress, hoping they were natives of Oregon. I figured it would be safe enough to go over and engage them in conversation about Mt. St. Helens. It was a very friendly and interesting conversation. They were so willing to talk to a complete stranger and happily give up what information they had. They said they weren't affected personally because they live on the west side of the mountain. They said they didn't even hear the boom. I don't know how far west they lived, but the woman said everyone in her community went out and covered up their pools. The sky was dark and gray and stayed overcast all the time. Another woman at their table joined in the conversation and she said she saw a "lightning bolt" when the mountain exploded. She said the ash was so thick one couldn't sweep it away; it was so light it would fly everywhere. They discovered all they had to do was wet it down and then shovel it. That must have been awful, but how fortunate they were to be on the safer side of Mt. St Helens. I can't even imagine!

Driving on toward Roseburg, South Oregon, we notice the closer we get to Crater Lake, the larger the mountains become. The Umpqua River is right next to us, on this scenic route, and scenic it most certainly is. We always tried to take the routes on the map that are marked the scenic route as they were the most beautiful. They were usually also the most difficult, with sharper curves and smaller roads, every bit worth it! And yes, they took a bit longer to reach a destination.

The trees are tall and remarkable, covered with a beautiful bright green moss. Further on, the Umpqua River shows off its rapids topped with white and bubbly foam. We are trying to go to the North entrance of the Park across Route 138 and then drop right down into the Park. There are deer crossing signs everywhere, but we kind of have a standing joke. As soon as we see a sign that says deer crossing we yell to each other "watch out for deer, get the camera ready!" Because we haven't seen a deer at a crossing yet! Sure enough, once we are way passed that area we see deer! Amazing! How do they know?

There is a large camper in front of us, quite a ways up, and Russ points in the sky and says, "What is that—is it an eagle?" I'll be darned, it was, and he was following along with the camper, so we sped up a little to get a little closer to the camper so I could get it better on tape. What a shot! He's so graceful and I'll bet his wing span was at least six feet. *Wow!* Beautiful! His bright white tail would flash in the sunlight against the beautiful trees that lined the road. He stayed with us for what we thought was an unusual length of time. The eagle is Russ's most favorite creature in the world. Just about every shirt he has, has an eagle on it, and he has quite a collection of pictures, statues, and a clock in his office donned with an eagle as well.

Every time we see another car approach from behind and that wasn't very often, we'd pull over to the side of the road, as soon as we could find a safe place, We'd let them pass, because we wanted to safely resume as typical gawky tourists and take pictures without worrying about getting slammed in the rear.

It is beginning to sprinkle lightly, and getting darker as evening falls. It is also colder, and the snow is packed everywhere except on the road. We were worried that the road would begin to ice over, since we didn't bring snow tires or chains. We really never thought there would be snow out here this time of year. That goes to show you how much we know about the west.

I sure wish there was a bathroom around here. We've been on the road a long time now and enjoying the heck out of every minute of it. But there comes a time when your body says, "I gotta go!" I see no other options in sight except to pull over and let Mother Nature take her course. But I'm scared to get out of the car, we really are out in the wilderness, and I'm scared to death something will come up behind me and I won't know it until it is too late! I didn't want to get caught with my pants down! Russ convinces me it will be okay and he had my back. He promised he'd watch diligently while I "mark my territory!" Ha ha. And why wouldn't I trust my darling husband of 37 years? So feeling safe and secure, I go do my thing very close to the car, and when I get back in the car there is Russ reading the map! Now, how on earth could he watch my back if he wasn't even looking! *Men!*

The road sign says we are at 5,000 feet in elevation now, and the curves in the road are sharper than ever, if that is possible. It is to the point where you can hardly see the lines in the middle of the road. Sometimes we are crawling at 5 mph—déjà vu! I was beginning to think we must have taken a wrong turn, and the lodge wasn't even here, but there was no place to take a wrong turn. So I wonder; are we lost? This movie is getting freaky! But it looks like it is going to be a repeat of Mt. Rainier; the road is snowed over and certainly not prepared for tourists travel. Russ manages to remain his calm self as I keep repeating, "Go slow, slow down, honey, no…slower. Watch out for that, is that ice, be careful!" He knew how scared I was. Many of the little side roads were gated off and I kept thinking, what if we have to turn around and do this all over again, just like Mt. St. Helens. Only it is later in the day now. But we have come to the end of our rope. The road is snowed over and we can go no further. So we have no choice but to turn around and get back on Route 230 and go south to the south entrance. We are losing a lot of time because we were really hoping to get to Crater Lake before dark. If we hadn't stopped so much to take pictures of the spectacular scenery around us, we would have not been so late, but I don't know how anyone could pass up all this beauty and not stop and wonder in it.

Sometime later, we end up in Union City, which is beautiful as all of Washington is. There is a sign at the junction for a restaurant called "Beckies." Good time to take a break, let's eat, and at least we won't end up in a place with a closed restaurant like we did last night.

Actually, Russ has a "thing" about eating at Ma-and-Pa-type restaurants. He always says if there aren't a lot of cars in the parking lot, the food isn't being moved fast enough to be fresh. Well, so much for that theory. When that's all you have, you stop and eat bananas and slim fast again. We pull up to the little parking lot, and there sits a heavily whiskered man with a big beard that goes down his chest and an old hat (the kind you see in the old pictures of a horse pulling a cart and a straw hat sitting on the horses' head.) The man is clothed in overalls and big boots, and I was wondering if he was going to pull out his ukulele and start playing it any minute. Because then we surely would have started running for Mona. Taking all this into consideration, I thought sure Russ would turn around and get back in the car, but he didn't. He really must have been hungry…and not for bananas. There was a big sign on the door that says OPEN, but when we stepped inside, we did ask a woman who had a very gruff voice if they were still open. She said, "Well, we usually close at 8:00 p.m., but go ahead and have a seat, folks." It was two minutes to 8. I guess our stomach's time clock is sitting on 8 or something. Anyway the lady was very gracious and kind. Russ got a turkey sandwich and I got chicken fingers. The sandwich came and it was huge, piled high with lots of meat, lettuce and tomato, the freshest bread and looked like a sandwich your mom would make for you. Both the sandwich and the chicken fingers were scrumptious, so see, sometimes you really can't judge a book by its cover.

While we ate, the gruff-voiced lady swept the floor and prepared for locking up. I was thinking how kind it was of her to let us in to eat. I know she was planning to close as we got there. She was sitting on one of the stools at the bar when the ukulele player came in and sat next to her. Apparently they were a couple. We thanked her most graciously for her kindness and hospitality and wonderful food, and left her a generous tip for her service.

Back to the road again, having eaten took some of the edge off, giving us a chance to settle down a little and take our minds off the snow and think about our stomachs a while. What else?

The road is bad, it is still drizzling, and it is difficult to see far ahead. My legs are getting antsy, and I am about to put a hole in the floor where I keep putting the brake on for Russ. Anyone who has ventured out to drive these roads in the winter can understand. My feet are pressing hard against the floor board and my toes are wiggling, which I always do when I am in pain or uptight. As we came around a sharp curve, it appears to go nowhere; we just can't see any further. Russ is going very slow and I keep saying, "Stop! Don't go any further." Poor Russ, he truly understands how afraid I am and just tolerates me. He said he thought he saw a light ahead, so we crept up the road (to comfort me) and went behind this huge pile of snow. My stomach got butterflies, like when you're going to go on a scary ride at an amusement park, in this case, go off the edge of the road. The lodge had plowed the snow onto both sides of the road into these huge 10-foot-high mounds. But sure enough, just a few yards ahead, there stands this huge lodge. We were so happy to see it, so we pulled Mona up into the lot in front of the lodge and Russ went in to see if there was a room. It's 10:00 p.m., and I'm sitting in the car, still shaking. Honestly, this really is not like me to be such a sissy! You can tell I am a city girl, not use to being out in the dark or the wilderness for that matter. Now I'm thinking, what if a bear breaks in my window and drags me away! This is a sad state of affairs! Since Russ didn't come right back out, this is my signal to go ahead and go into my little routine and get our cameras, maps and all together and be ready to go in. So far we have not had a problem with getting a room in any of the motels, hotels, or lodges, but in the summer, I don't recommend trying this without reservations

I just hate to keep admitting I'm scared, but my knees are feeling very weak as we gather our overnight suitcases and "stuff," and I wait in the lobby while Russ goes to park the car. This is Crater Lake Lodge and like Paradise Inn, the lobby is huge. People are sitting around playing board games and reading in front of an assortment of enormous fire places. It is very cozy and inviting, but we are only interested in finding our room right now. Our room is on the 3rd floor, and as we get off the elevator, we notice a couple of huge windows. Of course, we had to stop and see if we could see the lake, but there are puffy clouds or fog, I'm not sure which, covering it from our view. Russ was really disappointed, but I told him we know better than to accept that, we know what can happen by morning. The manager said it snowed the night before and no one got a glimpse of the lake that day; no wonder it was so overcast. Crater Lake is one of the places that gets more snow than anyplace else in America, on the average of 44 feet annually. Snow removal here keeps Oregon's road crews extremely busy. I guess that snow fall had a lot to do with our not being able to enter the park from the north entrance because from the information we received in the park's little newspaper, the north entrance is usually cleared by late May.

Once we enter our room, for some reason, my head is spinning and it felt like the room was moving and uneven. I ran straight for the bathroom, put on my nightie, and climbed into the bed, which was *so* comfortable. All I wanted to do was to cling to Russ, my security blanket, and go to sleep.

It is bright and early and we are showered, refreshed, and I think we have come back to our senses! On our way to breakfast, we had to stop and take a sneak peak out of the two windows in front of the elevator, and there it was bigger than life, *exactly* like the post cards we saw! There were still a few clouds on the water but I just knew they would rise up and go away. The sun was shining and by 8:00 a.m., that was true, the clouds did lift up! The water in the crater was a gorgeous translucent, pure, royal blue (like sparkling sapphires), and there was snow all around it like a huge white picture frame. The sky was so blue and the contrast in the two blue colors (the lake and the sky) is indescribable. Russ's first words were "it looks like a blue jewel."

It is the deepest lake in the United States sinking to 1,962 feet and all 4.6 trillion gallons of water that fills it comes from rainfall and snow melt. The water is so clear you can see anywhere from 50 to 75 feet down. The temperature on the surface is 64 degrees and 300 feet down and beyond, 38 degrees. It rarely freezes over though, the last time it did was in 1949. And I think they swim here in the summer months. *Brrrr!* In summer months, they also take tourists for rides in a boat all around the lake and over to Wizard Island to fish. It is said the fishing is fantastic. That is one thing Russ would have liked to do. The observation deck is not open because of all the snow, but I can't imagine seeing this blue jewel any better than we are right now.

Gosh, there are so many volcanoes in the United States I wasn't aware of, this being one of them. Crater Lake was formed by a tremendous explosion of Mt. Mazana 7,700 years ago and later Wizard Island was formed (the small island within the lake). It is known as a cinder cone and so is the Merriam Cone, which is in the back end of the lake, but it is under water. It is all so magnificent; we stand there in awe of it that we are able to view it in our lifetime.

The mountains behind are trying to hide, gleaming with snow as is the rim of the lake and Wizard Island. There are only a few clouds scattered here and there. I just can't believe it could be prettier than this in the summer. Much of the lake is roped off because of the danger of the snow and snow drifts, and ropes and warnings are posted not to get to close to the edge. There are big pine trees, white bark pines and hemlocks. They are even thick on Wizard Island, like the Island is decorated with hundreds of little Christmas trees. As we walk along the snowy rim there is a huge dead-looking tree that is so big and unusual in its size and shape, all twisted and gnarled; of course, we had to take a picture of it. We must not have been the only ones who thought it was amazing, because later on I found a postcard with a picture of it as well. I thought it was my idea first…guess not. All of a sudden, the most adorable little blue bird flew up next to us. I think the theme of this park is the most stunning blues you could imagine. This beautiful tiny creature graced us with his presence for several minutes before he flitted off into the wilderness. He made our hearts sing…even more.

We decided to go inside for a short while even though it was hard to pull ourselves away from the lake. The lodge is huge, and Russ points out to me that each floor has exit doors to the outside of the building. How about that! He said if the snow gets that high, you wouldn't be able to get out on the first floor and even sometimes on the second. The beams holding the building up are monstrous with heavy duty hardware supporting it all.

Before we left Crater Lake, we took a last walk around and stood at the roped off area to stare for one last time and sear that awesome image into our brains. The gentleman next to me began to talk to me. He told me how one night he and a friend had snow-mobiled up the east side of the rim and got up on the huge peak. He said, "The moon shone across the lake and it was magnificent." He also said he lived in the area and was over at the lake constantly because he admired its beauty so much. He mentioned that yester-day a man was standing there and decided he wasn't close enough. So he climbed over the ropes to get closer, lost his balance, and fell all the way down. That sent slivers up my spine to even think of it and I backed away from the ropes. He seemed rather angry over the incident stating, "Some people just don't obey rules. These ropes are here for a reason." But the man was rescued, though injured badly, which seemed to disgust him. He said, "It would have served him right if he didn't make it." Such a terrible thought, but I understand his thinking. In a way, he has a point. Other people's lives are put in danger too, trying to save a careless person like that. But unlike this gentleman, I'm glad everything turned out all right, maybe he learned a hard lesson. I can only imagine what a very dangerous and vital job the parks maintenance crew has; deciding where to mark boundaries and remain safe on some of the ledges they have to drive on. They do an incredible job!

Russ and I turned and walked around the area a little while in the snow. It was great hearing the crunching of the snow under our feet, a sound you always remember, as we see very little in Georgia. The trees went on and on, as far as you could see, so beautiful and so serene.

An organized routine now, we loaded our car and prepared for our next adventure. How different the landscape appears in daylight! Millions of straight trees line the road, and the snow was deep at first, but once we got down in elevation, the snow was only 1 or 2 feet deep. The road is winding like a top but the mountains are turning browner in color and the snow is disappearing. The mountain side with brown and beige, forms what look like cones or tubes, next to a canyon. They are called fossil fumaroles according to the informa-tion sign in front of the canyon. Very interesting. Then we see more waterfalls and Upper Lake Klamath, which is huge. All of this is snuggled in the Cascade Mountains. It took us all of 15 to 20 minutes to come down from Crater Lake, a remarkable ride that only the night before was a treacherous and dangerous hike. A nerve-wracking 4 hours, to be exact!

Another choice destination of mine was to see the Golden Gate Bridge. And that is where the rest of our movie will resume. So... *California, here we come!*

CHAPTER 8

Golden California

This is not one of Russ's favorite places to go, he is doing it for me, but I figure once we get there, he will enjoy it. We have a pretty long ride before we get to San Francisco. We probably won't be there until dark.

I can feel Russ's mood, at this point, maybe he is tired, or impatient, or just doesn't care to do this. You know, you can't be with someone all these years and not pick up on all the little clues of what is coming next, whether its irritation, hunger, I'm tired, lost, nervous, his glance, when he starts whistling, his attitude, or even the tone of his voice. Kind of like how a baby sends messages. So I pull out my ammunition, our music, our good ole faithful tapes. Don't forget Mona is old so she has a "tape" deck and not a CD player. But when we bought Mona new, I thought I was "uptown" having a tape deck. I put in one of our tapes, and it got him happy and smiling again. Pretty clever, huh? Easy!

It is 1:00 p.m., and we are in California! We stopped and had lunch and fed Mona. Gas prices are up compared to when we started our adventure. When we left Georgia, gas was $3.50/gal, and now we just filled up at $4.56/gal. That is quite a difference for one month. It's not even that bad today.

I believe the mountain we are passing now is called the Shasta Mountain and then we pass a large beautiful lake. But it will be a bit before we are in San Francisco. By the time we got through, the *Lion King*, and the *Jungle Book*, we were closing in on Oakland. Seriously, how much more uplifting can you get than with that kind of music?

What a difference in climate; from snow to sun-shiny California. Don't get me wrong, it is cold but no snow. We decided to look for a motel so we could move on with our day and wouldn't have to worry about that later, but much to our dismay, we couldn't figure out where to get off the expressway to find one. You see, California has these high walls and trees next to the expressway on both sides, and you can't see what is on the other side. Plus, we didn't see any billboards, either.

This is where I pick up all kinds of signals from Russ. *Deep sigh*, and then a little slap of his hand on the door rest. We have gotten off several different exits hoping to find either a restaurant or a motel, but no luck! Wow, first time we ran into this problem. Our vision is so blocked from the walls, it must be a law or something in California not to have high billboards, I don't know.

Russ is humming! Uh-oh! He is getting upset and impatient, that's when he hums, or if I ticked him off somehow, but that is not the case this time. We get off the expressway (or motor way as our English speaker on our GPS calls it), again, only to get right back on. Okay. We are lost! I admit it! We have gone too far, completely in the wrong direction. And why on earth wouldn't we stop and ask for directions? Squirming in his seat, leaning closer to the steering wheel *and* holding on with both hands, I know I better spring into action. I try some calming words, like, "It's okay, don't worry, we're in no big hurry or anything. We'll just turn around when we can." Finally we find a shopping center. It's getting late, and lo and behold, there is a restaurant straight ahead. Russ decides this is a good time to eat, and then we will resume our motel hunt.

On the way out of the restaurant, Russ asked a young man at the front desk if he knew where a comfort inn was and I couldn't believe my ears when he actually knew! Well, we found the inn much to our relief and decided to call it a night.

It is May 31st; we are rested and content and ready to resume our big adventure. I gathered a bunch of pamphlets on the way out of the inn, and we hit the road. We came upon the cutest little restaurant I've ever seen called "Mimi's." It is decorated like a dollhouse or a gingerbread house. Its roof has beige- and pinkish-colored tiles, with two little windows in what would be like an attic in a house (dormers), trimmed in royal blue with royal blue awnings, and flower boxes and flower pots under all the many windows. The little bushes around it are all blooming and ever so neatly manicured. The inside was even cuter than the outside and it wasn't so little either. It was almost like a little cottage with flowered windows, lots and lots of tables, antiques around and cozy little decorations on the walls and everywhere. It was a very comforting place and extremely busy, with smiling and seemingly happy servers as well as a happy and buzzing atmosphere. See, God knew right where to take us at just the right time. We had to wait a bit, but it was worth the wait until once again, we are full and content and looking forward to the next stop.

Being the adventurers we are, I dove into the many pamphlets we gathered. They are very helpful and informative about San Francisco. On our way through Oakland heading toward the Golden Gate Bridge, we came to another bridge. At first I thought it was the Golden Gate, because ignorant me…I didn't know there was a bridge you cross first to get *to* the Golden Gate. Well, this bridge is fantastic! I can't imagine the Golden Gate being bigger or more beautiful. The toll is $4.00 to get across. Come to find out this is the gorgeous San Francisco/Oakland Bay Bridge and it is known as one of the seven engineering wonders of the world. *Wow*, I love it. Also a bit of information…it was built in 1936, six months before the Golden Gate! Of course, I looked up all these little facts after we got home. This really is an added treat for me! The Oakland Bay is on our right and the San Francisco Bay is to our left. This bridge is magnificent. Can you believe it has *two levels!* We are on the upper level; it has five lanes and goes west. It spans 8.4 miles of dangerous and deep water. The bottom level which also has five lanes goes back to the east. How neat is that? It is built in two segments and right slap dab in the middle is a tunnel connecting the two. It is the largest bore tunnel in diameter in the world. The Bay Bridge, as the locals refer to it, carries 1/3 of the traffic of all the state-owned bridges combined.

Just to throw a scary fact in here, I found out that in 1989, San Francisco had an earthquake that reached 7.1 in magnitude on the Richter scale. A portion of the upper deck came unhinged and fell to the lower deck. I would say that was pretty good considering the span of this massive bridge. So at least we know now that the bridge can withstand such a horrible disaster because this is minimal damage considering the size.

I am still anxious to get to the Golden Gate, but in order to do that, we have to go through San Francisco and figure out how to find the entrance. This road is close to the ocean and it is hilly. The homes are multicolored and adorable. They are decorated in the Victorian style with balconies on the second floor. We can see there is a tourist route here and we will come back and go slower, but our goal right now is to find the toll plaza to the Golden Gate. The bridge is very visible from almost any turn. Finally, we find signs directing us to the bridge. We come across a small back street that has many turns, kind of like a back alley, in my mind. But, suddenly, right in front of us, here is the toll plaza, $5.00 this time and on we go. Just imagine, before the bridge was built, people would have to go over on a ferry. The bay has strong swirling tides and currents, the water is 500 feet deep and there are very frequent and ferocious winds at the center of the channel, not to mention blinding fog. Imagine the thought of trying to build a bridge in all that.

Both of these bridges, Oakland and the Golden Gate, are suspension bridges. The Golden Gate has six lanes, however. It is a brilliant red-orange in color because that is the color of the sealant they used in the beginning. So many of the locals liked the color, they persuaded the builders to leave it that way. The bridge cost a whopping $35 million to build and like I said before, it was built in 1937, six months after the San Francisco/Oakland Bay Bridge. At least now they realized it could be done. The cables are made of 27,572 strands of wire; they look to be about 3 feet around. This is the part that impressed Russ the most, as he encouraged me to get pictures of its structure. It must have been an enormous feat, and my research tells me that for the safety of the men, they built a movable safety netting beneath the construction site, which saved the lives of many otherwise unprotected workers. But sad to say there were still 11 men killed during construction. There is always a price to pay, isn't there?

As we drive across the Golden Gate Bridge, I notice there is a sidewalk next to me where people are walking across and on the other side bicycling over this monster. They say you really can't appreciate the size and structure of the San Francisco Bridge until you walk across it. Today pedestrians are walking on the east side, but that changes from day to day. If you peer down at mid span, you will be 220 feet up looking down at ships that appear to be small toys. The view is captivating, the sun is shining on all the sail boats and you can see Alcatraz from here. This is a fantastic experience and I'm so glad we came to see this wonder. I can see how people could leave their hearts in San Francisco. We'd like to visit the piers my pamphlets tell us about. One of the pamphlets has a great map of the layout of the city, and it makes life a lot simpler. *Hello!* Why didn't we do that in the beginning? Maybe I was just too busy gawking at all the beautiful sights around us.

I think we are now in downtown San Francisco. Well, if it isn't, it is busy enough to be. We find ourselves on Beach St. where there is a parking deck, which cost $20.00 to park Mona. It really wasn't hard to find a place to park. But remember we are not in the busiest season yet.

It is easy to see that tourism is the backbone of San Francisco economy. There are what seems like millions of people crossing the streets (and I thought Seattle was busy), cable cars, for which San Francisco is famous, are up and down this hilly city and there is an assortment of stores. From the elite all the way to T-shirts, 3 for $10.00, lots of souvenir stores, and small places to eat. I have to make a mental note to stop at the T-shirt and souvenir stores on the way back. Right on the corner is a Walgreen's so we stop in to get some more of my little disposable cameras.

As we approach the crossing at the corner, I notice the cross-walk signals. I haven't seen any like them in Marietta yet. The hand on the blinking light goes up for you to stop and then a visible count-down begins; to let you know how long it will be until you can cross. How impressive.

The sidewalks are crowded and buzzing with people. There are people everywhere, many at the road panning for money one way or another. Some are singing and dancing, one is playing a guitar, a little further up one is making cute animals out of little balloons, then a couple who are painted silver are dancing like robots (my favorite one), and the last one was a lady juggling fire. I just love that stuff and want to stop and watch, but Russ wants to keep going. He is at least 4 steps ahead of me and I am hanging onto his sleeve like a small child and my head is turned all the way around just so I can see all the acts. It is very obvious Russ doesn't want to be here in this crowd. He is giving me another sign: he is clenching his teeth. He kind of isn't listening to me right now either, because every time I say something to him, he says, "Yeah." "Honey, what would you like to see next?" "Yeah" "Wanna stop here?" "Yeah." "Russ!" "Here?" "Yeah." "Russ!" "What?" See! I don't even think he knows he's doing that.

Once we get down a couple blocks, we are next to the bay and just stand there by the waterfront for a while, and take in the uniqueness of the bay. There are beautiful sailboats with the Golden Gate Bridge in the background. What a sight to behold. Perfect! Then suddenly a young man comes right in front of us sail-surfing. That looked like so much fun, but hard to do, and I'll bet that freezing water was a shock as he went down.

We reached Jefferson St and go a little way and discover "Boudin At The Wharf." This is a restaurant and bakery where they bake sourdough French bread. We step inside and they have a little museum and bakery tour. Man, it smells luscious in here! Russ actually is interested in that sort of thing, so we do the tour and go upstairs to eat. This is fine dining up here, so we go back down stairs and order a sandwich, which is very interesting in itself. There are bread baskets hanging in baskets on conveyer belts running all throughout the restaurant. When we ordered at the desk, and the line is quite long, the little basket sails by the kids making the sandwiches and they just grab the kind of bread you need for your sandwich out of the basket. I had a chicken salad but I don't remember what Russ had. My sandwich was really yummy but Russ was disappointed in whatever it was that he had, I do remember that. Once we got outside, there was a large window in front of the restaurant and two men were kneading dough and shaping the bread into all different shapes, like teddy bears, alligators, turtles, and all sorts of cute things. It was fun and interesting to stand there and watch for a while.

I guess the most interesting pamphlet we had picked up, advertised Pier 39, so that is the pier we are looking for. There are many piers all along this street which is called The Embarcadero. They start around pier #47 and continue around The Embarcadero, ending with pier 1. It is quite cold, about 55 degrees and windy, Russ guesses the wind gusts are about 20 mph. I'm glad we weren't parked any further away. A horse drawn buggy, all in white, even a white horse, takes the stage, and passes us by. There is a shabily dressed man on the corner with a sign around his neck and I think he is preaching the Gospel, but right now, he is standing still like a statue with his arms outstretched in the form of a cross. He remains completely motionless as we pass and go on.

Shortly, we came to a pier with a huge circular sign in the shape of a ships steering wheel on the corner that says Fisherman's Wharf. We are at pier 39, and it almost looks like a shopping mall; it is 2 stories high and very long. There are all kinds of stores on each side such as: T-shirts, ice cream (brrr), restaurants, candy, a theatre of old movies, jewelry, clothing, and gold; practically any kind of shop you can imagine, and then guess what? I found a little shop with nothing but magnets. Wooohooo!

In the middle of the pier is a gorgeous carousel; it is a double decker too. Boy, San Francisco knows how to do it up right. I felt like a kid just looking at it. Beautiful colors, with lights all around and inside it, and the prettiest sky blue decorations around the top with scenes from San Francisco. The same color of blue contrasted with white drapes hanging down and wrapped around the poles. Children are waving to their loved ones standing on the sidelines; moms and dads are hanging on tight to the smaller ones with big and happy waves, wondering if their babies can see them as they go round and round. There are big smiles on everyone's faces as they go around and the familiar music reaches in and touches the kid in your very own soul. I do believe it is one of the prettiest merry-go-rounds I have ever seen. And I have seen quite a few in my lifetime. It is comfortable in here with our coats on, so we just stroll along until we get to the end of the pier where you are blasted with the Artic air; but what a great view from here! The bridge is gorgeous and Alcatraz is right in front of us and there are boats that will take you to tour it or just ride around it if you want. Did you know Alcatraz built the first lighthouse on the west coast in 1854? From what I understand, it is a national park now as part of the larger Golden Gate National Recreation Area. This certainly is "an inescapable experience." Ha, ha.

This is as far as we can go on the wharf. I am so happy Russ's mood has changed and he is his old self again. Our pamphlet tells us that Fisherman Wharf has been the home of San Francisco's colorful fleet for 125 years, and there are hundreds of fishing boats all around the wharf. There are pelicans flying overhead and seagulls walking on the pier and to our left, there are anywhere from 10 to 20 wooden platforms floating in the bay loaded with sea lions atop. I bet there are hundreds of them in this "loafers lounge" and I can't help but wonder if the fishermen appreciate all these critters, because I know the lions must love their bait. Some of the lions are just dozing and others jumping up and down, on and off the platforms and aggravating the larger guys. I really don't understand sometimes how that blubber thing works. They say the blubber keeps them warm in these freezing waters, but then why am I so cold? We stayed a while and just watched their little antics, but it was so cold we decided to head back to the stores we saw earlier, with the neat T-shirts. Then, maybe after that we will go back and find the scenic tour through town.

The wind was going right through us on our way back to the car. By now I have my gloves on and my hood up on my coat. You could just see how cold everyone was, but not everyone had a coat. They all had their arms wrapped around themselves, were walking really fast, and you could see the warm air coming from their panting mouths. We did duck into a couple of the cute shops anyway. I bought several T-shirts, but my very most favorite was the Alcatraz shirt that said, "THE HOTEL ALCATRAZ—GUARANTEED ROOM WITH A VIEW—24 HOUR SECURITY—LIFETIME ACCOMMODATIONS—CATERING TO SELECT CLIENTELE—BARS IN EVERY ROOM—ALL DRINKS ARE ON THE ROCKS—SAN FRANCISCO." Isn't that the cutest thing ever? There goes that warped sense of humor again.

It took a while, but we finally came across the scenic route once again and started with the Presidia National Park. This park has been transformed from a military base, so it has small homes all in a row which look like they could have been for the military families, or small offices. As we go through the base, we come to a huge military cemetery. It is called the San Francisco National Cemetery. If you can call a cemetery beautiful, this one certainly was. This is where Russ gets teary-eyed, as he has such love for the men in the military as we all do. But this scene is special to him.

San Francisco is only 7 miles long and 8 miles wide, which made me think of how small Key West is. Having grown up in Miami, Florida, we walked that many times. Anyway, the tour winds around the small streets of San Francisco, with the cute little Victorian-style homes. Then we pass this beautiful domed structure that we were trying to figure out what it was. Later on, once we got to the motel, I found a picture of it on a post card. It was called the Palace of Fine Arts.

It is time to bring our San Francisco adventure to an end, and finalize our day, and this time we get to drive on the underside of the bay bridge.

Once we got back on the other side of the bridge, we took more pictures of it as the wind just howls. There are so many things to do in San Francisco, we chose only a few, but if you have more time or wish to make this your sole vacation, you could take a week or two and fill your days easily. We could have taken lunch tours, go to the aquarium, the wax museum, a motorized cable car tour, visit Chinatown, or even take a ride on a wine train to name only a few of those things.

But sadly, it is time for us to move on and yet not so sad either because our next destination will be Yosemite National Park. So we found our way back to the same motel and stayed there again for the night. It is so nice with a balcony and you could stand there and admire the city.

The inn's buffet breakfast was enough for us today, so afterward, we went and "gassed" Mona. As we drove out of Oakland, we passed fields and fields of windmills or maybe they are wind turbines. I'm not sure which. There are millions of them everywhere, beautifully lined up and turning so casually and dutifully, like soldiers all in a row. I really don't know much about Yosemite, but we are excited about going there. It is approximately 5 hours away. The land is rather flat right now, and we seem to be in a traffic jam which is slowing us down a bit, but that's okay. As we progress, the hills are becoming more obvious. We were going to go across Routes 120/108, but instead, decided to continue down to Merced and then cut across to Yosemite on Route 140, the scenic route and enter through the Arch Rock Entrance. Doesn't that sound enticing?

Our flat land is no longer flat, as we go up and then down and over and oh my, we are about an hour out of Yosemite National Park, the roads are sharp, S-shaped curves, and it seems like the mountains are small but that is probably because we are in them. At least it is daylight and it is not raining, a gorgeous day. The view is fantastic now, and it has become another "white knuckle" ride, with narrow, two lane roads. And here we go again with our battering back and forth. "Russ, slow down." "Okay." "Russ!" "Okay." "Slow down, honey." "Okay." "The sign says 15 mph." "Oh, okay." I know you are getting sick of hearing me say that, so imagine how Russ feels. It seems Mona had to chime in and she moans as we swerve around another sharp curve. Sometimes we are literally on the edge of the mountain and now the roads are a little bumpy. It makes me a little dizzy to lean out the window and take pictures, when we are so close to the edge like that. It feels like we are on a roller coaster. I'm so glad we had our brakes checked before we left the house, I just pray they don't let us down. I mean *down* literally. "Slow down, honey." "Okay." We pass a little creek and then Bear River, nestled in the Sierra Nevada Mountains.

It is Sunday, about 1:00 p.m., the first beautiful day of June. The entrance to the park is up ahead, but first is the ranger's station where once again we can use our wonderful national park pass. We are handed a map and a very useful guide booklet with lots of facts and information. According to our little guide book, Yosemite is one of the natural wonders of the world, about the size of Rhode Island, 95 percent being designated wilderness. Far in the distance we see a little white trickle falling over the mountainside. Already the scenery is like heaven—a magic land. We must drive under a huge rock in the form of a tunnel named Arch Rock Tunnel, where there is a small waterfall. It is spring and I'm sure it is snow runoff. We can't help it, we keep stopping to take pictures; it is such a wonderland here. But who cares, what is the rush? It's still *our* movie and we're calling the shots. How wonderful!

We still have our eye on that white little trickle in the distance which isn't a trickle anymore, but growing before our eyes to a huge and graceful fall. It is Bridal Veil Fall! There are signs saying you can get out and walk up to it to get a closer view. It wasn't a bad hike at all, only 0.5 miles round trip and there were several people walking up to it. Oh, my goodness, it's simply amazing. You could feel the cool spray of the fall on your face, in fact, enough to cause me to remove my glasses. Droplets from heaven! Bridal Veil fall drops 620 feet and the very top of it is rolling off the mountain like white foamy thunder, haloed with mist that looks like smoke, but indeed it is white water splashing all around it, whirling in the wind. Just a little reminder…do *not* do your hair before you enter Yosemite! We spent a pretty good while there where all your senses are heightened. The fresh smell, the touch of the sun and the droplets of water on your skin make it real. The thunderous sound of the fall and the murmuring of the onlookers close by with their mouths open and heads tilted way back. One could hear the *ewwws* and *ahhhs*, expressing the feeling of wonder and amazement. We seemed to feel as though we were one with all the other vacationers, sharing the awesomeness of the moment. As you exit the fall, almost as a finale, you cross over a small babbling brook way down at the foot of it. The trees by the parking lot are beautiful mixed with sequoias.

The Merced River is to our left, following right along with us, crooked and a stunning green color, also bouncing with white foam on top. Rafters are on their way down it and look like they are having a ball. That is a fun and exhilarating thing to do. We rafted down some of the Colorado when we visited our son one time.

The road splits now and we are on a one-way street called Southside Drive. Before us we see a gigantic rock and it is named El

Capitan. It is a granite rock, a summit more than half a mile high, twice as tall as the Empire State Building or 3,593 feet from the base to the summit. It is the largest granite monolith in the world. The booklet tells me that climbers come from all over the world to climb it and there is no permit required for those who dare. These monoliths attract lightening because they intensify the power of the air around them. You sure better be in good shape to try and scale this bold slice of granite!

We observe many bikers and hikers as we continue our drive. The park is extremely busy, maybe because it is Sunday. There is a detour sign in front of us and a very small bridge, single lane, crossing over the Merced. We are in a line with two or three cars in front of us. It is a little scary because the bridge is so small and seems like a temporary one. We are crawling and the Merced is raging beneath us. Once we get over the tiny bridge, we turn onto a small road. The roads are very curvy and squiggly with sharp curve signs every few feet and signs warning of rock slides. Finally, another sign, stating we are officially "in" Yosemite. We decide to pull over and enjoy this one small spot of the Merced. It is beautiful green, clear water; we can feel the coolness of it and hear the glorious sound of the rushing water. Gigantic rocks have placed themselves comfortably in the river. Russ is peering into the river where he can see deep dark holes and thinking of the trout he wishes he was fishing for at this moment. I would think for most people it would be a relaxing and peaceful experience, but instead, I feel a "rush" inside with an intense urge for more. Show me more! I'm loving it!

Back in the car and looking up—more falls. I believe this fall is called the Cascades. We spy yet another fall called Ribbon Fall; wow, smell that air! And then Sentinel Fall. It is never-ending and we are turning here and there taking it all in. Located nearby are three huge peaks all in a row. They are called the three brothers. Of course, we have our own names for them since we have three sons, but the "real" names were Lower Brother, Middle Brother, and Eagle Peak, rising up to 7,779 feet. I like our names better! Straight ahead another fall called Horsetail Fall, which goes on and on and on and just when you think it is going to end, it goes some more! Breathtaking surprises with every turn!

The mountains around us sit in all shapes and sizes with little trees jutting out of them. The wind is whipping around. Picnic areas are everywhere and people are out embracing God's mesmerizing world. Yosemite is very accommodating to its tourists, with clean bathrooms spaced conveniently, places to eat close by, cleanliness, informative signage, and friendly helpful rangers and employees. As in most of the national parks, the safety of the visitors seems to be their very first concern and the animals within for that matter.

Of course, we have been dilly-dallying along, so by the time we get to the Yosemite Lodge, they are full! But the lodge employees are very helpful and direct us to a lodge called Curry Lodge, which still has 80 rooms available. Russ asked (just to make sure) if this was a place where you have to bring your own linens, etc., because we did pass a camp called Housekeeping Camp. The girl at the desk said, "Oh, no," so we drove over there only to find out they had sheets on the beds, but there were *no* inside potties! Well, I had already let Russ know, if there were no bathroom facilities *in* the building and we have to go *out*side at night; there was no way I was going out in the dark. The answer is *No! No! No!* I mean, I sleep with a night-light in my own house; there is no way I am going out in the pitch-black dark of the night at Yosemite Park to meet a bear! I want to see one, but in the safety of my own car, thank you! Not as often as I get up! This is one time our spontaneity does not pay off! So we will move on out of the park and find something outside of it, which we did with no problem, right next to the dynamic Merced River. We could hear the sound of the river as soon as we pulled in the parking lot. The room was on the second floor (no elevators) but what a view! As we lean into our window, the river is just feet from us, with such a great roar we cannot hear each other speak, but we are basking in the beauty and sound of this powerful place. The room was huge with a huge bathroom that had two showerheads in the shower. Call me ignorant but I had never seen something like that before, but that didn't mean we didn't know what to do with it!

Oh we knew what to do with it alright. Well, Russ forgot his towel. The next thing I knew he was on the floor sliding passed me like he was on a slide at White Water! He crashed into the wall at the other end. Well, I almost burst out laughing, but, I didn't. Not until he got up and said he was fine in a rather indignant tone. Oh my, that man. Anyway, we slept with the window open, and I slept like a baby listening to that deafening river. But Russ had a hard time with it's roar. Tomorrow we will do this again, but more in depth, and try to see everything we missed today.

Today is another beautiful day in paradise, one of Russ's favorite sayings! The lodge offered a buffet breakfast that was wonderful. They were very busy. We needed to gas Mona because there is no gas offered in the park. For the first time, we are paying $5.10 a gallon! But we certainly do not want to get into the park and get stuck. Our plan is to look for Glacier Point and see Half Dome.

No sooner do we turn out of the lodge and we see another water fall. It is huge, I can't imagine how we missed this one. It is much wider at the top than the others, almost divided into two separate falls. It falls to a landing and then gets even wider plummeting onto huge rocks. It is so wide and white and it looks like spun cotton to me.

Heading back to Yosemite Valley, we passed several more falls and decided to look around in the Yosemite Lodge. The valley itself is seven miles long and one mile wide. It is assessable year long. All around is a paved path. Such a beautiful sunshiny day, how could anyone resist taking a little walk with El Capitan at one end and Yosemite Fall at the other? Somehow I managed to talk Russ into taking a little walk with me. I guess we walked about half an hour. A family with very small children walked by; the young'uns were sitting in the cutest little red cart.

Yosemite Fall drops in two parts, the upper and the lower, with a combined height of 2,425 feet, which makes it the tallest waterfall in North America. As we drive on to find Glacier Point, we will be able to see the Yosemite from up above and get an even clearer picture of it, I'm sure.

We walked only fifteen feet over and we could already appreciate the wilderness. We came upon a grouping of sequoia trees and the roots were coiled and spread out in gruesome shapes. I got the bright idea to go over and sit on one of the huge branches that was shaped like a seat, so Russ could take my picture. That wasn't too smart because I jumped up from there so fast, by the time Russ snapped the picture, I was almost out of there. Now I understand where the saying "Ants in her pants" came from, because there were ants all over me. *Yikes!*

Close by was a bridge. As we walked across, right in the middle of it was a gauge indicating the height of flood waters with a date of each flood. The flood from 1937 marks a height up to my knee caps. The highest number was at my eye level, the results of flooding that occurred in January of 1997, when a warm rain fell on an already deep snow pack in the high country. The water is so clear you'd think it was only a couple inches deep, but in fact, it is about 5 feet deep. As we stood there a little while we watched the serene dark-green water flow below us. The same waters that literally raged and roared passed our window in the night. The park has warned never to swim or wade near waterfalls. Sometimes water is deceptively calm, but may have a strong current. Our park guide says each year visitors are swept over waterfalls. In 2005, three such tragedies occurred.

Half dome is towering over us now, powerful and captivating, looming over a quaint little chapel. It is called the Yosemite Chapel built in 1879, the oldest structure still in use in the park. I believe we are in Curry Village now. Then a little ways up there is a gift shop, oh boy, post cards. The seats to rest on here are tree stumps that are just the right height to sit on. There is Russ, trying one out and looking like "a bump on the log." Ha ha.

We had lunch at a mountain burger place and sat at a round table, with a couple from close by here in California. They gave us a few tips about going to see Glacier Point. We had traveled all this way, it would have been a shame not to see something so special.

As we progress up this mountain, there are signs with a red bear on them every so often. They mean "red bear, dead bear." Cars speed through here all the time, even though the speed limit is clearly visible. Hundreds of animals are killed here by speeding cars along these winding roads and the red bear sign sadly marks the place where a bear was recently hit.

We are looking for Glacier Point; the view is like a dream. Beautiful deep pink flowers blooming to our left and butterflies are flitting all around them. Waterfalls continue to take the stage though, while astoundingly colored birds seem to show off their stunning color. Russ is laughing as I run around and try to get them on film, so we will always be able to remember them. One is a little black bird with a shiny blue chest, he poses for me as if to say, "You don't have to chase me. Here I am." It looks like he may belong to the jay family because as he turns his head from left to right for us to admire him, you can see the little crown on his head. Since we are out stretching our legs, we stroll a little and find a little cave. Russ's opportunity to pretend he is a cave man, squatting and acting like a gorilla. Oh, my! I cock my head to one side and put my hands on my hips and wonder if he'll ever grow up! Well, I do have to say…he sure is fun to be with.

We come to another visitor center and the rangers are there talking to people and we spotted one of the rangers we have seen on TV before. He is standing on the stairs of the building greeting and talking to visitors. He and his companions mounted their horses and rode off into the sunset. I must say…What a great movie we are in!

We pulled over at several viewing areas as we went higher and higher, realizing we aren't alone any more. Where did all these people come from? There is a small wall around this area about three feet high. Russ said I should go over and sit on it so he can get a picture of me with all this grandeur behind me. Well, he might as well ask me to jump off. The wall was so small! But I did manage to go slow and cautious and sit on the very edge of it for the picture. I thought that was very brave of me.

El Capitan is right in front of us and now we can look down and see the falls from above. There is snow all around, and right in the middle of it all we come to another tunnel. Once we pass through this very long tunnel which is pure rock and appears orange in color because of the lights, we can see there has been a fire here, with trees left black and straggly, silhouetted by the bright blue sky. Yet other mountains around us are rocky, tall, and cluttered with tiny new trees all clinging for dear life, literally. As if to say, "There is no stopping us. We are going to survive no matter what." It does make you wonder where on earth they store their water and where their nutrients come from.

Sixteen more miles until Glacier Point, it is a great ride; the curves are dangerous with a very small wall on the edges. We are enjoying a beautiful view of the rugged terrain, at 5,000 feet elevation, when out of nowhere here comes one of those mini yellow school buses zipping past us like there is no tomorrow. I'm sure glad there were no children on it. Many times we were right on the edge of the road. The way people are passing us you'd think we were on an expressway. It is so scary because some of the cars coming toward us are way over their yellow line.

Another panoramic view and there it is...Half Dome! Half Dome rises to an elevation of 8,842 feet and is 87 million years old. This is Glacier Point at 6,000 feet.

Here sits the little bus that passed us a while back and I just couldn't believe they went so fast as to get this far ahead of us. We are way high up now, about as high as you can get, and Yosemite Falls is so clear in the distance. Both the upper and lower parts are visible at one time. The vista here is mind-blowing. Standing near the edge of a wall, a small deer walks up to us and passes on by like we were old friends. He wasn't a bit afraid, so you can see that they are used to being around humans. We, on the other hand, stare at each other in amazement as this sweet little critter leaves his footprints on our hearts.

Off in the distance, there are mountains covered with snow. They are Mt. Florence which is 15 miles high, Mount Lyle and Mount Star King, which looks to me like the shape of a pyramid. Behind Star King is yet another snow-covered mountain called Red Peak. The "untouchables" which seem so near and yet are so far away. As we look way down, we can see the outline of the river snaking down and through the valley. No wonder it is so fast and furious by the time it gets down to our lodge.

After walking about the area for a while and taking in all this natural beauty all around us, we decided to head back down to the

Valley. It is getting cold, probably around 50 degrees and you can hear the wind howling in the camcorder. We are alone in our movie once again. On the way down, we get a great view of Royal Arches which is a huge mountainside with arches carved into its side. Time, water and sand have carved out a place of paradise here in Yosemite. We are so blessed to experience this remarkable land.

Half Dome Yosemite National Park

It is a thrilling ride as we descend; Royal Arches is right in front of us, just like a mural painted on the side of the mountain wall, and not far from there is another fall called Vernal Fall. It is very wide at the top and difficult to see much of the bottom because of the tall trees in front. The three rounded rocks in front of us are named North Dome and Basket Dome. Half Dome is close too and further down; oh my goodness, as we make a sharp turn half dome is right here on us. It could slap us right in the face, all 8,842 feet of it. I can't believe what a thrilling sight this is. It just seemed to appear right there. *Wow!* I never dreamed a mountain or a rock could stir such overwhelming feelings inside me.

Some of the curves on this mountain are so sharp we are literally going in a circle. At one point, we couldn't see the end of the road and it looked as though we would drive right off the edge of the world. We are praying the brakes are still in working order. Then these delightful white tubular shaped flowers (like a bottle brush) are on the side of the road. There are so many and we got great pictures of them—a flock of flowers!

Now that it is dusk we're seeing deer, only one stood still long enough for us to take its picture though. Two of the deer were walking right in the village where people were practically right beside them. Actually, we focused a great deal on the falls and rocks throughout our stay at Yosemite, but there is so much more to see and do. We didn't visit the museum in the valley for instance, or hike, or see the wide variety of flowers that grow in the vibrant high Sierra. There are tours, bicycling, rafting, fishing, and the wilderness center, just to name a few. I believe you could stay at Yosemite a week or more and still not see all this amazing park has to offer.

We decided to end our day at the cafeteria in the park, which was wonderful; in fact, this is the second night we have eaten here. It is a shame not to spend another day at Yosemite, but our dreams are big and we have much left to see. Our lodge is just outside the park so we must cross over our little detour bridge as we leave. Now we can look to our left and see why we had the detour. *Landslide!* Oh, no! It was a good-sized one too. I hope no one was injured. This is one of the things that happen at Yosemite—besides fire and floods. It is expected that when stone walls corrode and ice causes pressure within its walls, there will be landslides. It is all part of the natural process in this dangerous but fascinating world of ours.

The next park we visit will be Sequoia National Park, so we will spend another night in our beautiful lodge, listen to the exploding roar of our river, and dream of giants.

CHAPTER 9

Giants Everywhere!

Traveling down Route 99 and passing through a small town called Madera, we noticed there was a hospital right there, off the highway. Since it was time for me to have my blood drawn again, we decided to just drop in and see if the lab there would accept my doctor's order and my insurance. It took a little while before they decided they could and we were sent back to the lab where I was to sign in. I started to sign my name, but before I could even finish writing it down, they called me back. I looked up and asked if she wouldn't like me to finish signing my name, but she said, "No, just come on back and we'll get this over with." I began to realize what I had done and by the time I got to the lab technician I was giggling pretty hard. She wondered what I was laughing about. I explained I had started my name, and when she called me, I hadn't quite finished and left it like this…Virgin…That's as far as I got. I thought she was going to lose it. My name is Virginia, but I could (in my sick mind) only visualize what the next person would think as they signed in behind me! Of course, I had to ask the receptionist if she'd mind if I finished filling it in before I left. Oh boy!

Down in Fresno, we stopped for a quick lunch, took care of some business at the bank, and continued our movie onto Route 180 on General Highway. It didn't take long to leave palm trees and small mountains on this windy and scenic route. We're not too far from Sequoia, but you know how it is with scenic routes. At 1000 feet elevation, our ears are already starting to pop, and the roads are dangerously steep, sharp, and narrow. The scenery makes this next roller coaster ride well worth it. It is a glorious sun-shiny day blanketed with the bluest sky. In a few hours we were at 2000, 3000, and then all the way up to 6000 feet. No snow in sight, but California has a different climate so maybe we won't see any here. The roads are unreal. Going down one side of the mountain the curves are so sharp and dangerous, you can actually see the next part of the road curling right around next to you, like a hairpin. I have worn another hole in the floor helping Russ put on the brake.

There are only a few cars that passed and the mountains are whispering to us…explore me, enjoy me, see my beauty. And we are too, with this striking relationship between God, nature, Russ and me. What a grateful feeling to be able to share God's captivating creation with Him.

I had no idea we would be in the mountains at Sequoia. I thought we would just ride by groves of trees and that would be it. There are many over-views where we can pull over and gaze down into the canyon below. We figured we would go ahead and get a room and at least get most of our luggage inside. We wound up at the John Muir Lodge in King's Canyon National Park, and believe it or not, it was the very last room available! We are learning that most of the lodges do not have TVs or cell phone service and sometimes not even a landline. The lobby is beautiful and set up so one can sit and enjoy the huge fireplace, or read, play games, chat, or just daydream and get in your head about the reality of it all. We decided to take the room for a couple of nights since it was already getting late and it was certain we wouldn't get very far this evening.

With only a few hours of daylight left, we thought we would look for the General Grant tree, one of the top five largest trees on Earth, and the second largest right here in Grants Grove, near the King's Canyon entrance. There are several different groves in the park, somewhere around 75. I'm told King's Canyon and Sequoia National Parks are called "twin parks" because they lay side by side and both were founded in the 1890s.

The trees look like a cinnamon color to me, I would compare the color to our own Georgia mud! The first thing I notice, of course after realizing their immense size, is that each one of the trees has a teepee shaped hole in its base. It is dark and almost appears dug out intentionally, each tree with its own unique "teepee." Of course, I know now that these "teepees" are caused from fire. These Giants are members of the redwood family and nothing like I have ever seen in my life. Think about it, many of these beauties date back in time before Christ, some over 3,000 years old. Is that not a mind-boggling thought? These giant trees are very choosy about where they want to grow, too; only in the Sierras in our spectacular America because only here they can reproduce naturally. But not without fire! Go figure! The bark of the sequoia is around two feet thick. So the bark protects the tree while the heat of the flames causes the pinecones to explode and the tree can then reproduce. This is an electrifying concept. In fact, many years ago, the park rangers tried to stop fires to protect the trees, not realizing this is why the trees stopped reproducing.

Every year the sequoia tree adds one ton of new wood to its size. There are monsters here that grow up to 20 feet in diameter. They are the largest living thing on this Earth. After driving passed several trees, we parked Mona next to a group of them lined up by a wooden fence. She looked like a little toy in comparison to their size.

Finally, the General Grant tree! Wow! You almost had to bend over backward to look up into its huge branches. The branches alone were the size of a whole tree that lives in our yard. The General Grant, named after our President Ulysses S. Grant, stands 267.4 feet high and 107.6 feet around the base. What an elegant tree, not only in stature, but by its striking red color (Georgia mud)! We could look up to about 100 feet before you could even see a branch. Sooo tall.

It's really getting too dark to appreciate our walk, so we decided to go eat in their restaurant. Scott, our little server, was very personable. He had just gotten his helicopter pilot's license and was interested in opening his own business here in Sequoia. He seemed like such a nice person and his enthusiasm was so catching. We noticed some people that came in late and Scott offered them a boxed meal, since the restaurant was already closed. It made us remember our experience at Mt. Rainier when the desk clerk wouldn't give us a thing to eat after hours. It only confirmed what a considerate person

Scott was and I was thinking he would have no trouble with a business of his own, with a great personality like that.

It is very cold so we hurried to our room to relax for the night. I realized I forgot my robe I had put in my other suitcase out in the car, so Russ went with me to retrieve it. It was pitch-black in the parking lot and we could hardly see our feet in front of us, not alone find Mona. I can't believe how dark it is out here. The darkness is just creeping in my whole body, and I am hanging on to Russ's arm like a little kid and started digging in the back of the car for the right suitcase. Suddenly, a strange and eerie feeling came over me and I just knew we needed to go back to our room right now. You know that feeling people talk about when the hair on the back of your neck stands up? Well, that is where I was at, and I told Russ to just close the car up and let's hurry up to our room. He is never afraid of dark or much of anything else, so he insisted on finding my robe. I didn't care anymore; I started tugging on his arm and said, "Please, let's go!" He still kept looking and I couldn't stay. He finally heard the panic in my voice and we all but ran back to our room. I could just feel something watching. I don't know what was out there, but I felt it and I knew we were in danger, and I couldn't get in that room fast enough. You would think there would be some kind of lighting out there with all the critters roaming around.

Breakfast was great, but unlike Scott, the little girl who waited on us this morning had a sour look on her face and seemed sad, very sad. On our way out of the lodge restaurant, I tried to strike up a little conversation with her. Come to find out it was her birthday. I wished her a happy birthday and hoped she had a happy day. Now, we will be on our way to get a better glimpse of the General Grant in daylight.

The colors are even more dramatic in the sun. Next along the path was a tree called the Tennessee Tree. The most interesting characteristic about this tree was how it had survived its fire burns. The sign below the tree said "the living tissue of a tree called cambium layer, lies just under the bark. So long as some of this thin, living tissue connects the leaves above with the roots below, the tree will continue to live. This living layer will eventually heal the fire scars." Our Lord didn't leave out even one little detail, did He?

Continuing along a path, we see a small wooden cabin that was built in 1872. We've been taking so many pictures of captivating surroundings, Russ says he is getting a neck ache from looking up so much. Russ said they grow tall really fast and then every year they add about a foot in diameter. As people get near the trees, it only ensures you how incredibly large they are. The path is long and lined with a crooked wooden fence. There are several people in our movie now, strolling along with us, chatting and gazing upward in dazed-like delight. The tourists are of all sorts of nationalities, all of them with the same look of appreciation for the scenery surrounding us and all of them saying adoring things in their own native tongue. No, we didn't know exactly what they were saying, but we were sure by the tone in which they were speaking they were words of either won-derment, or praises to our Lord who made them for us to admire. What an awesome God He is.

We are practically struck dumb by the thought of water trav-eling up 300 feet, the height of a 27 story building! One sequoia pumps about one ton of water, they weigh in around 3000 tons and are wider than some city streets. Now that is a powerful wonder.

After much time gawking and ewwing and ahhing, it is lunch-time and we have worked up an appetite with all this walking, so we decided to go back to the lodge and have lunch. I began to talk to one of the other little servers so I told her today was Nichole's birth-day. (Remember, she was the little waitress that was so unhappy). What a tattle-tale! (I love it!) She said, "Maybe we should all sing happy birthday to her." And I said, "Yes, you should." I am such a birthday freak, holidays too. After a most delicious pizza, on our way out the door, we could hear a chorus of people singing "Happy Birthday, dear Nicole" from somewhere in the back. And we could hear Nicole saying "Thank you everyone. Thank you everyone." It made us smile; music to our ears in the middle of Kings National Park. How nice to end our day like this.

Our next drive was up toward Kings Canyon. It is cold, but sunny with bright blue skies and big puffy white clouds; still we have been wearing our coats all day. These are the same clouds that covered everything when we looked up, but now we are practically eye level. Approaching another viewpoint we can see snowcapped mountains in the distance.

We are in front of Hume Lake now in Sequoia National Forest in Kings River. We had checked at the Visitors Center to try to get a fishing license for Russ, but they were out and wouldn't be back for an hour, an hour we didn't care to wait. The lake is huge and so calm, spanning 87 acres. Activities here include camping, hiking, fishing, boating, and swimming. Russ is feeling a little disappointed. He should have waited to get his license so he could fish for some yummy trout. We are at 5,200 feet in elevation, and from where we are, we can't see anyone else in our movie.

Driving up higher, we can look down on the lake, a few of the trails are visible, and it is surrounded by thick patches of trees. And up even further, we look down and the lake looks like a small blue puddle in the middle of them. From here, we get a great view of the Sawtooth Mountain Range and it is very obvious why they call them that. They are jagged like a canine's teeth, sprawling out over 400 miles long and 60 to 80 miles wide.

Route 180 continues to take us higher and higher, and we pass a place called Yucca Point. I have never seen a yucca plant before, but they are everywhere and they are the highlight of this part of Sequoia. The base of the plant has a sword-shaped leaf, and the flower is white and reminds me of a giant bottle brush. Everything in this land is giant size, even the flowers. Such an elegant plant, I wish I could grow them in Georgia.

These roads are closed in the winter; you can imagine why. It is a dangerous and wild ride. We can look down and see the Kings River; it is about 125 miles long and raging down through the canyon. It makes me think of the movie title *A River Runs through It*. Right beside us on this narrow, sharp-curved road some of the mountain side is a bright orange in color and rises straight up. But the scenery in front of us (the Sierra Nevada's), as we round each curve seems to stretch into infinity.

Here we go, another curve and it is called Yucca Junction. Exactly as the name implies, we see so many more Yucca plants displaying their beautiful flowers, and huge bushes of the smaller bottle brush flowers scattered all over too. Continuing on this scenic byway, we can literally see the road we will be on below us, as soon as we get around this hairpin curve. After a few more minutes, we saw a sign for Boyden Cave. Looked great to me and we really wanted to see it, but come to find out the path *UP* was approximately 3,400 feet. On second thought! It probably would have taken me the rest of the day and we ixnayed that idea. Well, you can't see everything. Know your limits, right?

We find ourselves in the South Fork of the park and decided we would continue on this byway until we came to Grizzly Falls. In the meantime, there is a place to pull over where we can look at the Kings River and boy, is it ever boiling mad. It is white with froth, running fast and furious, and loud. Bubbling around rocks in the center. Just have to have pictures of this as it passes under a small bridge. It is snaking right along with us on our way. The elevation here is about 1,000 feet, but we are beginning to climb again. There is an island of trees right in the middle of the river, about six of them with rocks landscaped all around them. I don't know how they survive with the river raging all around them and the current so fast like that, but it is as though a gardener planted them right where they are supposed to be.

As the river pounds against the mountain side, it carves its way through and we have followed it all the way back up to 4,000 feet elevation. It has finally led us to Grizzly Falls, where there are a couple other families. Where on earth did these people come from? Okay, they can be in our movie. The fall is the widest we've seen in our travels so far. It is most dramatic and full, but only falls 75 feet. In the late summer, it is a single flowing stream of water but now is a wide series of foamy white over huge rocks.

At an elevation of 7,335 feet, we finally made it high enough to see our beloved snow. This is where we will turn around and head back to the lodge to have dinner and then we'll go down to see the General Sherman tree, which is all the way on the other side of the park. Actually, that will be Sequoia National Park. We didn't realize the two ran together like that at first, we thought we were in Sequoia the whole time, but after I was able to track our route on the map, I realized we were in Kings National Park the whole first part of our trip here. Yup, we really played it by ear, but what fun!

The winding road shows us sights we missed on the way up, with huge tall rocks on the side of it, uniquely shaped and waiting to be noticed. You can see far out with layers and layers of mountains in the distance. I might add at this point, that the park is very gracious in offering restrooms at several locations, picnic areas, phones, and lodging. That is always a comfort for all to know, I'm sure.

The General Sherman Trail is in front of us now. There are a lot of branches on the ground, and they are the size of a full-grown "normal" tree. A cute little western chipmunk is sitting on top of one of them. It is grayer than our chipmunks and has a longer tail. Sequoia trees everywhere, some the clay-red color and some are more on the grayish side. Every time we round another corner we say "look at this one, look at this one"! Here we go again, they said it was a trip of 0.5 miles, a 15-minute walk, right? *Okay.* It's a really nice trail. Stairs of 4, then a wide step about 3 feet, then more steps and so on, *easy!*

This place is called the Giant Forest. It is captivating and our eyes pop from one tree to another. Russ is filled with joy; this is where he wanted to come more than any place else. The General Sherman Tree is endless; it goes and goes and goes. It is the largest tree on the whole planet, topping out at 274.9 feet tall (not counting the base), the circumference at the ground is 102.6 feet. You have to scan your eyes up the Sherman 130 feet before you see the first branch, and the diameter of the largest branch is 6.8 feet! Don't misunderstand now, it is not the tallest tree, it is the largest, considering its mass or volume. It is said, the General Sherman is probably 2,500 years old and they figure it weighs in at approximately 2.7 million pounds. Every year it adds enough wood to make a 60-foot tall tree, measuring one foot in diameter, and it's still growing

The trail we are on now is called Congress Trail which is a two-mile loop, and I can tell you right now I never did two miles in 15 minutes! Not lately anyway. We are in the northern fringe of the park and this trail provides access to the majority of the big trees. The grace of these trees is so amazing, they are very straight, and once they begin to tip or bend, they go over because they are so heavy and their roots are not very deep. One of the trees is down and they have cut it out so people can walk through it. Once they begin to be top heavy, they are done. This trail is not only world class, but very informative. There are many signs with names and information about the trees. The path is lined with wooden fences to protect the trees, but very neatly done. As we make the loop we are ascending now and it sure isn't as easy going up as it was going down, taking into consideration we are at a 7,000-foot elevation. The air is so thin up here! It took us a good while to get back to Mona, we took it slow, and just stopped and took little breaks on the way back here and there.

We are about 29 miles out, so we better start back because 29 miles in mountain talk is a *long* trip back with all the curves and slow speed. Oh, there are deer up there, a whole herd; we will get lots of close up shots of them. More pretty yucca plants too. All together on the way down, we saw 19 deer. We came across the most beautiful bird flitting about in the bushes, so we stopped to film him. He is all black except his chest which is a bright blue. Russ said he is a western jaybird.

At this point, we weren't very hungry so we decided to stop off at a little market and pick up a sandwich and chips and share it in our room. While we were back in our room we studied the map and thought since we are so close to Mt. Whitney we'd take a look at it, but first, take a visit to the museum here.

Right in the heart of the Giant Forest is the Giant Forest Museum. That makes sense doesn't it? What an interesting place, describing how the giant sequoias survive, their growth, all about the groves; how big they are and how many sequoias are in each and every grove. Right out of the museum, there is a small dirt road you can drive on to explore the unparalleled beauty of the forest. I was filming with the camcorder and Russ is in his glory. He is so excited! "Get this one." "Look over there." "Here, on this side!" I was getting dizzy turning from side to side. Now this is more like what I expected to see, trees towering over us and placed perfectly every few feet apart. I finally had to tell Russ to slow down; I was getting the pictures as fast as I could. And with that, he threatened to not let me be in his movie. Oh, it's his movie now! I am shooting through the windows like crazy, when suddenly, a deer nonchalantly walks right in front of the car, proving to us he had the right of way, and we were in his yard. As we looked to our right, we could see the rest of the family he left behind nibbling on the tasty morsels on that side of the road. How cute, there were five of them in all.

A tree has fallen across the road and a tunnel has been carved into it. It is, once again, appropriately named Tunnel Log and claims to be the only tree you can drive through in these parts. A sign to the side of it states the tree fell on December 4, 1937. The tree itself is 275 feet tall, and 21 inches in diameter; the tunnel is 8 feet high and 17 feet wide. I would say the tunnel you drive through is only about 3/4 of the tree, and there is still a quarter of it over you as you go under it. Amazing. If you have a camper, there is an alternative path to go around.

Here we are in the middle of the forest and it looks like a fairy-land, with all the stunning dogwood trees blooming. Not even cowering among the giant trees, as their delicate white flowers embrace the great size of the giants next to them. The trees overshadow and seem to cradle them in their great strength. Russ and I feeling very much the same: small and meek in the midst of our giant protectors.

The next outstanding tree on the path is named the Buttress tree estimated to be approximately 2,300 years old and 21 feet at the bottom. Then Auto Log which is a fallen tree with a base diameter of 31 feet. Also, here stands a huge granite rock dome called Moro Rock. It is a quarter of a mile steep and 6,725 feet high, which has steps going all the way up for a fascinating hike. Some of these trees are badly burned, they are very black several feet from the base and yet some look as though they had never been touched. As gorgeous as this place is, we have reached the end of our little tour and begin our way out of the park. We have many sharp bends to go around again, this road is very rough, and not paved very well. However, the striking scenery makes up for any of the scary, hair-raising roads we have to endure.

We are seeing signs indicating there is a safe overlook, called 11-range overlook, so we will probably stop and check it out. This is certainly an overlook that is a wonderful treat for the eyes. We're glad we stopped. We get back on the road, which also offers a panoramic view as we round another one of those wild curves. In the distance, there is a place in the side of the mountain that looks like a *huge* ear engraved into it. Never know what you are going to see up here. Suddenly, some loose rocks must have hit the underneath part of the car and made a terrifying sound. I let out a little screech; I thought we were being bombarded by a landslide, which in turn scared Russ half to death. That made us both laugh. People are visibly slowing down, thank goodness, because the roads are so dangerous. They finally figured it out, I think. First we are on the edge, and then we are on the inside where the mountain is next to us. Sometimes I wonder how that happens. I definitely like the inside better; at least if someone hits us, we ram the inside of the mountain instead of being shoved off it.

Further out, we have spotted a very strangely shaped rock. It just juts out of the earth like the enormous head of some historic monster, complete with a huge eye. As I zoom in, I can see it is actually two holes in the massive rock that go all the way through the "head" and appear to be the eyes. The eyes have two slices of rock that go across the eye like a rectangular pupil. There are all kinds of treasures unfolding here with the use of a good imagination, which we certainly are not lacking.

Pulling over to another safe viewpoint, you can't help but hear the loud and constant chattering and chirping. On the tree in front of us is another beautiful bird, reminding us that there is much more to this rich land than mountains and trees. He has a white chest and he is also the size of a jay, with a black back and wings. There are white tips on his wings, the white encircling his large black beak and face, but the black circles his eyes. And a deep color of red is on the crown of his head. I don't know if he is a member of the jay family or maybe a woodpecker, but only our Maker could have created such a remarkable design as this.

It is a very curvy road on our way to the next small town called Buckeye Flat. It seems we are going in circles as we are going south one minute and the sharp curves take us north the next and then loop us back south, that is how sharp they are. Oh, but *so* beautiful with Yucca plants sprouting here and there, sprinkling the mountainside. We can look down upon the raging river, it is so green, and there is some kind of structure, a thick cement wall going across half of the river. The other half has a big, maybe 5-foot dip that looks like a small waterfall almost. Then we notice some kids coming along in a bright, blue-colored raft about to go over the fall. At first, I thought they were going around it but no, right down it they went and got stuck on a huge rock. One of them got out and after some time, managed to free the raft and on they went. We were wondering how on earth they were going to continue on with all the rocks, it really didn't look like they would be able to get through. I kind of felt like a peeping tom, filming them, and they didn't know we were way up here. Oh, how I love these *zoom* cameras!

The mountain view is thrilling. I guess the reward for all these curves is the grandeur in which we become consumed. Every single minute has been worth it for sure. We reached Bakersfield, did a few Wal-Mart runs, found an inn, caught up on the news and weather, and did a bunch of laundry. Gas prices here are $4.59/gallon. We decided instead of going to Death Valley first, we would go see Mt. Whitney first. Didn't want to be so close and not see the tallest mountain in the "lower 48." We sure are going out of the way to see it, though. We could have cut across Sequoia, but the road is a tiny mountain road, which probably would have been a spectacular drive, but it was such a dangerous and curvy route it would have taken a day just to get there. This way we are going in a huge "U," and this route (down 99, over 58 then at Mojave up 395). To our left, there are mountains, but not so big anymore. They look like dark brown sand with dots of dark green trees scattered all over them. Ahead, are millions of windmills all over the side of the mountain, as though they are now replacing the trees that once grew there. I think that is a fascinating sight, since we don't get to see that in Georgia.

The sky is a deep dark blue and the mountains may not be as big, but they are uniquely shaped. They have beautifully shaped layers with shades of red in them, hence the name, Red Rock Canyon, through which we are now passing. Next, we come to Chimney Peak which has an elevation of 7,990 feet. There are a lot of sage bushes on the sides of the road. Russ said these are the same bushes that become tumbleweeds after they dry up. Interesting. And with that, he begins to sing Tumbling Tumbleweed, for all you senior people out there who may remember that one.

In about 5 more miles, we will be in Lone Pine. Far ahead, I can see a bright glistening white line across the earth, like a halo; we can't figure out what it is. I don't think its snow because it is so warm right now. As we close in on it, we realize it is a mostly dried up lake. There is little water, but almost all of it is a salt flat. It is called Owens Lake and the sparkle of the salt really is beautiful.

I have to admit, we weren't sure which of the mountains straight ahead was Mount Whitney. Thanks to my wonderful and informative post cards we figured it out by looking at the shape of it and decided to get a motel nearby. We found a motel (the ones we usually stayed in), but the price was totally out of sync from the others we stayed at just like it. The scenery embraced us as we drove on to look for something else and we couldn't resist the temptation to pull over and adore it. In the distance we spotted an elk, so far out I wouldn't have known if Russ didn't point him out to me. We drove on and found Mount Whitney restaurant and then right in front of the mountain, a motel that was much more modest in price...so we unloaded and as usual planned to wait until dusk so the critters would show themselves! We are literally sitting right across from the shrouded Mt. Whitney!

CHAPTER 10

From the Highest to the Lowest

By highest, I mean Mt. Whitney, and by lowest, I mean Death Valley. Both are easy access from Lone Pine, California. Lone Pine, being named after a large pine that once grew nearby. We will start with Mt. Whitney, all of 14,498 feet high with captivating snow-capped spires, also known as needles, towering next to it. The peak alone rises 10,778 feet, or just two miles, above Lone Pine. You may see a difference in how high this famous mountain is, some references claiming it is 14,505 feet high. The reason being technology of elevation measurement has become more refined over the years. Mt. Whitney is named after Josiah Whitney, the state geologist of California in 1864.

We are right on South Main Street surrounded by the Sierra-Nevada Mountains, which is completely on the opposite side of the Sequoias and King's Canyon. It is a little after 7:00 p.m.; we always wait for this "magic" hour to tour the roads, as this seems to be the time the critters like to leave their safe shaded wooded areas and show themselves. Ha! We outsmarted them...for sure, because we have come upon a herd of approximately 12 elk, up in a large green meadow. They are just a-wigglin' those little bright white tails that look like the center of a target, slap dab in the middle of a beige circle (their behinds). They are beautiful and stately with pretty good-sized racks, too. Russ said they are called tule elk, a species found only in California. They are named after the tule they feed off of in the marshlands. Altogether, we saw about 9 up there, but as we continued on down the mountain back toward Lone Pine, near the bottom, we saw 10more. We pulled over to film them, Russ whistled very loud at them to get them to turn, so we could get a good front view. It worked! That's when we saw two more appear…elk everywhere. I handed the camera to Russ so he could zoom in and see them better. In the meantime, I am trying to find the binoculars. Russ starts chanting in his deep voice like an Indian, he does that often. I guess he is an Indian today, the other day Latino. I just shrug my shoulders and act like there isn't anything strange going on! A couple of the elk are just staring at him. You can see their heads peering at him, all the way from their chest to the top of their antlers, as though they are standing up on their hind legs or a cardboard box, to get a better view! Can't help but wonder what on earth they are thinking about this strange human. Can't you just hear it… "Pssst, hey, Elmer…haven't we heard that thar chant up in these here hills not too long ago?" "Yeah, but those Indians could stay in tune a lot better than him."

The elk are huge, with black faces and shoulders. The rest of the body is a medium brown and winds down to their behind, where the "beige target" appears. What fun to watch them, but they soon became bored with us and moved on, so we did too. As we moved on though, we spotted more elk out in the middle of a meadow, stretching their long necks up and over some long grass, peering at us like we were both crazy, but a motorcycle went by and spooked them. I'd say we scored on that great idea; 7:00 p.m. does seem to be the magic hour for sure! And all this is happening about 10 miles out of Lone Pine.

The sun is beginning to set with colors of pinks and oranges, bouncing off the tiny little clouds in front of us. They look like tiny, brilliant pink and orange fluffy pillows, almost as though someone is sending us smoke signals in color. The colors of the mountains are many different shades of greens, white, and silver, like a bowl full of salad. The backdrop is that of shaded mountains and gray darkening sky, but still the brightness of the white snow-frosted caps continue to shine through. It has been a perfect exciting day, with more beautiful memories to add to our treasure-filled movie. It is high time we little vagabonds head to the motel and call it a night.

It is a beautiful bright new day; I don't think I have seen a sky more blue! The continental breakfast at the motel was very filling. This was the perfect motel because we had a beautiful view of Mt. Whitney right from our room. On the way out of the motel lobby, there are just about always racks full of tourist pamphlets and information. One of the pamphlets informed us of an arch and a waterfall to be found at the base of Mt. Whitney. So we make another spontaneous decision to go explore and see if we can find it, then we'll probably move on after that. We started packing the car and the people who were parked next to us began to talk with us about their travels. They wanted to know where we were from and where we were going. He was a Baptist minister. It was fun talking with him and his wife. They were so friendly. He said he noticed the fish magnet on the back of our car which struck up the conversation. It is so much fun to meet other people and feel like there really isn't such a thing as a stranger.

Being able to see the mountain from here and then drive toward it was an exhilarating experience. The mountain is glowing and magnificent in the brilliance of the beautiful sun-shiny day. If you are heading north in Lone Pine, there is only *one* left hand turn intersection in the whole town, with a light called *"the"* stop light. *So*…we took it and turned left into a whole new world!

It is advertised that many movies have been filmed here. Most of the restaurants in the area have pictures hanging of the different scenes, and the casts such as Errol Flynn in "Kim," the "Lone Ranger," Roy Rogers and Gene Autry movies, *How the West Was Won*, *Charge of the Light Brigade*, and more recently *Tremors* with Kevin Bacon. Well heck, we are starring in our own move right now, so they're not so special. With all that in mind, we see the rocks to the right are a rich deep brown color and piled in a high stack. I can imagine the cowboys riding through all of this. To the left and ahead, the mountains are silver streaked with white shiny crevices of snow. All this dreamy landscape takes the stage against the remarkable blue sky. Around the next turn lie a couple piles of sand, like God had nothing else to do, so He bent down and simply sifted it through His Mighty Fingers. A little further up the road, the rocks are more of a beige-gray color and someone with a great sense of humor painted the face of a comedic dinosaur on one of the larger ones. Come to find out it is called "Face Rock"…cute! To the left there are several huge formations that look just like a foot, with eight toes sticking straight up in the air. They are a very dark-brown color, almost black. And next, another grouping of rocks with an imitation of "half dome" right in the middle. Then a small group of buildings at the foot of several rock mountains that look like toys against it.

At this point, we are now able to shoot some fabulous pictures of the giant mountain; gray-pink in color with patches of snow placed artistically about. In my opinion, these pictures are as pretty as any post card I've seen. If I were looking for perfection, I'd have to say I just found it. The combination of colors, shapes, and sizes here are just so absolutely striking.

And now, back to the white knuckle driving of curves, esses, hairpin curves, and very narrow roads. I couldn't help but let out a little shrick and Russ said, "Don't do that, Ginn. You make my legs quiver!" Some of the curves looked like we were going to drive right off the end of the world in front of us, and as you rounded it, you couldn't get much closer to the edge. At the end of this next curve, a huge rock jets out like a rocket about to shoot up to the stars, and if I didn't know better, I would have thought it was pointing us into the right direction. We decided to pull over and peer over the edge, and we could see the road below which appears like a large long white worm. Still, we are not close to the top. It does seem like the drivers are a little more careful here, and I'm glad because these roads seem more narrow than others we've been on so far. There are no signs directing us to either an arch or a water fall. This is one time when the words *beautiful* and *scary* seem to go together perfectly.

Yet another excellent shot of Mt. Whitney, only this time the lighting shrouds it in silver and white. It looks like a temple of spires framed at the bottom with the very green trees. What an elegant picture this one is! As I said before, every bend we go around is another beautiful sight. We finally got a view of the falls. It was like a little camp ground, with a couple small buildings all in a row as we entered. It is busy with people walking and talking and children playing and scattering everywhere, with their parents guarding eyes following them closely. Kind of like a town you see in the movies and you wonder where you might find a town that looks like that!

We parked and went over to the falls known as Whitney Portal Falls. Oh, that wonderful sound of the water rushing and gushing and the white foaming surface. We notice there are trees literally growing out of the rock in several different places.

Nearby, a woman was sweeping off the sidewalk where we exited the falls. We struck up a conversation with her and talked for quite a while. She had lived there her whole life and had only gotten to the arch about a month and a half ago. Sounds familiar, that's how we are in Georgia, too. As we turned to walk, on our way to the car, a gentleman came up to speak to her, so she introduced him to us as Doug, the owner of the small restaurant we passed on our way into the park. So small in fact, there was space for only two vehicles to park in front of it. He was so friendly and full of personality, with a huge smile that stretched from one ear to the other. As I peered into his pretty twinkling blue eyes, I could literally read how much he loved this place as he began to talk about it. He said most people overlook this side of Yosemite (the east side). Doug said he wished the government would re-evaluate the area and come up with a better plan because work there was little; meaning jobs, and the pay wasn't much more, so the kids are leaving to get jobs elsewhere. Basically, he was saying it was difficult to live there. He took time to give us directions to the arch, which he gave a name for us (Mobius Arch), but in order to get to it, you had to go down a sharp drop and then downhill for a good hike. Okay, I can go downhill easy, but coming back up is a whole different ballgame, especially in this elevation.

We decided to pass on the arch and move on to Death Valley. But first, we stopped off to fill our tank at $4.54/gal. (Don't forget this is 2008). Maybe gas prices are another reason for people not to live in this area. We pulled in for lunch at a deli, where pictures were posted all over the walls of the movies and people in-the-know in the community. One of the photos was of a young man climbing a mountain, donned in his hiking apparel, and I swear it was a picture of Doug back at the falls, when he was younger. I sure wish I could ask him.

On our way to Death Valley, the first thing we see is a huge lake, partially dried up, with a little water in the very middle. It is a 2-lane straight highway, surrounded by beautiful snow-tipped mountains, no cell service and no one else on the road, so we are the primary characters in our movie once again. Which, when you think about it, it seems it is quite unusual in all these prevalent areas.

Then, it feels like we are right back in the mountains at Yosemite, climbing up to higher elevations, and doing u-eees again. Snow covers the tips of all the mountains, and this is how it will be the whole way through Death Valley, except for a short strip where we actually came down and reached a straight-away, and then right straight back up again. I never in my dreams expected to see mountains in Death Valley. I just expected to see desert. *Not!*

Suddenly, we hear a very loud roaring sound, only to look up and watch a jet fly over us, probably some type of military practice since there is a base close by. What an echo! Once we are in the desert, we can see cactus on each side of us that look like little people waving both arms at us, some of them with colorful flowers. There is desert all between us and the mountains on each side, but we are going up again and driving on a windy, curvy road. We are on 190 east and have reached an elevation of 3,000 feet. I am back in my "slow down, honey" mode. Colorful rocky mountains are on each side…why are we going so fast? "Honey! The speed limit is 25!" "Okay." I can't get over all these mountains; we can see the desert as we look down and out. We are up 5,000 feet now on a straight-away, between two mountains and it looks like the road is going to go right off into nowhere in the blue sky. Got a beautiful shot of that! The mountains come in beautiful combinations of colors marbled with beige and cream. This crazy truck driver just passed us on a double line in a 20-mph speed zone, on a curve yet! If that isn't bad enough, it already feels like we could go over the edge any minute. Then as fast as we got up to 5,000 feet elevation, we have descended to an elevation of 5 feet! And here sits a couple of buildings at a historical site called Stove Pipe Wells, but then we blinked our eyes and it was gone. From what I understand, there is gasoline available here, but we did gas up before we hit the desert, especially not knowing that, just to be safe. Who wants to get stuck in the middle of the desert with no gas, right? This place is huge, the largest national park outside of Alaska with the darkest night skies in the US.

As we approach sea level, we can see sand dunes and a black two-lane road snaking along ahead until it is out of sight. The landscape in front of us is gorgeous against the blue, blue sky. Our signs tell us we are at minus 190 elevation now, one of the lowest areas in the US; however it does go as low as minus 282 feet. My research tells me that in 1917, Death Valley recorded 52 days with temperatures over 120 degrees and 43 consecutive days over 120 degrees. Their record high is 134 degrees in July, therefore, making Death Valley famous as the hottest and driest place in North America. Of course, higher elevations are cooler than the lower valley, known to drop anywhere from 3 to 5 degrees F. with every 1,000 vertical foot! That was pretty obvious to us as the air conditioner would come on in the valley and the heater the further up we went.

We're wondering where the heck is the desert? These mountains are beautiful, but certainly not what we expected to see in Death Valley! Maybe the Mojave Desert would be a different story. Up ahead we see what look like palm trees and a spread of buildings. We didn't stop but I wish we had. We stopped everywhere else. That is what we get for not doing our homework. Later, we found out that it was a beautiful place called Scotty's Castle. It was built in the 1920s in Spanish colonial style, right here in the northern part of Death Valley, about 3 miles out of Las Vegas. There are tours year around.

On our way into Las Vegas, we decided just to drive through because there was construction everywhere, and besides, we had been there before. But as we look to our left, there are mounds of golden sand with mud brown mountains behind them in such beautiful contrast. The scenery is pretty as ever and shows off its splendor with golden lace ripples throughout the muddy color and then a mixture of the two. They are calling out to us "look at me," "no, look at me!" Such gorgeous patterns, how fun it would be if I could paint. Then, here are mounds with stripes of beige and gray, beige and tan, and more gold in the rough ridges and beautiful formations. The darker colors at the top of this one particular mound, look like a lazy sleeping lizard with his legs hanging down over it. Kind of like when we were little and laid on our backs in the grass and made shapes out of the clouds, it's the same with these mounds and mountains.

The sign ahead tells us we are in Nevada; Las Vegas is just up the road. The road is changing to a double lane. The first place we see is Circus Circus. When we were here about 12 years ago, this is where we stayed. We had 3 children with us and couldn't have made a better decision. On top of the hotel, they had a carnival/fair, with roller coasters, rides of all kinds of fun for the kiddies and they just had a ball. That part was free if you were staying there. One of the floors had games, where you shoot at things, throw balls, play all kinds of games, and every few hours, they put on a show. We sat and watched a tight rope walker who was very entertaining. The food was great, all you could eat and very cheap with free drinks in the casino to entice you to stay and spend money gambling. We took turns staying with the kids, but I am definitely not much of a gambler. Gosh, it sure was fun watching people and walking up and down the main street to see what the hotels had to offer. It was fascinating to see the volcano in front of the Mirage go off every few minutes, too. *Wow!* Standing there with our mouths open wondering how they do that. It was *so* real, right down to the sounds. The memories of that scene will always be a great part of our memories. We also saw the pirates and ships staging fights in front of Treasure Island. We saw the dancing waters then and walked inside Caesar's Palace. Their costumes were great and we got to see Roy and Siegfried's beautiful tigers. Anyway, this time I am enjoying just taking pictures of new and old memories. Boy, it sure does pay to eat here though, looking at advertisements all over the place for barbecue ribs and shrimp platters for only $9.99! We got a motel outside of the busy areas. No we did not eat there!

Well, we couldn't resist being so close, so after dark, Russ surprised me and we drove over to the main strip where it is lit up like a huge Christmas tree. It really is disappointing though, we couldn't find a place to park, and we would have gotten out and taken another walk. Construction was everywhere and many sidewalks were blocked off. The volcano was shut down, many of the magnificent hotels were gone and in place of them were drug stores and fast-food restaurants, all decorated up, like that was going to make them different. And even Trump's building: the *T* and the *R* in his name weren't lit up! It reminded me of any mall in America with all the same places in it, but lit up with bright lights. We never got out of the car, but I had fun snapping pictures of the hotels anyway. They took the "las" out of "Vegas" and made a big mess, but oh well, maybe it's all fixed up and new looking again by now. It was a sweet and fun gesture on my husband's part to see it again, only because he knew I wanted to. He is such a blessing to me.

Today is Sunday and we plan to go to Bryce's Canyon in Utah. We missed it on the way out to Alaska because we had a deadline to get to the airport in Seattle and get to Alaska for our cruise. So after breakfast at Denny's (which we are becoming quite attached to, wish we had one closer to us in Marietta), we got to drive across a small corner of Arizona and back up to Utah. I am reminded every day that we live in such a beautiful country. Russ points to the side of the road and the dirt was bouncing around in a circle and Russ said it was a "dirt devil." Well, I never heard of such before, much less seen one. It looks like a tiny tornado to me. It just goes to show you, there are all kinds of things, simple as that, around here to see and discover. Now that was very interesting!

The overpass we see ahead, and are soon to drive under, is gorgeous. It is painted along the edges in rust, brown, and beige mosaic designs. It looks so clean and elegant as it frames the scenery in front of us.

CHAPTER 11

Rocks of Ages

We are now on Route 15. It will take us up to Cedar City just off 15 and then turns into Route 14. It looks like a short drive on the map, but being in the mountains and on a scenic route, it is not so short. As we round each curve and turn, a new and breath-taking view is revealed to us all wrapped up in the beautiful colors of the earth. It reminds me of a time in Georgia a long time ago, in the fall, when we were on our way to church. My youngest was so overwhelmed with the beauty of the fall colors he just blurted out in his sweet little voice, "God is an artist!" He took us all by surprise, but what a revelation for such a young one. How true it is, as I look out at the awesome colors of these rocks.

We just left 101 degrees at sea level, and now we are at an elevation of 5,000 feet and maybe 70 degrees, with snow on the higher mountains around us. We are entering Small Valley Junction, where a Home Depot sits to our left with an American flag waving gracefully, high behind the building. Probably an everyday view to the people who live here, but to Russ and me, it was an awesome sight. He said, "God Bless America" and then added, "This is for you, Sissy. I love you." That is my sister, who retired from Home Depot. That just shows to me what a wonderful, thoughtful man (and brother-in-law) he is. And right up the road is a beautiful lighthouse, red and white striped, in front of a building that I didn't catch what it was. Russ was driving too fast. Uh-huh.

We will soon connect with Route 89, go just a little further, and we will turn off to yet a smaller road, Route 12, which will take us right into Bryce Canyon National Park. We have another bright blue sky and a perfect temperature kind of day; it is consoling and relaxing. After lunch, we continue toward Bryce, the roads twisting in a continuous sway from left to right and then right again, smooth, and carefree with a lot of green and captivating mountains galore surrounding us and keeping us safe in their arms. Likewise, we are both quiet and serene in this dreamy landscape. We are driving through the Dixie National Forest. The mountain ahead of us is thick with green at the bottom, and as it rises higher, the trees become sparser and the top looks like a bald man's head. Then all of a sudden, the mountaintops are taking remarkable forms of tiny stone beige towers. The light-colored mountain walls are beginning to close in on the road and cuddle us as we make our sharp turns, trees lining the mountains as you look up. Far out and up to the left, is a huge square pillar balancing a small rock on the top of it. Now in place of the walls, the next turn reveals a street lined with majestic trees and far down at what looks like the very end of the road, is a gigantic wall of beiges and peach color. It looks like if we keep going we will run right into it, and it will block us from going any further. The sun is shining on this wall making it look even bolder. The closer we get to this wall, the brighter the sun shines down on it, the brighter the colors get, bringing out the oranges and rust tones. There go those footprints on my heart again!

All this time we are climbing higher and higher, while signs warn the truckers it is an 8 percent grade. There is a good bit of traffic here too, which surprises us and right in the middle of all of this Russ yells, "Okay, everybody look for gold!" I have no idea what he is talking about. He is such a hoot! Maybe he is referring to the golden colors or the mountains, who knows? He makes me laugh. I really like being in his movie!

The sun is fading a little, which means it is getting close to our magical critter time. Russ pulls over to take a few shots. He is looking for deer, I know. A sign tells us that in the distance is Zion National Park, such great information.

We are back on the road, and Russ is really gawking into the trees…meaning Russ's eyes are *not* on the road. Of course, he is being reprimanded by me, poor guy, and right behind that my comments are "Oh, look at that!" or "Oh, I wish you could see that!" Right after I just got through telling him to keep his eyes on the road! I have to watch that.

There is snow scattered through the trees like a sugar-covered cake and stately green thin trees decorating it. Remember, this is June. A huge meadow sits in front of the trees, which I think are Ponderosa Pines, and not one critter seems to be within sight. The curves in the road are quick and sharp and nonstop. Wow, look at this curve! Oh, man…I promise you…visiting a national park will never ever disappoint you! It is absolutely thrilling going around another ear-popping curve, with a small creek rolling down. Just to show us we aren't the only ones spontaneous out here, so is nature, never knowing what will show up next. This road really is dangerous though; in the winter months, it is not recommended to travel it, not only because of massive rock slides, but because of its steep and twisting roads. Plus the summit's elevation is 9,200 feet.

There are what looks like clumps of dark brown mud in a heap on the side of the road, so we pull over to check it out. It doesn't look like any of the other landscaping surrounding us. In striking contrast stand stunning white-and-black aspen trees and speckles of spruce. There is a sign with more information explaining that this is lava flow from long ago from steam vents, not an actual volcano. My research tells me a lava flow is a moving outpouring of lava, which is created by a non-explosive effusion eruption. When it stops moving, the lava solidifies to form igneous rock. And that is what we are looking at and we got a great photo of. There really is a lot and we found more as we went further.

Our next turn reveals a lake and all I can figure out is that it is the Panguitch Lake. Panguitch is a Native American word meaning "water with big fish." This lake has a history of good fishing; mostly trout. There are many ducks out there; I count about 31, enjoying its vibrant blue water at 8,217 feet in the sky. Now Russ decided to go "Quack, Quack!" incessantly and very nasally…Oh my. I'll bet that water is freezing cold, but I don't plan to hike out there to find out right now. Russ is standing here next to me and once again breaks out in song…something about looking at the sun? Gosh he's so funny! He just makes things up as he goes along, such a happy little camper. Tee-hee.

We are passing a very picturesque ranch house, painted a bronze color, with a white wooden fence all up and down and around it. All around there are mountains and the darkening deep blue sky behind it, a red truck in front and several horses a few yards away. I wonder if they know they have such a tranquil and beautiful "backyard," where they can graze and drink from a stream abundantly; a very alluring scene to say the least.

We are still climbing up and come upon another lake which Russ says is the Navajo Lake formed by volcanic action in the past. They maintain it as a reservoir and fishing purposes. It is nestled in at 9,200 feet elevation and seems to twine, twist, and turn just like our road in front of us.

The formations of the rocks are becoming more and more unique in their shapes, and the colors are getting darker as evening approaches. There is more lava flow and it is on both sides of the road, so I guess they just laid the road right through it. We come upon a critter in the road and we thought it was road kill, but as we approach it, we startled it and it took off. Russ said it was a marmot, another new thing to me but it was adorable. He said they are sometimes called large ground squirrels. He sure was cute: fat, with a tail, all different shades of brown and beige and a little gray on his face. He took off so fast I couldn't get a picture of his cute little self.

Our "magical hour" proves to be true as Russ is making a sound like ew, ew, ew, ew, or in other words (Russ language), he's excited and is trying to say "*Quick*, turn on the camera…deer!" *Woohoo!* What a beauty she is too. Altogether we see about 13 mule deer as we drive up and down and back up again. The roads up here are wonderful. We are about to go through a tunnel only 15 minutes before Bryce Canyon. Boy, if all we've just seen is simply a preview, I can't begin to imagine what the real Bryce will look like! Wow, in front of us is a huge tower of three different shades and a sign that says we are in Red Canyon, and is it ever! Looking up, there are strange-shaped rocks, two in particular that look like chess pieces. But since the sun is gradually setting, they are silhouettes in the sky.

We finally see a sign that says Bryce Canyon National Park. At last we have arrived at the park, but rather than stop, we just had to go on because after all it is our "bewitching hour" and we couldn't possibly miss out on that. To our right, there is a little path that has been following along for the past few miles with a very small cross-over bridge. All together we have seen 13 mule deer and about 30 elk. This is so much fun.

Ahead there are several critters by the road. At first we thought they were more deer, but Russ in his excitement blurts out that they are antelope. They are adorable, on both sides of the road, looking at us with curiosity. I find myself talking to them like they are little babies. Oh dear, I must be catching this from Russ. In a high-pitched voice, I hear myself saying, "Hi, sweetie, you are *so* pretty. Look at you. Don't be afraid. We won't hurt you. Is that your little baby there? She's just as pretty as you." So freaky.

It's a good thing it is time to secure a motel room; it seems we need a good night's sleep, so we turn back. It is dark and a deer darts out in front of us, thank goodness the guy in the oncoming lane was alert as well or we would have witnessed a tragedy right then and there. He was scared to death and ran for his life.

The Ruby's Lodge is way too expensive, so we headed across the street to the Bryce Canyon Lodge. It is very cold with the sun down, although we are only up about 8,000 feet. Tomorrow we will get some beautiful pictures, I know, with the sun shining down on these scenic wonders also known as the Hoodoos. Spooky, huh?

For breakfast, we went over to Ruby's Restaurant which turned out to be an all-you-can-eat lunch bar. It was very delicious. We decided a good start for the day would be to stop at the Visitor's Center. The entrance fee for this park is also $25.00, *but* this is where our trusty little Senior Citizen Pass came in to play. It is Monday, June 9th, and what an awesome place to start a Monday! The Visitor Center offers a video they show daily, it was already in progress, but what we saw was very interesting and informative. We learned geologists believe that Bryce Canyon's formation began at the same time dinosaurs were becoming extinct.

Getting back to the Hoodoos, which by the way is the name of the Bryce Canyon's little newspaper also, available to visitors for more information. Their descriptions of Hoodoo are many, one being a practice taken from the West Africans of sympathetic magic, and second being a natural column of rock in Western North America often in fantastic form. I sure like that second one, because the word fantastic is an understatement. In fact, I am having trouble finding new words to describe this unparalleled beauty! As we travel on, I will try to fill in a little history, most of it taken from their "Hoodoo" newspaper. Here at Bryce you can shuttle, hike, bike, and go horseback on their trails. There are ranger-led activities, camping, dining, cross-country skiing, and snow-shoeing in the winter, wildlife viewing, flower viewing, star talks, photography and fishing in nearby lakes. Name it, they offer it, but of course in the summer months, you may need reservations for camping and other activities.

As with Arches National Park, these weird and bizarre formations throughout Bryce are caused by a network of rivers and streams that have since disappeared, leaving behind this brilliantly colored limestone. Also, ice from sub-freezing temperatures at night and then warmth in the day, result in cracking and splitting, rounding of edges, running down the rim, and causing all these odd formations that are left behind. Of course there is much more to it, but we won't go into all that detail or this would be a whole different book. Just know that all this erosion in Bryce is not necessarily a good thing. It forms Bryce, but it will eventually destroy it in the distant future. Even today some of Peekaboo Loop Trail is not accessible because of the remnants of Hurricane Dean. A day of heavy rain saturated the plateau's edge below Bryce Point, leading to a large mud and rock slide that made it open only through a distant trail via the Navajo. And that is not the only closing while we are here. According to what one of the Ranger's told us, Paria Point is closed as well, because the whole point where the visitors stand had fallen off. He said this is the third time to rebuild. Fortunately, no one was there when it happened. So, always know, that there are dangers with nature. It is always, shifting, changing, eroding, and cracking. In 2006, a huge rock fall occurred in the Wall Street section of the Navajo Loop Trail. There were people there that witnessed it, but thank God no one was injured. The rock debris was estimated at 4 to 500 tons which covered an area roughly 60 feet long, 15 feet deep, and 15 feet wide. The Hoodoo newspaper says some of the rocks were as large as cars.

Bryce averages less than one fatality per year (not to say that that isn't one too many), usually caused by heart attacks, falling off cliffs, lightning, and vehicle accidents. However, hundreds of serious injuries needlessly occur from simply not paying attention to park rules and ignoring warnings. We must heed the parks warnings and safety rules to avoid such mishaps and totally ruining what might have been an awesome vacation.

It is time to start our adventure, into the world of vivid profusion of color and odd shapes that have the appearance of castles, cathedrals, and as Russ says "chess pieces." We have a little map to go by, so we are going to try and not miss anything along the way. It is a very simple guide that proves anyone can get to the different points and it will take you to heights of 9,000 feet.

The first attraction we will visit will be Sunrise Point. This point is mammoth in size and equally impressive in color. It looks like a wide stadium, with riveting rocks and spires, like a Jell-O mold, but uneven. It is in round and grated towers, with spires jetting out, all jagged and different than the one next to it, with exquisite colors of oranges, beige and terra cotta. Walking down the path and looking down, is a large hole called Natural Bridge. It reminds me of a castle gate, the top platform shaped like the top of a fort for men to stand and take guard. Actually, if we were in Arches National Park, it would probably be named as one of their famous arches, as it is formed the very same way. We are witnessing erosion, responsible from ice and water and cracking, with the end result being gravity finally pulling loose the weakened pockets in the center. Behind the bridge are almost white slopes, more a very light peach in color. Two of them look like you could slide right on in.

Continuing to look down, huge orange rock walls rise up and end in decorated points, some of them several feet apart from each other, but continuing on and on. These rocks are all basking in the sun which appears to be bouncing off them right back to us and some have fingers for tips that are pointing toward the heavens. Ponderosa pines are sprinkled throughout the rocks for decoration, with their bright green needles. It seems they are all placed perfectly, just like they should be. Its 65 degrees and quite windy and the blue sky seems even more blue with that bright, bright orange against it.

The next view looks like a huge city with a guarded fort in the back, and then Russ's chess board, and then a huge rock with huge stairs all the way up in a gorgeous Georgia clay red. Then more chess pieces plus a staircase that is individual, like step, step, step, and the same underneath, with maybe thirteen little steps in a row, stepping all the way to the bottom. You know, all along there have been people walking down in these "knights and kings," but we are so high up we didn't know it. Like when you're up in an airplane and it gets to the point you can't even see the cars anymore, but you know they're there. Russ zoomed in to the bottom of this "chess game" and there they were. People...hiking all through them. How neat is that? And not just people but trees are all around down there, too. Russ kept zooming until we could see each person's face and the color of their clothes, some with hats, visors, or ball caps to shield their faces from the sun; some with backpacks and some walking with ski poles for support and balance. I know I sure could have used those ski poles in Arches! I would have loved to go down there and explore with them, but then, there's *up*! Ummm, no, thanks, maybe next time!

This area we are in now, appears to me to be an Olympics diving stadium, with a huge wall in front, a very deep hole in between us and the wall and pointed jetties sticking out from this side, which looks like the diving platform. And all the colorful pillars and spires are the spectators. Oh, and next to the wall are light gray pillars and lots and lots of trees next to them. This is an imagination play land that can take you anywhere you want to be. But the colors are way beyond our imagination; they are all masterpieces of our Maker.

This next scene is a slope, filled with pines and pillars that look like they have been carved out of white stone, and they look like four snow people, one is holding a child, two look like chubby women and a bunch of lumps in between all of them, and then a small snow child. We continue to walk along the path and see more pillars of different sizes, ranging from deeper oranges all the way up to light beiges. It is an enormous stretch of pillars mostly flat on the top and zigzagging all over.

This is so convenient the way they have laid a path, complete with a fence to walk along. It guides you along the point so that you can see this drama of spires, walls, forms of rock people, and terra cotta colored dunes unfold. Maybe God gave us this opportunity to look down on this treat for the eyes, just for this moment in time, like He does.

Coming upon our next scene, I just love it. It is bright orange, and slap dab in the middle is a huge pillar balancing a small oblong rock. But what is so dramatic about it, is this little oblong rock is balancing another oblong rock that is six times its size on top of it! Just incredible! Russ said it looks like it is balancing on someone's finger or toe, and he is right, it does! This already has an official name; it is called Thor's Hammer. How appropriate! Got lots of pictures of that and even later saw postcards as well. But I must say that my pictures are just as pretty if not prettier.

We have already concluded Sunset Point and now are moving toward Inspiration Point. No trailers are aloud beyond this point. This is the other disadvantage to coming with a trailer, so if you are doing that you need to research your vacation carefully. As we look down on these hoodoos, we can see how the tops of these are flat and worn and are wearing tiny white rocks and stones. I would be inclined to say it looks like rubble. But they are piled within and on top of other rocks, surrounded by a cascade of rocks around them, forming a huge circle. Bryce's formations are so unique and captivating. I don't know why I keep calling them the voodoos instead of the hoodoos. I need to remember they are also known as tent rocks, fairy chimneys, and earth pyramids. Really tall, thin spires of rock that protrude from the bottom of an arid drainage basin or badland. Maybe that makes more sense.

Inspirational Point is like a huge amphitheater in three layers of castles scattered everywhere. Hmmm, inspirational! Its grandeur is almost overwhelming, and the brightest orange yet, with such intricate formed spires packed in, row upon row; unending. Russ claims it is so big we can't get a shot with all of the points in it. It is said you can look toward the silent city, near Sunset Point. The scene is shadowed by Boat Mesa in the background. The lower parts of these formations are a light salmon color and even lighter at the top. There are more barren slopes here too, sprinkled with Bristlecone pines. The steep cliffs here are very dangerous at this point, because they are formed of crumbly rock, slippery slopes, and sheer drop-offs. We are now at an elevation of 8,100 feet; the wind is blowing louder than ever in our camcorder.

As we leave Inspiration Point, we will drive onward next to the Rim Trail and enter Bryce Point. There are many pasture-like areas, so we pulled over for a full view, and when Russ zoomed in, we captured an elk far out in the field, grazing and ignoring everything else, right in broad daylight, too.

All the different views from the different points are magical, but I think I love Bryce Point the best; talk about an amphitheater! It captures the fullest view which seems endless. It is an electrifying orange; even if the color wasn't bouncing off the sun, you would probably need your sunglasses. This is the place most photographers want to be for a sunrise view of the sun highlighting these Hoodoos. It is the canyon's namesake, Ebenezer Bryce, who lived here for a short time. All he is known to have said concerning this point behind his home is: "It's a hell of a place to lose a cow."

Bryce Point is even higher in elevation at 8,300 feet. All of a sudden, I hear, "Hey!" and I turned so quick, almost losing my balance, only to see Russ looking at me and I could hear him speaking into the camcorder saying, "That was Buddy. She cut me off." He got a good shot of the back of my head as I walked right between the camera and his good shot. Uh-oh… "Sorry!" I better watch myself or he is going to fire me from his movie!

This point is almost surreal. There are spires after spires, in rows of millions and then more rows sporadically lined up behind those rows, with dark-green trees scattered all between the rows. Some have flat tops scattered with stones and some come to points, either way they look like rows of graceful castles for the King. The rock directly in front of me looks like a weird critter. It is lighter in color than the rest with sunken in eyes and a short neck and big bumps on its forehead.

We have spent a good amount of time here and will drive on back and down to Farview Point. Paria View would be the next closest point, but as I said it is closed right now. Somewhere in here we went past Swamp Point, I don't know if we missed the sign or what. Up until now, the signage has been outstanding. I do believe it was a smaller area than the others. I guess that is what made our drive so much longer from Inspiration Point. From the car, we see a lot of green land; Russ says they look like they could be farms, which is probably right if Mr. Bryce used to live in here. Farview is appropriately named because of the captivating far away views. Among the pillars and in the back are pink plateaus called the Aquarius Plateau; in fact, my information tells me you can see as far as the North Rim of the Grand Canyon and 160 miles to the Black Mesas in Arizona. And this is all because of Bryce's high air quality. We have traveled a good distance up, because Farview is at an elevation of 8,819 feet. Trust me I feel it, I thought it was just me, but even Russ seems out of breath when he speaks in the camcorder.

Suddenly, here comes a helicopter through, I bet someone is taking an overhead look at this unbelievable landscape. Russ says the rocks in front of us look like another bridge, but to me it looks like a cave down there. Further on the trail, there are benches, which are actually trees split horizontally, with the flat side up, which I thought was so perfectly suitable for this area. Russ took a break from his busy movie to sit down on one for a little while and take in all this world class beauty. *No*, I don't mean me!

The view in front of us is a huge mountain, which really appears to be a sand dune, but of course isn't. It has a few pillars on the left and in the middle are three rocks that look like the three little piggies. Then to the right of them it is rather barren, but behind it is pure dark green grass and more trees than you can count. Right in the middle of all this is a beautiful bush of flowers; they are pale yellow with a tiny touch of green, five to six petals and bright yellow stamen.

I tried to find out the name of them but couldn't; however, I got a good picture of them anyway.

We have returned to Natural Bridge, because when we saw it before it was turning dark. Before we see the bridge though we see a huge pillar holding a huge rock on top of it, and I don't think we saw that before. It is mid-center, standing out like a sore thumb with all the greenery behind it. Russ figures the wind is blowing anywhere from 20 to 25 miles an hour in gusts. He is usually right on.

We are going up again to 8,800 feet elevation where we arrive at Agua Canyon. The first thing that draws our attention is another balancing act and this time it is a tall pillar, wide on the bottom and then narrows as it rises. It is bright orange with a gray rock on top, that looks like it just landed there out of nowhere, but it is con-nected. Russ said it looks like it belongs on Easter Island. To me, it looks like a dragon lifting his head way up over the cliff to see what is going on up there. The overlook here has several "parts." To the left, is a large gray "fort" and it is named The Hunter. Why, I don't know, but underneath it has a Georgia clay-colored base, then more gray and more clay, and it seems to continue to alternate the colors. To the right, is another completely different tower, wide and huge, almost a giant vertical square with a giant gray square rock sitting on top. It was named the Rabbit or the Backpacker. Either way, it doesn't look like either one, hence the park stopped naming these prominent hoo-doos because many have either fallen or eroded away and they look nothing like what they were named in the beginning, anyway.

Russ said, "If this is Agua View, shouldn't there be water some-where?" That is a good question. There probably was at one time many years ago and that is what formed all these odd shapes. And look out because if it rains here, you definitely don't want to be caught on those trails below. It certainly would sweep you away.

The Navajo Mountains sit behind all of these remarkable sights, but right now taking center stage, is a really true balancing rock. It looks like a bust; Russ says it is of Caesar. It is literally sitting on a pointy tip of an orange pillar that is wide on the bottom and narrows into a point. This bust is teetering there and it is not even centered. As windy a day as it is, you would expect it to topple right off, and not only that, it is completely white in color contrast. *Wow!* Bryce is surely one of God's greatest works and still changing with time.

A few steps more and we are looking down into another hole. After each point, there is a little drive to the next point. In this case, the next point will be Ponderosa Point at 8,904 feet. The drives are as beautiful as the points, the roads are good and the scenery thrilling.

Ponderosa Point is so spacious with the huge mountain range behind it. The gray cliffs are wider and wander more, too. On the floor of this canyon, there are huge Ponderosa pine trees, therefore, the name of the point. There are also Blue Spruce, and Douglas Fir. It makes me think of when I was a little girl and we'd go looking for a Christmas tree, and we'd look at the Blue Spruce which Mom liked, but were too expensive.

We have now driven on to Rainbow Point at 9,115 feet and the shirt I am wearing is very appropriate because it says "Got Oxygen?" I am also wearing a stupid looking hat and Russ is too, we purchased them in Alaska to keep the sun off, and we both look like Goobers. I don't know how Mona recognizes us! Oh, what a hoot!

Somehow, we drove past Black Birch Canyon, so we will catch it on the way back. This is the southern end of the park. Yovimpa Point is right across from here as well. Now we see the park recommends this is where you should begin your tour of the park—at the south end. They recommend you drive all the way to the South end first and then work your way back, so that you begin by viewing the entire park from this position. Well, too late now, we are viewing the entire park now and it is just as overwhelming at the end as it would have been in the beginning. Just spectacular! But that is what we get for not reading this information ahead of time. I'm sure they know what is best, but walking down still further, you get an overwhelming look of what they call the Grand Staircase. That name makes sense. The bright orange rock appears to be a huge staircase all the way around and up. We may be taking pictures galore and using the camcorder like mad, but the view of this vibrant canyon is something we could never have imagined. It feels like we got a little peek of a piece of heaven prematurely. In fact, I believe this is heaven on earth now.

We are standing on top of the Pink Cliffs still in Yovimpa view point. Bryce is so wonderfully organized with the signs, the roads and the way it is set up. You can drive so conveniently to each viewpoint. I am so blessed to be able to experience all of this, because like most young people from my generation, vacations of this caliber did not exist. Most of the people I knew could not afford such. Usually, we visited relatives, a lake or mountain close by, not to say there is anything wrong with that, at least we were with our family. Happy. And we were leaving our home town, but Bryce and Arches and all the rest…never in my dreams and a very untouchable one at that.

Well, back to reality. Thank God the parks are great about restroom facilities along the way. Another plus for our national parks in the good ole US of A. Russ is reading information that states this ridge was once connected to the ridge way far out in front of us, about thirty miles away. This big split is due to earthquakes, rock mountains pushing through and seismic activity. This is the highest elevation of the park and you really can get the bigger picture from here. There are more trees at the end of this point than the others and a trail beneath called Riggs Spring Loop Trail, which is a strenuous 7.5-mile loop for anyone who is able. Behind that and under the rim is a trail called the Under-the-Rim trail, that reaches out 23 miles all the way back to the canyon.

And that is exactly where we will go, but it is hard not to stop and take a few more shots here and there. It is a lot to take in, all in one place. There are more white rocks in front of us with all the spires behind, standing at attention in beiges and oranges, with trees surrounding and you can see so far out. The pile next to those look like a huge snow man and it pops out at you with the brilliant and deep green trees behind it. I love the next scene of the wooden fence in front of us and right behind that is a dead tree, silhouetted by the blue sky and foggy-looking mountains behind that. This is one of my favorite shots. It is hard to pull ourselves away as we keep looking down and out over the rim. As I let go of the fence, I get that queasy feeling in the pit of my stomach, like I am falling and practically fell over. Not over the fence—just over. Meaning down on the ground, I am standing on. You know the feeling I mean. I couldn't stop laughing at myself because I don't think Russ got it! Oh my! Russ is still filming, I guess the more you film the more you see to zoom in on.

We decided to stop off at the Visitors Center one last time to see if we could catch the end of the movie they show about the park and wouldn't you know, we walked in the exact same place in the movie as we did the first time. So we decided to go ahead and have lunch.

Driving out of Bryce, in the distance against the shadows of the darkest green, are glistening snow-capped mountains. Just because we are leaving Bryce, it doesn't stop the colors and formations from coming. This is the northern portion of Bryce and we have arrived at Fairyland Canyon at an elevation of 7,758 feet, and it is located one mile north of the national park entrance station. So from the south end to the north end, we have already traveled 2,000 feet down. Out in the woods, is a deer having a field day, running on over to the meadow out in the open. As we walk into the area to view Fairyland, there is a jay, colored the prettiest blues; I believe it is a western jay. Our blue jays are a very pretty blue, but don't have the golden beak and those royal blue colors.

This section is comparable to a factory. It has a large umbrella looking formation of peach-colored rock cascading down into pillars, forming a wall. Then underneath many separate pillars, some in pairs, which look like piping and workers. Ponderosa pine are scattered all over at the top here too, and a couple rows coming down the middle. Here we can view the hoodoos on an eye-to-eye level, and we find ourselves about 5.5 miles north of Bryce Point. As we drive out of the park there are tee pees on our left, I guess they are available to camp in.

The view is that of bright terra cotta dunes with scattered trees and then before we know it, we are exiting through the twin tunnels. You might say we are literally "winding down" this beautiful scenic road and get a better picture of the two balancing rocks we saw on the way in. Only then, it was starting to get darker. They are even prettier as they demand our attention in the daylight. And I still can't get over how green it is here with the white-mountains in the background. It is an up-close view and yet so far away—if that makes any sense.

Mona is doing a great job at getting us to our next destination. We are back on Route 89 heading north. Most of the pictures I take and filming I do, I am doing right through the wind shield or the window, and yet the pictures come out so well. The ones taken off the camcorder are a little on the blurry side, but we do not own a digital camera. We have looked at them, but Russ is the type to research things out first. In this case, I think his problem was procrastination.

The rocks are instantly turning from the bright oranges and salmon colors to brown. We are back to Route 15, also known as Veteran's Memorial Highway, and continue to go north. There is actually ice on the road. We've driven a pretty good while, and are passing a beautiful dark red ranch or farm. We plan to drive until we find a motel and then we will pack it in for the night. We stopped to have dinner, but Russ only wanted an ice cream cone. We came to a Quality Inn and seemed to be in some kind of trance, pondering over the high lights of the day, which were many. It is time to get to bed and dream of the next wonderful place we will land…the Grand Tetons!

CHAPTER 12

The Three What?

It is Tuesday, June 10, 2008. We decided to have the continental breakfast at the Inn, packed up Mona for another day in our movie and headed out to get gas. We are facing yet another beautiful, bright, and sunshiny day. The temperature is 68, and I know I keep saying it, but we figure life can't get much better than this. We are traveling toward Salt Lake City and hit a couple little sprinkles of rain and now we can see the lake in bits and pieces as we travel along, still on Interstate 15. Ohhh, back to reality again as we run into a bunch of construction. Progress, right? Interstate 84 has joined us and we are now entering Brigham City, where we are getting a beautiful view of the Great Salt Lake.

We've just crossed over the state line into Idaho and pulled over to the Idaho Welcome Center to get some yummy tourist information. Boy, talk about a green state; it is so pretty and the view across the street is awesome, with the mountains and snow. Well, that almost sounds like a contradiction, with green and snow in the same sentence. But it is so true, so beautiful, and so green. It is very cold and windy here this morning. The difference in the temperature in just a few miles is amazing, because it is down to about 55 or 60, not counting the wind chill factor. We are passing Devil Creek Reservoir, a pretty greenish-blue color.

Continuing on Route 15, we'll soon cut over to Route 26 which will take us into Wyoming. Russ is such a character, the star of course, because now he is singing Sonny and Cher's song…"and the beat goes on"…and the beat goes on. I think he got that in his head because

183

while I was recording on the camcorder I said, "And the beautiful green grass goes on and on." Trust me, I know him…that *is* why! Too funny!

For lunch we stopped off in Pocatello, Idaho, at a Burger King, something new and different. There was a little shopping area there with a beauty salon and I told Russ I really needed a haircut and I know he sure did. I can't believe he agreed. He has never sat himself in a beauty salon in his whole life, even though nowadays, men do that all the time. We had so much fun, I don't know if Russ was cutting up because he was a little nervous, or what, but those girls were just a barrel of fun. We talked and talked of our adventures this far and had them rolling. I would definitely count that as one of our favorite things we did, mostly because I never got to go with my husband to get a haircut. This was definitely something new and different. Oh, my!

It's such an enjoyable ride in this emerald green state. Next, we are coming across a farm with several silos; everything just looks so clean here. The green expands as far as your eyes can see and of course, the mountains as background props, far away. We keep driving on and the snowcapped mountains are on both sides of us now; we see farms along the way in the midst of all this beauty and then a sign saying Palisades Reservoir. And then, boom, we are in Wyoming passing over the Snake River, which will follow us for a long time. There are these huge "mounds" on both sides of us, maybe every quarter of a mile. I say mounds because I don't know what else to call them. They are each as long as a football field maybe, but very narrow, like possibly it is a storage area or something, because I can see a door on the end toward the street. They look like they are made of dirt and there are sporadic patches of grass growing all over it. They all seem to be the same size, but we never did find out what they really were. Immediately, we are back on a scenic route, and you know what that means, more turns, and ups and downs and the most picturesque scenery ever. I can't wait to see what happens next!

It may seem like it didn't take long to get here, to Wyoming, but it is already 6:00 p.m., so we have been on the road all day. I see why they named this river the Snake River, because it is doing just that; acting like a snake and winding itself right next to us as we likewise wind around this mountain. It is beautiful and Russ keeps saying, "Get a picture, Ginn. Get another picture!"

I'm surprised to see so much traffic, but people are really out and about today. The greenest green I've seen is surrounding us, like new sod in the form of a carpet, soft and plush. And then God came along with His dreamy landscape ideas and scattered yellow flowers everywhere. I want to get out of the car and get in the middle and sing The Sound of Music while twirling around and around until I can't anymore. And just lay down in the middle of it, out of breath and panting and laughing at the beauty of it all, staring up at the sky and giving thanks. Ohhh, so breathtaking, so breathtaking! These flowers look like bright yellow daisies to me, but they are called arrowleaf balsamroot. They are everywhere, a delight to the eyes! It seems like such a long sophisticated name for this beautiful wild flower.

Then, practically right next to all this lively green and wild flowers, we find rows and rows of dead trees that make this section of scenery look almost wintry. But these trees have been burned, either by the rangers or maybe a lightning strike; in any case, not unusual for the national forests. Just as drastic a change as the burned trees; we are back into the rolling and soft-green-blanketed mountains, with long shadows looming over them as we approach the evening sunset. Our friend, the Snake River, serenely follows and the oncoming cars are turning their headlights on. The shadows are getting longer and looming down the sides of the mountains; it will soon be dark. To the right, is a very pretty and soothing scene of the winding Snake River, with a very small reddish-colored bridge going over it. It has about 5- or 6-foot rails on each side of it, coming from out of nowhere and disappearing into nowhere too, because there are a group of trees covering the other end of it. This is really a great adventure and at least we know we will have a nice warm room and a heater inside, unlike the lodges at Mt. McKinley and Crater Lake. The wind gusts have picked up to seventeen miles an hour, which could be worse, but it sure makes the cold colder! As the sun goes down so does the temperature, so we find a motel named after me (HA), The Virginian, and settle in. We are on W. Broadway and Virginian Lane and will stay in Jackson Hole for the night. We must bring in our two suitcases we packed for Alaska, so we can trade off for heavier clothes; like winter coats and long johns! After we got all the luggage in, I admit Russ did most of it, we sat around a while to warm up. Then we ran out and got something at Wendy's because everything else was already closed. The newscasters tell us the temperature is going to drop to 40 degrees and by midnight to 28 with a possibility of rain and snow in the morning. Woohoo! And here we are right in the middle of a winter wonderland! It's so exciting, but it is also scary, Georgians don't know how to drive in snow, and we are in some of the biggest mountains I've ever seen! Good thing Russ grew up in Pennsylvania!

The name Jackson Hole refers to the valley region surrounded by mountain ranges and highlands; according to my national guide book the parks give out. "Jackson" is the name of the town at the southern end of Jackson Hole, only four miles away from the Grand Tetons.

As much as I dislike waking up every night at about 4:30 a.m., this time I didn't mind so much because I peeked out the window to see it was snowing! But this morning, we are determined to get on to the mountains and get a good look, so after breakfast at the Virginian Restaurant (which was excellent by the way), we hit the trail. But before we leave, there is a pick-up parked right in front of us with the name "Jim" on it, so, of course, I had to take a picture of that for our friend Jim, to let him know we were thinking of him and his wife Sandi. As we leave the little town, we go through two lights and then come to what we call, "The Square" in Marietta; here they call it "Town Square." There, parked on the corner was a stage coach and driver waiting to take a willing customer for a ride. The coach is bright red in color in the sunlight, but as it pulls into the shade, it is more of a brownish-bronze and the driver is sporting a big ole cowboy hat. Each corner of the square was uniquely decorated with a large arch made completely of antlers. The arches are huge, thick and tall. This is the corner of North and South Cache Streets; we will turn left onto N. Cache. No sooner do we get a few miles, when a coyote trots right out in front of us, it seems not to have a care in the world, making our day right off the bat. It happened so fast I didn't get it on camera, and I know coyotes are all over the US, but it is the first time I've seen one in the wild like that. We drove down Jackson Hole Highway to the visitor center in Moose Junction, called Moose Visitor Center, *duh!* Of course, I had to get post cards and a magnet which always makes me a happy little camper. The ranger handed us a great information booklet and a map of the park. We always appreciate that, so we can try to see everything and it is just full of wonderful information. I noticed a ranger outside raising the flag, I thought that was a captivating sight and got a picture of him, and it just brought all the patriotism out in me. Love it! Of course, my next favorite sight is that of a small post office, so I have a place to mail my postcards. Moose, Wyoming is printed on the side of the small dark brown building.

We come upon a lake with a rugged wooden gate, with big geese and their cute little babies following behind. There are so many of them, three or four adults and about seventeen little guys—*so* cute. Our guide book tells us some of the best panoramic Teton views are found along the Snake River and we are beginning to find out just driving down the highway gives way to the most striking views of all. Soon we come to the Chapel of the Transfiguration, just north of Moose Village. The chapel is snuggled in the valley, outlined with a log gate and a beautiful view of the Teton Range behind it. There is a little A-framed roof entrance, fully open to walk under on a wooden side walk, that welcomes you to this impressionable and peaceful place. The church itself is made of logs, with a cross on the top of the A-framed roof and a cross inside on the altar as well. Our guide book tells us this historic chapel was built in 1925, by the residents there because they had so far to go, usually by buckboard, to town. Episcopalian services are held there in the summer months, but they leave it open for you to go inside and enjoy the simplicity of this tiny chapel. It has seats inside and out with a few pews that might hold maybe fifty parishioners. As Russ takes my picture in front of the chapel, it is beginning to snow a little.

There are many places you can pull over to view the scenery and as we do, we find a skeleton of a critter. I'm guessing this is a small elk, probably hit by a car. I imagine that is a common occurrence here; there are so many critters around. Today is kind of an exploration day, to see what kind of trouble we can get into, so we decided to continue on to Jenny Lake, about eleven miles from here and right behind the Grand Tetons.

In the beginning, some parts of the shoreline of the lake look like a little swamp, but then we walk through and find sidewalks with gorgeous pines all around and outlined in the background, is a very foggy mountain. It is still snowing lightly and colder than the dickens. But we wanted to go as far as the pier and boats that take you across the lake, just to check it out. Looking over the sides of the pier, the water is crystal clear, we are able to see the bottom, which looks like it is right there, but it must be about five feet deep at least. All in all though, the lake is estimated to be 423 feet deep and encompasses 1,191 acres. So I would say it is a pretty large lake. It is considered to be one of the major focal points in the park, with many hiking trails, scenic boat rides and a quick access to the major climbing route into the tallest peaks of the Teton Range. They say the Jenny Lake trail, which is 7.1 miles and loops around the lake, is a fairly easy hike, since the altitude gain is "only" 700 feet! But the altitude increases drastically once you enter Cascade Canyon. The longer we stay the foggier it gets, so we decided we'd check the shuttle boats out tomorrow and maybe take a ride across. For now, we decided not to go any higher, as it was getting more windy and the higher we go the colder it gets. You couldn't see the mountains anymore for the complete cloud cover and fog and the snow is starting to stick to the ground. We are not going to stop at anymore overlooks, either. But I have to admit, the roads are great with a gradual up grade, except the road by the lake. On the way back, it looked like someone had an accident because there were several emergency vehicles.

The park offers many overlooks and turnoffs, for viewing and picture taking. The signage is very helpful and in most places, when you pull over to take in all this beauty, there are information plaques which are very educational and you learn about your surroundings. There is also much to do here as in most of the parks, like hiking, fishing, campgrounds, horseback riding, boating, biking, bus and boat tours, and in the winter months, cross country skiing and much more. So you can certainly keep yourself entertained, when you are not busy simply enjoying the thrilling view.

We have come across the Jackson Lake Dam and Reservoir and stopped to take pictures of it. Traveling from the park's south end to its north boundaries is 56 miles. We plan to go back on the second route, since there are two roads around the mountain. Of course, we had to stop and take pictures of a bouquet of the bright yellow flowers, as the snow begins to fall heavier. As we pass a few lodges, we find a place called Flagg Ranch, which has cabins and a restaurant, so we decided to stop and have lunch there. A big window was vacant and we chose to sit next to it and eat. I felt if anyone was looking from the outside in, we would look like an advertisement, in a huge frame, the snow outside, and our faces shining with joy. What a delight to sit and watch the snow fall, so very soothing and bright.

As soon as we got back on the road, an elk and her baby walked right in front of us, how adorable. I'm glad Russ hadn't picked up speed yet. The road led up to elk plats and we filmed herds of them. As we venture on, it is getting harder to see. I could see the shadows of something out there, probably an elk or a moose. As we continue to drive to the motel, there are herds of buffalo out in the fields, some lying down, they are enormous even lying down. Also known as bison, these giant creatures weigh in at 2,000 pounds at *least*! Actually they are the largest animal in North America. They are declining in number, but they are protected in the national parks. A couple more miles up the road and we come to a herd of elk. Some of them are lying down as well; guess they are all settled in for the upcoming storm.

The snow is sticking and the trees are heavy laden. Snow drifts are forming on the sides of the road. Rain, thunderstorms, and snow are in the forecast, so we hunkered down with our playing cards, post cards, and TV, for an evening of relaxation. We also have lots of new adventures to think about and plan. Not to mention all the adventures and beauty we have to discuss already.

When we got up the next morning, the sun was shining bright and we could hardly believe it. This hotel couldn't book us another night because they had reservations coming in for the weekend.

Don't forget we are doing everything spontaneously, so that is to be expected once in a while. So we went to another motel and made reservations for the next three nights. So there! Then, we get a call from the previous hotel apologizing and saying they made a mistake and the room would be available after all. But it was too late, as we decided we were so close to Yellowstone; we'd just keep this room since we had secured it already. Sorry!

You can tell it is a beautiful sun-shiny day by the amount of people out sight-seeing. We passed a building that had beautiful statues of a heard of elk. I think it must be some type of museum, we will have to check that out another time. We pass one of the stage coaches, as though we see them on any ordinary day. Just before we get to the Teton peaks, we spy a sign for the Jackson National Fish Hatchery. Being the sportsman Russ is, he wanted to go take a look. It is a pretty good hike from the parking lot and it really doesn't look all that big. There are only about four very long buildings, which are called raceways and a small pond or lake in the middle of a huge property. The land is the National Elk Refuge, a protected feeding area for elk in the winter. Some men are busy working down there, so we figured we'd go take a look.

There are millions of very young fish inside one of the long buildings and they are kind of divided in different sizes of fish. The next building has fish that are bigger and the main building has eggs and female fish. This hatchery produces fish for an 18,000 square mile distribution area in Wyoming and Idaho. The only species of fish they rear here, is the Snake River Cutthroat Trout. Jackson Hatchery is only one of 70 National Hatcheries in the United States. They were established in 1950, and it is a self-guided-walk-yourself kind of visit. Over to our far right though is the pond, so after watching the men work a little while we decided to explore it. We only stood there a few minutes in this peaceful little place, when all of a sudden birds started whizzing by. There were only four or five, but they were darting about so fast, we could hardly figure out what was going on. They were just average-sized birds, but its underside and wings were the prettiest aqua-blue! The rest of the bird was a silver color and I tried to get pictures of them, but they were going at such a great speed, it was almost impossible. They would dive into the water, after bugs I guess, and they were just so precise, like the Blue Angels. One would fly right behind the other, so perfect and never missing. Maybe it was some kind of a swallow-like bird, I don't know. Just as we were turning to leave, in flies this beautiful bright-yellow bird! Oh my goodness, the beauty of these colors! His face and chest were bright yellow, except right next to his beak, which was a little rusty yellow. His back was an olive green/yellow and there were stripes on the tips of his wings and tail. This little guy was willing to sit still long enough for me to get a shot of him though, and Russ, well, he is standing there thanking the bird for letting him catch it on camera! And in the lake, clear as a mirror, there is a huge trout at least two and a half feet long. I just don't know how anyone can not know there is a God.

I tried to find these birds on line but couldn't. The closest I could come on this one was maybe, some kind of a warbler. But they sure made that little side trip worthwhile. Such captivating colors.

The mountains are still hiding behind the clouds looking like a blur, with the dark storm clouds behind them, but what a great puzzle picture that would be to put together. We hear the rangers have closed the east gate into Yellowstone because of the heavy snow, which is practically right around the corner, so to speak. On the left of us, is a mountain partly covered with snow. It flashes a picture of what looks like a face at us, the way the snow is positioned there. Russ thought it looked like an old man and I thought it looked more like a baby. I guess it is all in the eyes of the beholder.

A new day and it is a sunny and care free Friday morning, a Friday the 13th, at 36 degrees. It is expected to warm up to 64. We are on our way to another exciting day in Wyoming. It is such a gorgeous state! There are some beautiful flowers outside the motel. They are a deep purplish-red bush with tiny pale pink flowers. My pictures hardly do this plant justice, as it catches everyone's eye as they pass it, I'm sure. I had to look this one up too, and the only thing I can figure is it is a species of the "Smoke Tree." *So* perfect. We have a smaller variety of that in Georgia, often used as ground cover. There is just so much beauty and wonder around us we don't want to miss a thing, no matter how insignificant it may seem.

Coffee sounds good to us right now; oh, how convenient, a McDonald's! Mmm, mmm, mmm. Can you just smell it? They have the best coffee!

Driving along there is a hawk sitting on the fence post, got a blurry picture of it because we were just going too fast, and still a little further, a herd of critters way far out in the field, probably elk. And then we spot a herd of buffalo out there in them thar hills! Next, a huge herd of elk, two of the young ones are so cute. The one on the right is reaching way over with his neck to the one on the left, as though he is giving her a little smooch. Buffalo, buffalo, elk, elk, buffalo. And that is the way it went for the whole ride. There is an elk next to the fence and it looks like she wants to jump over it, to get back on the inside. We keep watching and she keeps edging closer and closer to the fence. We keep thinking she's going to do it. She's going to do it, *jump*! But, no, I think she is frightened with us so close, so we kind of gave up on her and started to move on toward the mountain.

We have reached the Tetons, clear as a bell and grand and bold. Russ was so amazed and he took such a deep breath of awe, he scared me. The Grand Teton, of course, is in the middle and rises the highest to 13,770 feet. Each mountain has its own name. To the immediate left of the Grand Teton is the Middle Teton, and next to that is Nez Perce. To the immediate right is Mt. Owen and next to it is Teewinot. Of course, the range goes on and on. Right now we are practically at the base of these powerful beauties, except there is a small lake in between the mountain and the road, then a good bit of land and then a fence about six feet from the edge of the road. There are absolutely no foothills to block our view at all. There is a cloud the whole length of the range, long and narrow, close to the bottom of the mountains. But as we sit there and watch, the cloud very slowly begins to rise until it is up and over and almost gone. The white of the snow is a striking contrast against the very bright blue sky. Another fulfilling sight, to just stand and stare and lose yourself.

The Grand Tetons

The Grand Teton's name comes from the tallest of the three mountains in the middle of the range. But, the actual naming of the Tetons came from a group of French fur trappers-les trois tetons, which means the three teats, or nipples, or breasts. Hence, the title of this chapter. Really? Now where were they're heads? There are more elk out in the field, and they don't seem at all worried we are there watching them. I'm sure they are used to us weird humans standing there, gawking at them all hours of the day. Little do they know they are the stars of Russ's movie right now! Suddenly, Russ lets out this shrill, loud whistle, which I wish I could do, and the elk scatter like there is a bear in their midst. Come to think of it, Russ does sound a little like a bear this morning, like his voice is changing or something. It is raspy, but I'm thinking it is because of the altitude. Then the birds begin to sing like there is no tomorrow, and we can't concentrate on anything else besides the calm, the view, and peace. WOW!

Jenny Lake is right around the corner and we can hardly wait to explore and see what is on the other side of the mountain. I'm surprised Russ didn't blurt out that song! As we walk around to the sidewalk, we make our way to the lake and a little tiny critter ran in front of me. Russ had the movie camera, and I couldn't believe it, but he got him on camera. He was so cute as he scurried off the sidewalk, into the grass, and sat right up on his hind legs to take a look at us. Russ is clicking his tongue at him and he just keeps looking. He stayed there a pretty good while, too, as if to say, "I may only have a small bit in this movie, but someone is going to discover me and I am going to be a star someday!" Russ called him a ground squirrel. It made me giggle.

It was a nice walk up to the lake, but it is very cold. I can tell Russ is cold because his shoulders are raised and his chin is down and his arms are clasped around his chest. Not to mention the air coming from his mouth. Nonetheless, he looks really good with the back side of the Grand Teton behind him and the long boarded walk over the lake.

We stood and watched one of the boats back in. But the bigger boats were tourist boats, with large canopies over them and many seats to accommodate the tourists and carry them over to the other side. There was a woman in a booth selling tickets and boy, did I have some questions for her, like: how difficult is the terrain, how long will it take to get to the falls, does she think a women my age with breathing problems already, can do it? And her answers were very simple…"Easy, not long and yes!" She said, "Well, I did it myself and it was really very easy. It is only a half a mile." She didn't look a whole lot younger than me, so we went for it and bought a ticket. But I should know better by now, that when these people say something is easy, or its only one half a mile, or "I did it, not a problem," what they really mean is: It's straight up all the way, it's probably a mile or more, not a half mile. And yeah, I did it and I'm not a hiker means: I'm 22 and it wouldn't matter if I was a hiker or not. And they usually live there, so they are acclimated to the mountain air.

But in spite of all that, we boarded the boat with several other people, with a goal of reaching the falls at the top. Hidden Falls is the name of it. I'm not sure, but I think it is the only falls here.

I got pictures of the lake, as we crossed: of the impressive pristine, blue-green water, and of the people on the boat. Well, of the back of their heads that is. And of course, the stately lodgepole pines and the wake the boat was leaving behind us.

Once we arrived to the other side of this beautiful lake, most of the people jumped off and took off like a bullet up the path, which was okay with us because it seemed like we were alone again and had the mountain all to ourselves. We just took our time, and Russ and I got busy taking pictures of this neat path. It started off with nice concrete steps, a lot of steps and then proceeded into a winding trail. We are presently at 6,000 feet elevation. The path is about 4 feet wide. There are medium-sized rocks on each side with snow. The snow wasn't sticking yet. No wonders everyone was already out of sight and that lady at the ticket booth thought it was so easy. I thought; this is going to be great, that lady was right, this should be a breeze, not like arches where it started out so nice and completely disintegrated into dirt, rocks, and hardly no path at all.

The sound of water was off in the distance, so we stopped and took a little break. As we continued on, we could hear the sound of water. The water flow was from the falls and was white and foamy and just a babbling. We got more pictures of the water and the snow in the woods and as a hiker passed us he informed us that a black bear was seen in this area the day before. Don't ask me who was out here in that weather, but maybe they meant the day before that. Now we are really on guard, but don't know what good that will do. But I can tell my ears sure are perked up a notch! They say you should talk and make noise while you're walking, to ward off a bear, but heck, I'm just trying to breathe.

The slope is getting a little steeper, every now and then people would come and we'd step aside and let them pass. The boat continually goes back and forth bringing and taking tourists. And remember that nice path, humph. Now it is mud, ice, and snow and about a foot and a half wide. Women are coming down toward us, four of them, and they said they were afraid to go any further, it was getting too hard for them. They were in our age group. I offered them to come with us and we could all help each other, but there was no way we could convince them that they had come this far, why give up now. I think we are about to find out, it is an hour into our hike.

We stop again to catch our breath; we are actually getting warm from all the exercise, so I take my coat and wrap it around my waist, and take some more pictures. The brook is getting louder, but the scenery around us is spectacular. We can only see the scenery immediately around us, because of all the trees, brush and humongous rocks that are obstructing our view. It is very rugged terrain now, with lots of trees, some of them fallen, and a good bit of snow, slush and ice and stupid me with tennis shoes on. We both left our hiking boots in the car, since it was only going to be an easy half mile hike. Figures, right? All of a sudden I have this cramping in my belly, you know the feeling, gurgling, crampy. Oh, I gotta go! I looked at Russ, and he knows my looks as good as I know his body language. Uh-oh. What on earth do I do now? I looked all around. Oh, dear, *where?* Then I saw this huge rock, maybe I should say boulder, much bigger than me and I thought that is all I can do. Russ helped me climb way up, the boulder was about six feet up. The snow was deep there and it was pretty close to the edge, where the brook was flowing from the waterfall. Well, I was desperate! All I could think about was that bear they saw up here the other day! I felt like I was marking my territory and I was going to have to fight for it at any given moment. One little slip and I'd be in that pretty babbling brook, and mind you it was traveling at a pretty good clip. I hate to say what could have happened if I landed in that. With the speed it was going, all the rocks to bump me around and oh yeah, the temperature of the water! But I can tell you this, I would have gotten down to the bottom before anyone else, dead or alive, I don't know. And I didn't know if where I was standing was stable or not either. You know, you can't rush these things, and oh boy, talk about *cold!*

I was so afraid someone might be going by on the path and they would see me. Thank goodness, I had a napkin in this little purse I had with me. My foot slipped into a little crevice full of snow, and I was praying it wouldn't get stuck in anything. I was also worried about something coming out of those rocks and biting my bare and very cold bottom! Then I had to get down, which is twice as hard. Going up I had a sense of urgency, but coming down was just plain scary. When I got to where Russ could extend his hand to me, I was up pretty high. He said, "Jump!" Are you kidding? I just knew I'd go sliding right on down in all that ice. I kept standing there, scared to death; I really don't know how I got up there in the first place. People were coming passed and looking at me trying to get down and I just know they knew what I was doing. Finally, Russ just wrapped his arms around my knees and lifted me off the rock and back down to earth. Then we had to sit there just a minute, because as you know like at Arches, I had those shaky knees that just wanted to give way. I don't know why I keep doing these things; I don't think I ever will again. By the way, I told Russ I wouldn't write about this, for some unknown reason I guess he was embarrassed, glad I didn't promise.

Well, now the path is more hazardous, maybe a foot wide, definitely a single-file path, and now it is ice and we have been hiking an hour and a half. To go up, and the slope is steeper, we literally had to kick our feet into the snow to the side of the path, so we could dig in and move forward and up. Then, my world fell apart again. In front of us was a bridge we had to cross. A wooden bridge about four feet wide, okay, maybe it was five, and twenty feet long, covered with ice. *Nothing* to hold on to, no railings going over this brook, which didn't seem like a little brook anymore and was about eight feet below. Why on earth isn't there a railing to hold on to? Even that would have been scary! In my mind the water beneath was more like a powerful river, because both the sound and the strength of the flow had increased mightily in its intensity. Didn't I just say I wasn't going to do these crazy things anymore? Russ is trying to convince me it will be okay. I'm like a frozen pillar standing there. Russ says, "I will take your hands, get in front of you and hold on to you and I will walk backward and take baby steps. After all, that beautiful falls is not far from this bridge now." Why I thought that sounded sensible *or* safe, I don't know. I can't believe the words came out of my mouth, when I said okay. So off we go, I'm holding his hands going forward and he is going backward baby step by baby step. I am staring intensely into his eyes like I could climb into them. But I felt like if I didn't look on either side, I wouldn't be as scared. Oh, and did I mention the bridge was going up at a slant as well? I think if any one tried to go around us, I would have had to get on my knees and simply crawl across. I wanted to scream, "*Don't get near me!*" God bless my patient husband.

Once we got across the bridge and it did take a long time, since we baby-stepped and went at a snail's pace, we ventured on. The conditions on the ground were worse and we weren't there yet. We began to wonder if we missed a path or something. So we began to ask people coming toward us where the falls was. A young boy, no more than eleven or twelve years old said, "Well, there's another bridge up there, if you turn left, just before you cross it, you will get a great view of the falls. But, be very careful it is very icy up there." The key word in that sentence to me was, "before you cross it." Thank goodness we didn't have to cross another bridge. We went on and found we were very close to the second bridge. Then we had a hill to get up to a landing-like area, to observe the falls, about forty or fifty feet. I'm talking a steep hill, again covered in ice and snow. So we did the kick-into-the-snow-with-the-toes again in order to get a foothold, Russ always in front of me with a helping hand held out to me to grab. I guess I thought this was nothing after baby-stepping across the ice bridge. As we were climbing up, there was a log sticking up out of the snow that looked like a little seal sticking its head out to watch us climb pass. Russ paused to take a picture of it. Now can you imagine him doing that while we're in the middle of climbing up ice? I'm just thinking this Hidden Falls better be worth it.

At last, we did make it to the top and the ground was flat. Icy, but flat. And up here, they at least had a guard rail so you wouldn't fall over. The fall was spectacular, but I have to admit after having seen Yosemite, we were spoiled by the sights of many falls and most of them higher. The thing is though; we didn't attempt to climb to those. We took many pictures, even of the height of the Teton itself. I found out later that had we gone further, we would have come to a huge area where you could literally sit and have a little picnic, if you wanted. But we would have never made it back to the boat in time, and I don't think I could have done it. Going further also meant a second bridge! No, thanks.

Blue skies are in our sight overhead, the tip of the mountain is remarkable and it brings to mind, the passage in Isaiah 55: "The mountains and hills will *shout out* His Name," and trust me, the Tetons do just that. You can't help but think that very thing, when you see their grandeur. After a time, we continue admiring God's beauty as we descend and we see an animal on the rocks, but Russ couldn't film it fast enough. He said it was another marmot. It was a pretty good size too, like the size of a big ground hog. There is a lot of snow to either side of us, fallen trees all about, and rocks…big rocks, everywhere (maybe I should say boulders). The path up here is covered with ice and snow, but we have won the battle and made it to our goal and will slowly hike back down and feel a great sense of accomplishment.

Don't let anyone tell you it is easier to descend than ascend, because sometimes I think it is equally as hard, if not harder, going down. It didn't seem possible that we got up some of those rocks. I almost had to sit down and then slide down to the next rock to continue on. Now to go over the ice bridge once again and trust me I went back over it the same way I came, except looking only at my feet this time, step by step. It took us two and a half hours to do that trek and another hour to get back to the boat. Russ always stayed in front of me, with his hand extended for support. My knees were trembling a bit from doing things I certainly am not used to. It is beautiful and the air is crisp. It fills our lungs and our hearts with the true wonder of it all.

Jenny Lake is in sight, the boats are coming and going to pick up the fearless hikers, and I use the word *fearless* loosely! The lake is so calm and blue and the sky is a sight to behold, with a host of fluffy clouds and again, snow-crested mountains, outlining the edges of the lake on the other side. We see beautiful trees here, with moss hanging from them and pretty pink buds. It has taken us almost a whole day to accomplish our hike, and I have to admit it felt so good to sit down again in the boat. That was the longest half hour hike ever!

On the way back in to town, we decided to stop in at the museum, well, we thought it was a museum, but it turns out it is Jackson Hole and Greater Yellowstone Visitor Center. We passed it every day and kept saying we were going to stop. Beautiful mountains surrounded it and there was a big totem pole off to the side. The visitor center was interesting and filled with a herd of elk that looked so real. Maybe they were, real that is, just not alive. There were several wildlife exhibits there and information about plants and animals and the geology of Jackson Hole, the Grand Tetons and surrounding areas.

That evening, we went to a barbecue place and had some delicious and tender brisket. Yum! Then we returned to our motel and collapsed on the most comfortable, soft, warm bed in Jackson Hole.

Our dream now is to head out to Yellowstone, which is a place we both want to see in the worse way. I think ever since childhood, when you see movies and read about Yellowstone and its uniqueness in your geography classes, you want to go there some day. Well, our day has arrived and I can hardly wait to see Old Faithful!

But, on the way out of the Tetons, and probably for the last time in our life, pass the great buffalos out in the pastures. We are alone in our movie, as we exit this beautiful and unforgettable country. How fortunate to be able to see the Tetons, hike them, and live next to them for a short while.

CHAPTER 13

Did We Just Miss Planet Earth?

It was exciting to wake up and think about finally making it to Yellowstone National Park, especially knowing it was practically right around the corner, only minutes away. We will keep this room in Jackson Hole for one more night, because we did make reservations starting tomorrow in Yellowstone. So we quickly did a stop at Mickey Dee's and got right on route toward the south entrance. Due to the snow the past couple of days, the entrances were closed off, but we felt sure that today, that would not be an issue. Way up ahead of us we could see a coyote run across the road into the brush, and to our left, stood the beautiful Tetons grand and tall. I thought that was really ironic, because the first thing we saw entering the Grand Tetons is a coyote and now, the last thing we see leaving is a busy coyote. Kind of like a hello and a goodbye as we move on to our next exciting adventure.

Did I mention today is Flag Day? Well, God bless America! Such an amazing and beautiful country we live in, and we can testify to that as we continue our journey, because if you're looking for perfection, here it is.

The snow is melted down in the city, but since we are going up again, in elevation, that is, there is snow on the banks on each side of us like bookends. We have finally come upon the Yellowstone National Park sign. I am so excited to finally be here, and of course, we must take pictures of it, to remind us we are atop an active volcano! The Snake River is here to greet us in its care-free fashion and the lodgepole pines, which are the most common tree in the park, are surrounding the landscape. But this time Momma duck is there with her babies too, watching the river make its slinky snake-like turns through this dreamy land.

Much of Yellowstone sits inside a giant caldera, and the Yellowstone caldera is the largest volcanic system in North America. We are crossing over what is called the "approximate caldera boundary." Oh boy, I really had to look into this one. Caldera is taken from the word cauldron, which of course is a large boiling pot. That's appropriate, since Yellowstone is one *huge* active volcano! The approximate boundary indicates an unofficial region or area, which according to maps, seems to be marked as a pink dash and make a complete, but uneven, circle around the whole park. So we will probably cross it again as we go further north. But back to the caldera which is a cauldron-like volcanic feature, usually formed by the collapse of land following a volcanic eruption. The collapse is triggered by the emptying of the magma chamber beneath the volcano, sometimes leaving a collapsed ring. It can occur from one or several eruptions or even a series of eruptions and can be hundreds of thousands of square kilometers.

You can see these on the Moon, Mars, and other planets including other parts of our own world. Some are explosive and some are not. Hopefully, we won't see that theory tested today! There is comfort in knowing there are several seismometers all over Yellowstone keeping vigil. Scientists check these regularly. There is so much information to share, and I will do that a little more as we go, just to be able to understand a small part of this huge force in nature.

Next, we cross over the "continental divide" at 7,988 feet high. This is surely putting my geographical skills to task! Just for the sake of good information, I thank Wikipedia so I can explain in simple and short terms. A continental divide is a drainage divide on a continent, such that the drainage basin on one side of the divide feeds into one ocean or sea, and the basin on the other side either feeds into a different ocean or sea, or else is endorheic, meaning not connected to the open sea. I believe there are six altogether in North America, also known as the Great Divide. And so much for information on this subject, which I believe should satisfy most curious minds.

Route 89/287 will take us straight to Old Faithful at the south entrance of Yellowstone Park. It really isn't very far, and it's not too crowded at this point either. But we are still saying goodbye to the bison. We approach a huge lake, Lewis Lake, and on the other side of it, you can see what looks like smoke signals in the distance. No sooner do we turn the corner and there is a sparkling falls ahead, appropriately named Lewis Falls. I'm wondering how far and how high we were going to have to climb to get to the bridge this time. But it wasn't far and I am so grateful, since I am really feeling our hike from yesterday in my thighs. We took our pictures from there, by the bridge. There was quite a way to go to the trail and hike up higher if we wanted a better picture. It was gorgeous from there, a wide cascade falls, 30 feet high called Lewis Falls, named after Merriweather Lewis, as in Lewis and Clark, the expeditioners. We are halfway to Old Faithful so we decided to keep going after a few good photos were taken.

Just a couple miles before Old Faithful, we come upon some beautiful cascades called Kepler Cascades. It is about 40 feet wide and drops approximately 150 feet over multiple drops, the longest being 50 feet. The name came from the governor's 12-year-old son of 1881, Kepler Hoyt.

We are now at the south entrance to "Old Faithful," and when we approached the park it was like we were in a totally different world, hence, the title of this chapter! Oh my, it truly did feel like we fell off of planet Earth. And now, somehow, here we are in a most shocking and dramatic change in scenery. From green and trees and snow-capped mountains, to a flat land of smoke, steam and bare neutralized colors. We just turned our heads and looked at each other in amazement, standing there, trying to adapt, to this impressive and overwhelming change. Seriously, this was definitely a jaw-dropping moment. Like zombies in a trance, we kind of wandered over to where all the people were, some standing and some sitting on long benches, anticipating the eruption of Old Faithful. We had arrived!

I guess we waited about 35 to 45 minutes for her to perform. Words can't even express how amazing it is to think she goes off every 90 minutes, "*Faithfully!*" Did you know from year to year that time frame varies by a few minutes? It is just mind-boggling to think, as I sit here and write this, she is still performing! In fact, she has not missed a performance in more than 120 years. Right here, where we stand, in this dream and almost science fiction landscape, is the world's largest collection of geysers. It includes some that are even bigger than Old Faithful, more regular and even a few that are more spectacular! Some geysers are named for the shape they have built around themselves. Like Beehive Geyser and Castle Geyser, which I'm sure your imaginations can fill in the blanks on those.

While we patiently wait, we take shots of the geysers behind her and all around her that are spouting off. I never in my wildest dreams knew there were other geysers at Yellowstone, so you can imagine my wonder. Old Faithful is a cone geyser, which means it erupts in a narrow column, like a fountain. The eruptions last anywhere from a minute and a half to five minutes and spouts as high as 106 feet to 180 feet. She spouts anywhere from 3,700 to 8,400 gallons of water per eruption, depending on the length of the eruption. Just prior to eruption, water temperature at the vent is 204 degrees. These amazing facts are from the *Yellowstone Today* newspaper, the official newspaper of the park. I might add that after each eruption, a park ranger records with a stopwatch. He records the height, volume, and temperature of the water, then he posts a sign informing the visitors when the next eruption is likely to occur. And from what "Readers Digest" reports, the ranger is rarely more than ten minutes off the mark.

At last, she began to perk a little, each time going a little higher. Then a short lull and she'd perk a little more. It was as though she finally got the hang of it and let go full blast and all the people ewwed and awed over it. And rightly so, as this was our first time, to see her do her impressive act. Everyone applauds her and some whistle loudly. How thrilling, to watch and try to digest this totally new terrain, full of all these fascinating features, some very unpredictable. We watched until she was simply "letting off steam." Practically right next to Old Faithful is a marshy, steamy, dead area called the Black Sand Basin. It's full of water, some dirty looking and some a beautiful blue and it was lined all the way around with dead trees. We decided after that we'd visit the gift shop and save the rest of the sights for tomorrow.

Grant Village sounded like a good place to have a late lunch. We were both completely worn out from our hike yesterday, which finally caught up to us. We will head back to Jackson Hole for our last night there which will take the rest of the afternoon. But on the way back, passing Lewis Lake on the way out of Yellowstone, the most colorful sunset embraced us, with its oranges, tangerine, peach, gold and yellow colors. A breathtaking event, with another perfect ending to another perfect day, and I gotta tell ya, when we got back to our room, we went right to bed and I fell asleep first, which is very unusual! I think the rule is the one who falls asleep first is usually the one who snores, which, of course, is almost always Russ!

Gosh, we both slept until almost 9:00 a.m. today. It is Sunday, June 15, Father's Day! I surprised Russ with a Yellowstone shirt and some Indian music, which he loves. I already told you this is how he sings: hi wa ho ya hi wa ho ya hi wa ho ya. In his deep voice, which he seemed to make deeper when he did this. It actually sounded kind of soothing when he keeps on and on and on and on. Too bad I didn't have my little drum with me. No, I do not really have a little drum! Well, we have until noon to be out of the motel, so we just took our time. After Mona was loaded up once again, we decided to have breakfast at a restaurant right here in town up the road a ways, as we say in Georgia. I won't say the name because as you might have guessed, I don't have anything nice to say about it, and like we tell our kids: "If you don't have something nice to say, don't say anything at all!"

As soon as we got into Yellowstone, there are seven elk hanging out in the field, plus we had to get another picture of us in front of the Yellowstone sign. Someone was nice enough to take one of us together this time. Yellowstone, by the way, is the world's first national park ever. It is a magical and bizarre place, with the most unique landscape one can imagine, the landscape is rich with mountains, rivers, falls, canyons, plains, and wildlife, not to mention the spews and splashes, bubbling and colors; and perpetual spouting. The geysers, fumaroles, hot springs, mud pots, and oh-so many, many more baffling and dazzling sights.

As we pass Lewis Lake, there is a fisherman out there and he is in an inner tube-like thing. Fishing! He comes toward us and gets out and it looks just like the inner tubes you sit a child in with a place for his legs. He and his buddy were out there having a very good time. That is the first time I have ever seen that, and I found out they are called "fishing float tubes." You wear fins with it and go to places sometimes a boat cannot. I bet it is like fishing from your most comfortable chair in your living room.

Since we didn't see the West Thumb Geyser Basin yesterday, we thought we'd start there. West Thumb is located on Yellowstone Lake's shore. It is believed that a massive explosion may have formed West Thumb many years ago. The trail is only about 2/3 of a mile long and makes a loop around several hot springs and pools. It is also a caldera within a caldera. This walkway overlooks the west side of Yellowstone Lake. Altogether there are about seventeen highlights that the walkway crosses over including pools, geysers, springs, cones and mud pots. Each has its own individual personality, so to speak; each one mesmerizing in its own right, demanding your complete attention.

Yellowstone marks the hottest pools to be greens and blues, the most striking colors of all. These colors are usually below 140 degrees. Some of the beautiful colors here are created by heat loving microorganisms. What a treat to be able to view these unforgettable sights, after all, Yellowstone preserves the largest collection of hydrothermal features on the whole planet. One must really take caution not to stray off the walkway, unless otherwise indicated, because some of the crusted earth is so thin, you could go crashing into some scalding water and get severely burned. Since all thermal pools are near or above boiling temperature.

The walkway is in a kind of odd oblong circle, parted down the center, with features on both sides of it. It is built so that you are walking about three feet or so above these phenomenal attractions. Come, and walk with us.

The first feature we see is the Seismograph Pool and Bluebell Pools, which are a beautiful blue-green in color and known as the Blue Pools. They are quite big and not separate, but run in together by a foot or two and then split off into another huge pool. Apparently someone thought this pool might help measure the intensity and time of earthquakes. It is somewhat muddy on the edges of the pools because of the runoff of nearby mud pots. They are both surrounded by bright gold and orange colors and are steaming ferociously.

The Thumb Paint Pots look like miniature mud volcanoes, exploding as high as 3 to 4 feet and steam escapes from their fury, sometimes leaving what they describe as little mud chimneys. The mud looks silky and smooth and has a pinkish tint to it, but the consistency of the mud varies. They say the water is more acidic here than nearby pools. It reminds me of grits when it boils, and I know from personal experience how hot that gets and how it hurts to get splattered. Imagine what these little bubbles will do. What an unforgettable experience to stand on this boardwalk and look down at all this pure wonder around us.

We thought we'd go straight up the middle of the walkway path, since starting here, there are features on both sides. Then make a swing to the outer platform, to get back where we started. Surging Spring is the next stop and to our right side, which has an average temperature of 167 degrees F and steaming. This is a large, dramatic blue pool and I guess it is called surging because it overflows, sending waves of water surging into the lake.

Again, to our right is Ledge Spring. It is a smaller pool, very deep, deep blue in color and has a ledge all the way around it. It looks like an upside down or backward comma. The earth around it looks like it must be very delicate and crusty and there is very little steam coming from this pool. This spring fluctuates from hot, blue, and overflowing to cool, colorful and half empty.

Hot springs are really deep channels. Water flows below, even though the pool is deceptively calm, flowing from the molten interior of the planet, closer to the surface in Yellowstone more than anywhere else on earth.

The next two pools are on our left. First, is Collapsing Pool because it does look like it simply collapsed into the space which contains it. It has the same description as Ledge Spring, except the shape of it is more round. It is also steaming and has a ledge around it, from the collapse I'm assuming. Second, is Thumb Geyser, which is totally inactive and lies covered by the runoff of other pools. There is a bigger view from this viewpoint and steam is rising all over the place. But, Thumb Geyser is a pretty blue in many different sizes of puddles, all contained in a large area.

Turning back to the right side, we approach Percolating Spring. It used to bubble constantly and vigorously in the past. It makes you think of the old percolating coffee pots. This spring is multicolored with a marine green in the center, rippling out to yellows, deep golds and bordered with a rusty-colored crust, almost like a pie crust. It is very captivating, since the marine color in the middle makes it appear as a deep swirling hole, but it isn't.

Still to the right, is Perforated Pool, which is in the middle area of the basin that all seem to share a common plumbing system. This is a smaller pool that appears to me to be a rounded off exclamation point, filled with that beautiful marine blue color of water, also steaming. These secondary clusters can be drained of water when some of the major features are in the active phase. How interesting is that!

To the left side, is Ephedra Spring, formed in a small and almost perfect circle. It also has a crusty ledge but is not steaming. It is an ugly black and brown combination in the center and a dark brown on the outside edges. Not far up from that, is Blue Funnel Spring, on the right. In appearance, I would describe this spring as a backward question mark. The curvy part of the question mark is what I call diarrhea green, with a rusty color outlining it. The dot part of the question mark is about four times the size of the curve and is that ever a beautiful swimming pool blue. When Abyss Pool began to erupt in the winter of 1991–1992, the water in Blue Funnel, Perforated Pool, and Ephedra Spring, cooled and sank well below the rim. Then the four features appeared to exchange energy: Abyss stopped erupting at the end of that winter, while these features were rejuvenated.

The next is Twin Geyser, one geyser with two vents, which has short periods of dramatic eruptions and longer periods of dormancy. After a 23-year dormancy, it began erupting again in 1998; its last known eruption was in 1999. This geyser has a two-part event, the west vent erupts 70 feet, and the east vent erupts more than 100 feet. They are both steaming and also look like a comma in shape, the upper part is larger than the bottom.

Coming to the end of the walkway, right on the edge of the lake is Abyss Pool. This pool is one of the deepest hot springs in the park. It descends 53 feet and varies in color from turquoise-blue to emerald green to various shades of brown. It is rippling, magically serene and a beautiful turquoise blue today.

As we turn to go back on the outer walkway, we come upon Black Pool. The pool is sky-blue today, but it is said at one time it was black, due to the lower water temperature. During the summer of 1991, the temperature rose, killing the organisms. Black pool erupted that summer and several times the following winter, making it one of Yellowstone's most beautiful pools, like Abyss. The outer crust is a coppery color, with white unattractive mush mixed in.

Now we are really seeing something different, jutting out into Yellowstone Lake called Big Cone Geyser. It looks like a flying saucer, all made of the crust of the earth, floating on the lake, with a huge hole in the center. Eruptions are rare from this geyser, and when they do happen, they only reach heights of one foot or less.

Fishing Cone Geyser is Big Cone's buddy, right up from it. It is shaped exactly the same, except its outer part is rigid and steaming from the center hole and Big Cone Geyser is smooth and not steaming. This geyser was fun to read about, because it is said that mountain men told of a geyser on the shore of a high alpine lake, where one could catch a trout, swing the pole around, dip it into the boiling pool, and cook the fish at the same time, without taking it off the line! They actually did allow this when the park was new, but anglers often injured themselves while straddling the boiling water to have their pictures taken. *Ouch!* Fishing is no longer allowed there!

Rounding toward the end of this incredible adventure sits Lake Shore Geyser. Accounts from the 1920s and 1930s, tell of this geyser erupting up to 50 feet. It consists of 3 separate holes. But it is described as two geyser vents, the smaller generally not exposed until mid to late August. The smaller is to the right and deep blue-green, the middle one is a bronze color and the one on the left is also a deep blue-green. So maybe the middle bronze one is nothing. Lake Shore Geyser boils vigorously and almost continuously and often erupts a few feet; its last known eruption was in 1970. There is a large crusty area around it, in tans spackled with white, and it truly is right on the shore of the lake.

The last feature is Lakeside Spring. It is a round blue-green pool of thermal water, that drains into the lake. It is steaming hot and has a green run-off like a tail. This has been a feature attraction here at Yellowstone. I have to say I feel as though we have been struck dumb with amazement.

I'm thinking I am never going to be able to match all these pictures we have taken to each individual sight! Every single one of these features is picture perfect.

We decided maybe we'd better go ahead and get our room, at the Lake Yellowstone Hotel and Cabins. This is one place Russ did make reservations, but not until we actually got on the road. We couldn't find it at first, apparently driving right passed it. I think the sign said lake area, but nothing about the hotel. This hotel is right on the Yellowstone Lake, and of course, it is yellow in color. It has several sections, the largest or main section is the lobby, I believe they call it the sun room and I understand they have a string quartet there some of the time. Then off that, in an L fashion, are cabins and then further down they had lodging, almost like camping. I found out this is the longest standing hotel in the park and is listed on the Register of Historic Places. It is huge, with the front of the hotel facing the lake. It is so beautiful, with gigantic white pillars which gave it a very majestic appearance, and a porch with chairs and rockers to sit, and enjoy the sunset and the Yellowstone Lake. They even give tours to provide you with the history of the hotel. While Russ registered us, he also bought some tickets for a bus tour for tomorrow called,

"Circle of Fire" tour. This tour offers different times and different lengths of time as well, we chose the half day bus tour. They also offer many different kinds of tours, such as photograph safaris, fishing trips, sunset tours, stage coach adventures, and wildlife expeditions, just to name a few. Of course, in the winter some of that changes, to such fun things as snowmobile touring, ski tours, and much more.

As we brought Mona around to park her closer to our room to unload, two *huge* buffalo, or bison as they seem to like to call them here, were standing there, one on each side of the little road. I don't know why we didn't think we'd see any more buffalo after leaving the Tetons. What a sight to see these monstrous critters, who seem so content to have people in their home. These tame-looking monsters can weigh up to 2,000 pounds and can sprint at an impressive 30 miles an hour. At one time, these creatures were on the brink of extinction, but today, have established a stronghold within the park. Friendly? Tame? No! Beware—one never knows when they will take a wild notion to take its horns to you. That is one of the things I really admired about Yellowstone is when you arrive at the park, you are ushered into a room to watch a film about the dangers at the park and the safety precautions you should take. In the film they presented, a story was told of a young girl that got really close to a bison so her friend could get a picture. The bison rushed her and wound up throwing her through the air and killing her. So caution should always prevail.

I really have to mention here, talking about the buffalo, one of our most favorite movies was *Dances with Wolves*. And if you remember, when Kevin Costner finally became friends with the neighboring Indian tribe, he learned that the name for buffalo was "Tetonka." Of course, I am not familiar with the correct spelling. But I love it! It became one of our favorite words each time we saw a buffalo. *Look!* Tetonka!

We will go have dinner here at the hotel and then take our usual "critter ride" to see what we can explore next. I decided to call my camcorder my critter cam, why not, we've named everything else! Well, no sooner do we get on our way and we notice there are a lot of cars parked on both sides of the road. One of the ladies standing there said there were bears spotted. *Darn!* A day late and a dollar short. Oh, Yellowstone, we can't wait to see all the thrilling adventures you have to offer.

Anyway, it seems like we missed all the action, so we continued on our merry way, observing more "tetonka" and a coyote. The coyote crossed the road, so Russ did a youie and went down a little further. We came back up and got on that side of the road, so the coyote was coming toward us now, right toward me on the passenger side of the car. That coyote just kept walking toward me, allowing me to get the best shots ever. No worries, I had one leg in the car and one foot on the ground, filming through my open door window.

It is getting late and the sun will set soon. We are parked in a place where we can see the whole horizon. There is rain just pouring down on one side of us and the sun setting over the mountain on the other side, lighting up the mountain like it was alive and on fire! Psalms 65:8 (emphasis added) says, "The dawn and sunset *shout* for joy!"

As we were retreating to our room, we came to a place where you can pull over, and we did because that ball of sun and the sky surrounding it, were literally a brilliant and illustrious bright red. This unfolding of perfection, right in front of our eyes! Just how many perfect days will there be here?

Tomorrow, we are going on our bus tour around the park and see the highlights. I'd say we are off to a pretty good start. Relaxing in our room now, I can hear a coyote or maybe a wolf, howling in the distance. Such an eerie feeling; we certainly are not in our element by a long shot. But laying there listening to the sounds of this extraordinary world, we fall fast asleep.

Our bus tour was to leave at 9:30 a.m., and we were supposed to be there at 9:15, so we had an early breakfast at the cafeteria. We are all to meet in the lobby and I would say we are a part of maybe 20 or 25 excited tourists. Our bus driver or tour guide was a little late but got us all seated except for a couple that had an issue where they were to be seated. Apparently, they wound up split, and I can't say that I blame them for being upset; after all I want to sit with my husband. But they got really ugly with the driver, no one would move, so they exited the bus in a huff. It looks like this day is off to an interesting start.

The driver explained in explicit detail where we were going, what we would see, why certain things were the way they were and we found out he was full of interesting and sometimes shocking stories. Our first stop was West Thumb, where Russ and I were yesterday. Now we will take more in and get better pictures, and learn more from our most informed guide. This dynamic place (maybe I shouldn't use that word here), does nothing but provoke wonder; even a second time around. I have no words for our excitement!

The tour takes us back to Old Faithful and we watched her show off again and spew out her fury. We had time for lunch and then back on the big yellow bus. We come to Isa Lake, which straddles the continental divide at Craig Pass. Everyone knows what that is now, right? Isa is a very small and shallow lake, oblong in shape and rather dreary in color. It is known for draining into both the Gulf of Mexico and the Pacific Ocean. *Backwards!*

Next on the agenda is the Midway Geyser Basin, which is maybe 16 miles from Old Faithful. Just as Isa lake is small, Midway is the smallest of the basins. It may be small, but it contains two large features and is located next to the Firehole River. In the 1800s, it was referred to as Hell's Half Acre and still is sometimes today. Firehole flows 21 miles north through several geyser basins. It contains 3 falls and as you gaze down the river, you can see steam popping up here and there. Despite the beautiful bright orange colors on its banks, caused by the chemicals in the geothermal features runoff, including Old Faithful. Both Brown and Rainbow trout love these waters, as do the fishermen.

The first of the two large features within Midway Geyser Basin is Excelsior Geyser, which is a 200-by-300-foot wide geyser and pours over 4,000 gallons of water into Firehole River. It is a beautiful brilliant blue crater, steaming like a regular pot of water at 199 degrees and also has a lot of run off. Its last eruption was in 1888. It hisses loudly and smokes excessively.

The second feature is Grand Prasmatic Spring, which is 370 feet wide and 121 feet deep. This is the largest hot spring in Yellowstone and in all of the US. It is the most intense sapphire-blue, with bright, bright yellow, orange and gold colors completely wrapping around it. Grand Prasmatic Spring is the most identifiable, not only by the rotten-egg smell, but the awesome bright colors. It sits at 147–188 degrees.

looks like burnt drift wood Yellowstone National Park

Red Spouter is loudly hissing like a very large snake and is composed of two big muddy, gray, deep holes with reddish-brown tints. On the edges, sit what look like drift wood; burnt and seething. Sure is a lot of loud steam-blowing going on here. To me, this is a very eerie and threatening sound. It is a very odd and peculiar sight and yet on the other hand, beautiful at the same time. All of these geysers are on the Fountain Paint Pot boardwalk. There are many paint pots around, all of which are a reddish-gray, dismal looking, seething, and some are bubbling like a witch's brew.

Down by the end of the walkway and way over by the lake, is a beautifully colored geyser of greenish-blue. It is called Clepsydra Geyser and it has been erupting continuously to heights of 45 feet. Its name comes from a Greek word for water clock, because prior to the 1959 Yellowstone earthquake, it faithfully erupted every 3 minutes.

Great Fountain Geyser is without saying, a fountain geyser located close to both the Fountain Paint Pot and the White Dome Geyser. This fountain amazes me, because it consists of a series of bursts (up to 7. It's like this fountain has a mind, because about 70 to 100 minutes before each eruption, water begins to overflow from its vent. One half hour later, bubbles appear along one edge of the pool. The boiling becomes more violent until the bubbles are 3feet high. This is only the start. Suddenly, it may become very quiet and still. Then the entire surface of the geysers pool will dome upward (like it is alive). As soon as the steam reaches the surface, the water explodes outward and upward. The first burst is the tallest and strongest, shooting up to 75 to 220 feet in the sky lasting over 2 hours sometimes! *And*…this happens every 9 to 15 hours *and*…is pretty darn predictable too! Whew! I just can't get over how amazing and sometimes surprising each individual attraction is.

Continuing north, we adventure upon Fountain Paint Pot. Its name deriving from the awesome colors of blues, oranges, and yellows. This walkway takes you all around to the different attractions here, from the bubbling mud pots to awesome sapphire pools, all bubbling and steaming. You would think they were boiling, but in truth, it is the gases causing the mud to bubble and pop and there is steam and hissing sounds all around. Carefully placed signs warn of danger of the very hot waters, and thin crust of the ground, that could give way easily if you step off the trails. The striking colors, the dull grays and beiges of mud, the deep cool blues and reds and yellows are all breath-taking surprises to behold.

White Dome Geyser, is a cone geyser quite big, like a giant beehive, grayish-white in color, expect for one side which is a rusty color. We are told that is caused from magnesium oxide. It is only a few feet from the Firehole Lake. Its cone is 12 feet high and is one of the largest cones in the park. Its eruptions are unpredictable, but generally occur between 15 minutes to3 hours and it can reach heights of 30 feet. And we were privileged to watch her blow!

As we were strolling along the walkway, Russ looked up, and sitting right there in a perfectly round hole, sits an adorable and curious little bird, who seemed very interested in what we were doing: he was watching us watching him. He is so beautiful. We can only see the front half of him. His chest is a snow white, and his head is a bright blue-green color, like he is color coordinated to match some of the springs and geysers! There is a black line from his beak around his eyes and his head is cocked to one side. Russ zoomed in and got a great picture of him. Russ said we should call him "Knot head"... Awww. I have to wonder how many people noticed him sitting there, because he is so small and almost looked like he was planted there on purpose. Well, I guess he was. He was like a little topping on this beautifully decorated cake.

Spasm Geyser is in front of Clepsydra Geyser. Its name is obvious, as that is exactly how it behaves, spastic and unpredictable. This is a very spacious area, looking out forever with steam and beautiful lodge pole pines popping up here and there. Some of the trees are laying on the ground in clumps, like piled up sticks and deer are comfortably browsing and nibbling the grass in the distance. There are cracks in the crust of the earth and then a small puddle with a gorgeous color of blue-green water inside, or a mound that is probably a small geyser. This particular one I am looking at, is a big hole sitting sideways in the earth, with a huge mouth that looks like it wants to swallow something and has deep green liquid inside. It is colored all around its lips with deep gooey yellow and gold colors and seems to be sprinkled with powdered sugar. This is a spot you don't want to trip, or you might be that thing that gets swallowed up. There are many geysers on the shore of the lake, in shapes of abandoned tires, all of them seething and smoking, like this whole world just got over a huge dowsed fire. I still say it is an eerie and wondrous place to see and very unusual to say the least. What a Creator we have!

Now we are driving along Firehole Canyon Drive, which is a hidden jewel among the pine trees. The Firehole River is beside us to our left. This is a 2-mile, one-way drive and it will take us through the outstanding canyon, right to Firehole Falls, which is a 40-foot drop. We parked here for photos, and we are walking around at an information station just outside of Madison. There is also a swimming area there for you if you like, but one must be very careful since there is no lifeguard here.

Back on the bus and traveling through Madison, while everyone is peering out their windows, cameras ready; you can feel an air of expectation with every few yards we gain moving forward. We are to the left of Nez Perce Creek which is named after the Nez Perce

Indians along Firehole and then next to Gibbon River. Both the creek and Gibbon are excellent fishing places, especially for you who like to fly fish. The next sight we were to see was Artist Paint Pot, but for some reason, it is closed. I would love to have seen that because we are told it is full of color and beauty. I have to admit, I did ask a clerk at one of the shops why the Artist Paint Pot was closed. He told me one of the boards on the boardwalk broke when a large person was walking on it. He said she fell through and her legs were badly burned. I don't know, I'm just saying that is what I was told.

Most of the park's thermal features are concentrated right here, in the west-central part of the park. There are buffalo to our left, on the edge of the road, walking in the same direction as we are going when suddenly, the herd veers in front of the bus. Why did the buffalo cross the road? Right, to get to the other side! Ha ha! Our little rendezvous continued on, until we came across Steamboat Geyser. It is a huge geyser, said to be the world's tallest active geyser. It has frequent, unpredictable eruptions, reaching 3 to 40 feet. Both a short water phase and a longer steam phase occur, lasting up to 12 hours. *Wow!* This is such a rarity though.

The big yellow bus takes a turn to the east, and as we drive thru wild meadows and hills, we see buffalo all over the place. They are such awesome creatures, but there is something lying on the ground and it almost looks like a dog, wagging its tale and taking a little siesta. But it is a baby buffalo/bison or calf, reddish-brown and small and cute. Who would ever think this little guy was going to grow so enormous and, sorry, but…well…he really is downright *ugly*. Momma's not far away as she guards her "beautiful" baby. Then there is a huge bison casually walking down the side of the road toward us. He probably knew where he was going, since Yellowstone is the one place where they have lived since prehistoric times and are allowed to wander freely. The buffalo that are out in the pastures are nibbling green grass and you can see steam way out in the distance, adding mystery to all this intense activity.

As we pass a large meadow up on a hill, our tour guide begins to tell us a most terrifying story. He said, "A tourist was driving down this very same road one day and looked up on the meadow and noticed a tripod set up there on the hill, but there was no one around. Several hours later, that same person returned back and noticed the tripod was still sitting there, but still, no one seemed to be up there. So they called and reported that to a ranger. When the rangers arrived on the scene, the tripod was in fact sitting there with a camera atop. They started to look around for its owner when they saw blood stains on the ground. They followed them until they came upon a gruesome scene of a dead woman, who had been bleeding profusely. The rangers took the camera, and later when the film was developed, there was a picture of a momma bear and her two cubs. The bear must have felt threatened and thought she was protecting her little ones. It makes me shudder to think of such a devastating thing. You really should never go off alone in the wilderness; it is a risky place, where every safety precaution should be exercised. I will never forget this horrible story.

Suddenly, the driver slows down and warns us that it looked like a large herd of bison were going to cross the road right in front of us; yup, they're going to get to the other side no matter what. Kind of like the pedestrians in Atlanta, and they're not going to look first either! It was a pretty steep slope on both sides of us, but no matter, this huge bison takes the plunge and another and then another and right up the slope to the right side of us. For such huge animals, the big guys seemed very sure-footed and confident. They just assessed the situation and off they went. Then, here comes a baby, and she is very hesitant about going down that big ole hill. She/he starts, then hesitates, then starts again and maybe, very cautiously, but no. But you know, if my mom looked at me like that, and she looked that mean, I think I'd know, I better get down there now! He stands there a good while, the big bison next to him stands by (must be momma,) and finally, charges down and then back up the other side, and many more follow. The driver says, "Watch the little ones. They are so cute when they play." Sure enough, the ones that made it across started to kick their heels up and jump around in circles, as if to celebrate their triumphant challenge. I guess no matter what creature it is on this earth, babies just tickle your heart and your funny bone.

Well, now that traffic is backed up a pretty good ways, we will move on to our next destination, Canyon Village, which is one of the most majestic areas found at Yellowstone. Again, we stop at a visitor center, where I pick up my usual postcards and magnets, and we decided to enjoy an ice cream cone too. We are heading east, toward the other side of the park. It is also one of the most popular features in the park, featuring two falls and the Grand Canyon of Yellowstone. All of this is located right in the center of the park. Out in the field, we spot a huge buck, nibbling away, but he is ignoring us.

We are on a bridge now, and I am able to get some really good shots of the river as we cross. It is the Yellowstone River, and it looks quite swollen and full. But what a beautiful picture this is of the curving water and the thick trees and the snowy-topped mountains. Soon we near the canyon and the falls at the end. It is the most dramatic change in scenery yet. There is a wooden walkway and stairs to take us to the top of the canyon; this is the Grand Canyon of the Yellowstone. Yellowstone seems to have many faces, and I don't think I can really put into words the wonders that my eyes are seeing right now. For starters, the canyon is so colorful, alive, with rich rusts, oranges, yellows and beiges, all created by hot water acting on volcanic rock. It is roughly 20 miles long, 800 to 1,200 feet deep and 1,500 to 4,000 feet wide. There are trees scattered along its elegant walls and snow patches randomly strewn in various places. There is a gentle breeze, causing the trees to sway from side to side. This is such a treat; this place of endless discoveries. The river below is racing at a quick pace, foaming white and bubbling along, twisting and winding itself furiously to unknown yet intentional designations.

Both the falls are contained here—the Lower Falls and the Upper Falls. The Yellowstone Lake comes crashing down over Lower Falls, which is higher than the Upper Falls. That does sound backward, doesn't it? But that is because Upper Falls is 1/4-mile downstream from Lower Falls. Upper Falls is only 109 feet tall whereas, Lower Falls is the biggest waterfall in Yellowstone. The way the sun is going in and out, it makes shadows of deep maroon-ish colors on the walls of the canyon, with silvers and bronzes and dusting of small fallen stones. Lower Falls drops 308 feet, almost twice as high as

Niagara Falls. And one last fact: It is impossible to see the two falls at the same time because of the wandering river. I thought you'd enjoy just a little bit of mind-boggling information to rattle your brain a little.

To see the Upper Falls, we climb some stairs for a better view. This falls gets nowhere near the attention as its sister, Lower Falls does. Maybe, because it is wider and somewhat prettier. It is beginning to rain, so we all board our bus and drive south toward our next big stop, Fishing Bridge and all the endless discoveries in-between. We pass over the bridge again, only this picture is taken with no sun, which caused it to be a very pretty green-shaded photo.

Our first burst of excitement comes when we see the Mud Volcano area. Notice it is not simply mud pots any more but "volcano" area. Here sits a huge bison, naturally they're always huge, right next to the Mud Volcano. The first feature is the Sulphur Caldron, which is highly acidic, but at one time, long ago, this volcano shook the ground until the earth trembled, and slung mud to the tree tops, until one day it blew itself apart. Today it is not active. It looks like a big round circle full of mud angrily boiling. It is surrounded by dried, cracked mud in a uniform fashion, as though someone tried to lay a brick patio down in the caldron. This mud is more of a silvery color than brown, but just as smelly. Its temperature is 184 degrees F and it is 17 feet deep.

We drove another quarter of a mile up to visit the Dragon's Mouth Springs. For this; we get off the bus to experience another new personality, as each feature does seem to have its very own. This is one of my favorites. It is a cave 16 feet deep and smoking and steaming at 170.2 degrees F. This is a turbulent hot spring, which someone with a good imagination named perfectly, because it does appear there could be a dragon in there forcing all this steam out of its mouth, threatening to expose that dragon at any given moment. The walls of the cave are shiny and slick, silvery and green with white. The water is mucky and well, looks like mud. But the water rushing out has formed a round pool and all around this pool the mud looks dried and cracked.

Back on the bus, it is so hot on here, but who is complaining? We are all hardly able to wait for what is in store for us next. Naturally, it is a buffalo; but what is neat about this guy, is the way he is standing to nibble on the grass. He is on a slope and his 2 back legs are at the bottom and his giant head is at the top, so he doesn't have to bend down. I wonder if he is smart enough to know to do that on purpose. He only has half of his outer coat left on his back, as this is the time of year they are molting. Every time I see these big creatures I can't help but remember the time when I was a little girl and my parents took us to the train station in Buffalo, New York. In the center of the station was an enormous statue of a Buffalo. I can remember thinking about that big head and those strange horns, they were so frightening. Next to him is another bison, drinking very muddy, greenish-colored water, but he is not as smart I guess, because he is backward or upside down. And his front legs have sunk deep into the muck.

We slowly drive passed more hot springs, usually bubbling and steaming, some places appearing as though there is a fire coming from the forest, but it's always a fumarole or a hot spring or even a geyser. There are also bison venturing along or grazing, sometimes alone, or taking a stroll along the road. Something different up in the woods. We think it is a gray coyote—no, I want to say it is a wolf. Its legs are longer and it's a little bigger. They are very hard to see, mostly because they keep a very low profile in the day hours. But as I look at the developed photo, I think it is probably a coyote. As we continue to travel on now, there is a herd of antelope far out, but then, as we get closer to the group, it is easier to see that they are molting too.

The final destination is in sight and is called Fishing Bridge. This one is easy, as this was the name of the original bridge in 1902. It was a popular fishing bridge in those days, but today, this is the home to a campground, a visitor center, a store, and a gas station. It is located at the north end of Yellowstone Lake. There is nothing like hanging over the side of a bridge railing and yelling "I see one!"

We are through with our tour now, oh my, it was so informative, exciting, and quite the adventure. It always amazes me how much these tour guides know and how enthusiastic they are about sharing their own private experiences in the parks.

We are back in our own little Mona and turn that air on! Talk about ole faithful, she has certainly been that. Thought we'd sit here a minute and cool off and figure out where we wanted to have dinner. We decided to stay with the cafeteria in the park, it is so cheap, only $13 for the two of us and they had a large selection of delicious food. I thought the price was amazing, considering we are sitting in a national park. Mostly teens worked there I noticed and in other areas we saw senior citizens guiding, helping with directions, working in gift shops, the centers, and the museums. They hire for the season each summer and winter and you can even live there for that period you work. What an adventure that would be for a young person to do over their time off from school and get to see these parks on top of it. Just think of all they could do, like take advantage of the trails, sky high mountains, falls, and other benefits of these geological wonderlands. I believe all the national parks offer this, too.

Woohoo, it is time for our critter drive and I must add, this is also our sunset tour as well. We went to our room to freshen up a little, and as we walk out the front door, here are the brothers Billy Bob and Bubba Bison waiting to say hi. Yup, had to name them so we could get up close and personal, uh, no, not up close.

The sky is becoming an exquisite pale pink and yellow. I just have to sigh and feel so happy to be in this place. It is like being in a place where God is every single minute. The mountains are a misty pink, peach, and charcoal gray and the further out you can see, the mistier it is. As we drive off, there is a buffalo standing on green, green grass in front of the baby-blue lake, a perfect silhouette against it. What a sight to behold! He seems to have a really long beard compared to the others we've seen. I wonder if that has something to do with his age. We spied more buffalo and antelope and a lot of snow melt, resulting in tiny little falls along the road. We are up pretty high, so there is a ton of snow and the trees cast long dark shadows over the bright white. In some spots, the snow looks blue from the shadows.

We found a place way up on the mountain and just stood there to watch the sun bid adieu for another day in Yellowstone. Here the lodge pole pines are silhouetted against the pale colors of the sky and the now pink clouds. It is like a light show, as the sun slowly sets, leaving in its illustrious trail of golden orange linings, peeking out from around each cloud. The sun itself, is the brightest most brilliant of whitish-yellow, as it begins to hide behind the black mountains. It's interesting as more and more people gather, some with cameras, as we are literally shrouded in the warmth of the very last feature of the day.

After an experience like today, it is very difficult to go right to sleep with all the sounds of the geysers, the falls, the mud pots, oh my, still in our minds. We can hear the coyotes in the background (or wolves), and Russ and I lay there reminiscing over all our adventures, and thanking our Maker for such a world class, exhilarating and thrilling experience.

It is a new day, the 17th of June, and we have our sights set on driving out to see the Mammoth Hot Springs. Billy Bob and Bubba Bison are here to wish us a good morning as usual. Don't you just love it! It is a gorgeous fresh airy, lung filling day, with blue sky and plump and fluffy white clouds.

Mona has already delivered us high up in the mountains. There is snow and right now I am freaking out, because we are right on the ledge of this mountain, in the middle of a U-turn. I guess I will never get used to this part, but oh my goodness, what a view. This area has many trees that look like they have been burned, they are like skinny sticks all along the road. On the left and on the inside of the curve, there is a 3 and 1/2 to 4 feet of snow the plows have piled up, to clear the roads. We find an overlook spot where we can take some pictures. When we look up, there are three deer struggling to walk through the snow—two females and a baby. First, the one adult is stuck, apparently hitting a soft and deep spot, and both her hind legs are all the way in the snow. But she manages to free herself and then the baby lands on its chin and its rear is in the air. So so cute. The thing is, there is a dry area right below where they could pass with no snow. But when you think about it, wildlife really has to struggle in the real winter months here. Maybe they have a certain path they like to follow each year, no matter what, I don't know. I know the buffalo travel the same paths from year to year. These animals are not just leaving their footprints in the snow but in our hearts too, such a beautiful sight. The vast scenery is unending and unforgettable.

Yellowstone National Park

The curves are very sharp and the snow drifts are higher and higher as we go up, but the streets are safe and clean and they sure do have Georgia beat. One little snowstorm in my hometown and we are pretty well snowed in for a couple days. We've come to a section where all the trees are dead. The national parks report, that some fires do occur from human activity, but most often lightning strikes are the culprit. Afternoon thunderstorms occur frequently here with little rain, so dry lighting is not uncommon.

Oh, now this curve is practically coming to greet us. By that, I mean the road going in the complete opposite direction is right next to us, practically kissing me on the cheek, this is a big youie if I ever saw one. But as we round it, out of nowhere, there are more green fields with three bison scattered in a triangle position. We are alone in our movie again and I just don't know how we manage to do that, it's very humbling. Being out here in this vast country does make one realize how small and reliant we are. Like Thomas Wolfe said, "This is the one place where miracles not only happen, but where they happen all the time."

Yellowstone is divided into five "countries," so to speak. There is Geyser Country (Old Faithful and other thermal features), Lake Country (Yellowstone Lake and Fishing Bridge); where we are staying, Canyon Country (Yellowstone's Grand Canyon), Roosevelt Country (Tower Falls), and Mammoth Country (Mammoth Hot Springs), where we are going next. Each and every one of these countries is as unique as the other. Yellowstone is shaped in a figure eight; the tour took us around the bottom part of the eight, so our goal today is to explore the top part. So we are going north from the bottom right side of the 8 first. We will have to go up and through canyon village again, where we were yesterday in order to round out the top part of our 8 to the left and see Mammoth Hot Springs. I hope that makes sense!

Looking to our right, stands a beautiful young buck, with his proud head held high, just posing for us. We have seen many more elk and antelope than deer so far. This is known as Roosevelt Country; a rolling countryside covered with sage brush, every tree imaginable and beautiful sparkling streams loaded with trout.

We have parked Mona, and started hiking toward Tower Falls. We are now approaching a little commotion ahead, I don't know where all these people came from, a ranger is standing there, and we ask him what is going on. Come to find out, a momma elk just gave birth to the sweetest little Bambi twins (I know, Bambi was a deer), but these babies are just as adorable, with white speckles and they are so wobbly on their feet. Momma has managed to get up to her feet and the babies are all over the place, trying to get their balance. Momma tries to hide them from us, so we get the message and leave her alone with her two little miracles. Surely, we have been blessed with another true bonus for our day.

We can hear the falls and finally it comes into our view. This powerful falls is very pretty, tumbling down 132 feet. It was named after the towers and pinnacles that surround it. We climbed to the top in order to look down at this white foamed fall. It is framed by eroded volcanic pinnacles, in a misty narrow, gorge and then it hastens over another series of ledges in the Yellowstone River and roars through its own canyon toward Nevada. It is fast, foaming and bubbling over large boulders and trees. It has formed all types of eerie-looking shapes and left them behind in its winding trail. These shapes are anywhere from 50 to 100 feet tall and worn into every conceivable figure, very delicate and easy to crumble. Some are standing like sentinels guarding the fall at the very brink of it.

Back in the car and once again on a very winding and bumpy road, with a tall wall next to us. This wall almost looks like a man made fort wall, in uniform shapes. It is gorgeous and heads straight up the mountain side. I found out that the "wall" is called Sheepeater Cliff, named by a Shoshone tribe long ago. Once we get passed the rock and can see pasture again, we look out in the distance only to see a huge deer resting leisurely under a shady tree. Russ said it is a mule deer with a very large rack. We will park Mona and walk over where there is a petrified tree. This is an ancient redwood in the center of an iron clad gate. Something moving up on the hill catches our attention and we realize it is a nosey coyote, looking to see what all the clamor is about down below. How fun it is to see these awesome critters walking around, like it is just an everyday thing in our life. Oh…look…another coyote…ho hum, but really, it is so exciting to be able to embrace all Yellowstone has to offer!

We did a pull-over to view the side of the mountain. Scattered all around are the most delicate, pure white flowers, which I finally identified as Phlox. And not far from there, I tell Russ, "It looks like something is moving in the woods," pointing to the right, only to discover it is a big black bear. He is just meandering through the woods enjoying this beautiful day, but in all our excitement, somehow we managed to get some great shots of him by zooming in. We are very thankful for a breath-taking sight of him and even more thankful he is going in the opposite direction!

There is all kinds of activity out here today. Wow, here come a few people on horseback and not far behind them a horse-drawn stage coach, bright yellow, carrying about 12 people, at a guess. Looks like a fun ride, appropriately placed in our movie. This is turning out to be a most interesting road, because as we turn the bend, all the trees here are burned, dark, and straggly.

Our movie is getting a little crowded now, as many people are pulling over taking pictures of the elegant mountainside, covered in every shade of green, with dips and crannies, careful not to give up all its little secrets. And then on the next big mountain, not so green, but rocky and gray and white, with beautiful shades of tan and burnt orange, allowing us to peek at the big-horned sheep that almost look like a speck or a rock themselves. The binoculars brought them to life for us. Whenever there is a "sighting," cars are pulled over and there is a chatter of excited, loud voices as people point in the direction for you to look! If you can't see what they are pointing at, just say "where?" and someone from the crowd will enthusiastically and with great pleasure tell you where! Like 4 o'clock or 2 o'clock or between those two large rocks by the tree! I thought, how very interesting it is that we humans don't want to see anything alone, we want everyone to see it and share it and participate in our excitement.

Our next adventure will be Mammoth Country, where we will explore Mammoth Hot Springs. We are traveling on the Grand Loop Road, on the extreme north end of the figure 8, I spoke of earlier, where just a few miles before the springs, we find Wraith Falls. It is only a 0.8 of a mile round trip, an easy hike, to see this 100-foot streaking cascade fall. The view is a treat for the eyes. I don't know why, but for some reason I didn't even get a picture of the falls, but less than a mile from here is another falls called Undine Falls.

Well, we can't find Undine falls because some of the roads and trails are blocked off. We don't know if its construction, bear warnings or bad road conditions or what. But we are just a few miles from Mammoth Springs and the border of Montana.

My goodness there are elk everywhere. We are at the Mammoth Hot Springs Hotel, and they are scattered all over the lawn, calmly nibbling the nicely trimmed lawn. I wonder if maybe they are the ones who keep it trimmed. They are all over, like they are the tourists and not us. Some are crossing the road right in front of us. Many of them are so big and some have little fawns. They are browsing in the sage and a field of greenery.

We have passed all the business of the busy elk traffic. Now we are passing beautiful green valleys and mountains loaded with thick and tall trees, in an intricately painted background of blue, blue sky. In the far distance are more snow-covered mountains and the rolling hills are fading into the beiges and greens at the bottom. Then the colors sink into a small river that is zigzagging here and there. The roads buddy up with the river and curve around more beige and gray mountains, just waiting for us to see what sights are around them. Some of the spikes are taller and submit to more uniform ridges, as we cross over what I think might be Gardiner River. This river is taking us right over the border of Wyoming and into Montana as we pass through a huge brick arch. This is known as the Roosevelt Arch.

The Roosevelt Arch was erected under the supervision of the US Army here at the North Entrance, which was the first entrance to Yellowstone. Its cornerstone was laid down by President Theodore Roosevelt in 1903. Clearly inscribed on the top of the arch are the words, "For the Benefit and Employment of the People," which doesn't make a lot of sense to me. But the most exciting fact to me was that the cornerstone that the president laid, covered a time capsule that contains a Bible, a picture of himself, local newspapers, and other items.

This small town is called Gardiner, Montana. There is a sign just north of here, where the road crosses Gardiner River, that says 45th Parallel Bridge. This marks the 45th parallel of latitude, which is an imaginary line that circles the globe, halfway between the equator and the North Pole. Then, a little further south of the sign, is a place called Boiling River, where bathers are allowed to go in the water at strictly specified times. That sounds life-threatening to me, but I suppose it wouldn't be allowed if it wasn't safe. I sure would dip my tippy toe in first, very delicately!

We will turn around and go back through the arch on the other side back into Yellowstone, but this is my sneaky way of being able to say we were in Montana. As we near the Mammoth Hot Springs, we come upon a huge mound which is named Liberty Cap, and stands 37 feet high. Our literature tells us its shape resembled the worn peaked caps during the French Revolution; hence, the name. At one time, the pressure in this cone was strong enough to spit water to great heights, but now it simply towers the earth, alone and silent.

Ah, at last, Mammoth Hot Springs, where mineral-laden scalding water from deep beneath the Earth's crust, seeps its way to the surface and builds tier upon tier of cascading terraced stone. It sits on a hill of travertine and hot water rises through limestone, rather than lava. The water cools and deposits calcium carbonate. Mammoth Hot Springs deposits about two tons of travertine limestone (calcium carbonate) in one single day! It really does appear to be a porcelain-like terrace, surrounded by a never-ending walk way and many stairs. It is huge.

We decided to have lunch here first and then tackle the walkway. It's amazing how Yellowstone provides such conveniences for its visitors such as, food, lodging and restrooms and not too far apart.

Mammoth Hot Springs lies outside the caldera boundary, but scientists believe the heat from the hot springs comes from the same magmatic system that fuels other Yellowstone thermal areas. Mammoth Hot Springs is completely different and unusual compared to the rest of the sights, so far. Yes, there still is steaming, bubbling, flowing water, gurgling everywhere, but the shapes and colors are so different. Dramatic terraces that look like wide oddly sculpted steps, with water cascading and steaming delicately down them with captivating colors of white (almost crystal), pink, and rust. This terrace constantly changes activity, shape, and colors over time.

It is time to tackle this enormous walkway and get our adventure started. The first named feature is called Minerva Terrace. It is so pretty, shaped like individual big blocks of ice pushed together in different levels of steps. It is a crispy, seemingly crystallized white color, but as you walk along, it becomes a reddish-brown. It is beautiful, but it sure does stink. At the very top, it looks like it is overflowing with thick icicles and they look more frosted than the icicles or stalactites you would see underground in a cave. Water is over flowing from the top as well, gently flowing down to form small waterfalls.

Sitting right in the center of it all, is a large dark gray-colored rock and it is called Devil's Thumb—all of this towering as high as 6,735 feet. As you walk along, everything turns into wonderful pastel colors, with a brand-new name of Cleopatra Terrace. It is much the same, other than it is smooth and the colors are almost striped, ranging from greens, pinks, peaches, and white. Just like an artistic tapestry moving slowly past us, as we continue our walk. As we look in the distance, we can see smoke coming up from behind another geyser and I'm thinking, we really are on another planet. From the height we have climbed to we can see far out. There are beautiful green trees dipping up and down the rolling hills. We can also see Mammoth Village, until it becomes darker and further away, then there are snow-tipped mountains, which is the Gallatin Mountain Range.

The walkway covers about 1.75 miles and it is zig-zagging this way and that, all the while going *up,* with benches placed ever so cleverly and just in time. Wow, I am taking advantage of a bench right now and I look over the side and it almost feels like I am sitting in the middle of a snowstorm and ice, because I am surrounded by white. We have been exploring the lower terraces; as we continue to climb higher, we will explore the upper terraces. This seems to be a gray dismal rocky area, with ghoulish and terrifying faces carved into it. I believe this is called Mound Terrace and some of the faces look like they are screaming in agony, as though being tortured. This is a really freaky and spooky section, that somehow seems misplaced in the midst of all this color and beauty. In one spot, pieces of the rock had peeled off and it was pure white underneath. It made me think of a coconut, once broken open and how white it is inside. Another small fall is trickling down and as pretty as it is, it also smells of rotten eggs! Ugh! Then, everything gets bright orange and tall. The color is caused from the bacteria and this is called Orange Spring Mound. We are at the top and again the view is captivating. Grassy Spring is bubbling and spilling down a surface of travertine deposits. It is living proof that this feature is very much alive. It is a beautiful orange color.

This is where a gentleman approaches us and tells us of the Upper Terrace road, which is about 1.5 miles long. He said, "If you go back down and out of the terraces, there is a one-way loop where you can explore by car, and travel around the back into the woods, where you can see impressive thermal features that are not visible from the main road. You can also access the lower terrace boardwalk from there." Now he tells me! So, heck yeah, we went and got Mona and drove back up. What a beautiful overlook. We could see everywhere we had been and everywhere we wanted to go. I think we didn't read our park information very well. Just ahead is a little cone spring, which stands a foot tall, but it is 3-4 feet wide. It is called Prospect Spring and is dormant gray and white, as most of the area around it is, which is known as Prospect Terrace, because you can see great distances from here. The water on top is a beautiful blue and looks like a big flat pond, but it is deceiving in its looks, as it is dribbling down the sides of the terraces with its offensive odor. I am trying to be careful where I am walking and when I look down, right next to my foot, are the most beautiful wild flowers, in almost any color you can think of—all within the same area. There are some 1,350 species of flowering plants in Yellowstone. Mixed in with the green grass, gray pebbles, large gray rocks, bright pink stems, and oddly shaped pieces of wood, it appears to be a well-planned dream landscape. That is, aside from the burnt dark black trees standing amid the ivory white of the hot springs and the orange floor they are sitting in. It actually makes them beautiful against the eye-catching contrast. I assume the heat of the steam and the different minerals surrounding them, demands more of them than they can handle. Standing right in front of us, like he is supposed to be there and he probably is, not us, is a young buck. He is licking the heck out of a little tree stump which seems to demand his most undivided attention. It doesn't matter one bit to him that we are standing there watching him because he is determined to get every bit of whatever it is in there out. Maybe the lime or the calcium carbonate; anyway he'll have good bones and teeth when he is done. A few more feet from him is another hot spring, which is beautifully dressed in oranges and peaches. It drapes down its staircase which is pure white, with water trickling along too.

More elk join us but seem to be more interested in their own very green tossed salad of grass.

Well, I think our thrilling adventure at Mammoth Hot Spring has come to an end, and thrilling it was. So we'll proceed on the loop and out and disappear into the spectacular scenery ahead. The mountains are gray, brown and in odd shapes, which makes them is all so interesting, especially with the shadows falling on them, as the sun will soon go down. Ahead is an intriguing bridge, called the Golden Gate Bridge, which is completely wrapped around the mountain. It is named after the color of the mountain, that lights up like gold in the daylight and it is such a sharp curve you cannot see the end of it. Then we see a falls, which is beautiful and a surprise, since it just appeared so abruptly. There is a turn out where you can park though and get some good pictures. This is Rustic Falls which is 47 feet high. Not everyone thinks so, but I thought it was one of the prettiest of the falls because of its uniqueness and its delicate shape of a fan. I believe we were really fortunate to see this fall, as I have read that in the summer, it sometimes dries up completely. That's kind of hard to believe the way it just flows on and on into a vibrant little creek.

Golden Gate Bridge leaving Yellowstone

The elevation is 7,300 feet and about 16 miles from Norris, as we head South, with the Gallatin Mountain Range to our right. First, comes the creek (Fan Creek), then lots of grass and forest with the mountains in the far background, snowcapped, of course. The sky is the most breath-taking color of deep lavender. And all I can think of is "how beautiful the spacious skies...the purple mountains majesty!" This is definitely a picture that should be on a calendar. Stunning!

It is so peaceful out here, as we pass Swan Lake and then Sheepeater Cliff for the second time. This is the wall of unusual rock that looks man-made, with piles of old lava laying in heaps from over 500,000 years ago. This is our favorite time of the day, when the critters like to appear, and the clouds look like little soft tangerine pillows. In the next pasture, there are elk everywhere amid the many silver fallen trees. And then a few miles up, a couple of buffalo doing the same; just love it. Some of them seem to be so huge. Right behind them are more geysers, with steam everywhere, like there are little fires behind them, but it's not smoke, its steam. Although I've seen in different pictures of Yellowstone, how the buffalo have figured out to keep warm in the winter. Some of them get by the hot springs to keep warm, where the crust is too thin and so do the antelope.

The banks on the side of the road are turning reddish-brown in color. Then, we see a large area of steam pouring out of the ground and crevices on the side of the bank. Over the tree tops, the yellow moon is beginning to sink, as we pass Nymph Lake. This is a very small lake and is one of the most acidic in the park, being the reason there are no fish in it. The way the moon is shining down on the lake and the surroundings, makes the sand look pinkish in its glow. Oh, and by the way, it stinks badly here, too.

We are still on Grand Loop Road and approximately 2.5 miles North of Norris Junction. Before we can get to Canyon Village, which is about 12 miles and turn south again, we must reach the middle of our figure 8. But once we enter Norris Junction, we remember Steamboat Geyser is there (the one we saw when we were on our bus tour). We just had to look at it again, it is so huge and alive...

It seemed to be huffing and puffing our welcome, with an odor of course, but we don't take it personal.

There is good phone reception here and I might add, one of the few places it is, so we stuck around and Russ picked up all his Father's Day wishes from the kids. Our drive has become a crisp moonlight drive, but we see a sign for Virginia Cascade, which was one of the falls we wanted to see, especially since it was my namesake. I really didn't know how Russ expected to do that in the dark, but the roads have been really good and once again I agree to a crazy idea. So we turn off our course onto a one-way road, which kept getting smaller and smaller and the edges didn't seem very safe to me. Once again I am in panic mode, because it is really dark back here. We can hear the thunder and splashing of the fall as we close in on it and it seemed like the water was right next to me. I know we drove on that little road for about 2 miles altogether. Spooky isn't even the word for it, we can't see very far ahead, we can't hear anything around us because of the deafening sound of the fall, and I'm such a fraidy-cat. I am not moving from this seat right now. Finally, we can visibly see the white foam of the fall, so Russ starts taking pictures, which never came out. I was just so glad to get out of there. We still have a pretty good long drive before we get to our room, but it is okay. Just as we were rounding the corner to our room, a beautiful big elk ran right in front of the car. Who on earth wouldn't long to be where we are; driving home with a Yellowstone moon?

It is a beautiful new day, June 18, 2008, and it is Wednesday. It was about 11:30 p.m. when we got home last night, so we got up late. I forgot to mention our room is a place with everything you need, not want. There are no televisions, no radios, no air-conditioning, and no Internet hookups. Not to mention, little cell phone service; I suppose in keeping with the natural surroundings of Yellowstone. We should be used to that by now. And oh, the sheets and curtains are yellow too. I decided to take a few pictures of our beautiful hotel. We didn't see Billy Bob and Bubba Bison this morning to greet us as usual, wonder where those guys are? So I got a picture of the post office across the street, the back entrance where we went into our room, the little cabins on the other end, and in the front of

Yellowstone Lake sitting in front of all the beautiful snow-topped mountains framing the lake.

Can you believe June is more than half over and there is still snow on the ground? We really weren't hungry yet, so we went straight to the marina, where Russ could check on fishing permits. He also checked out a place we visited earlier called Fishing Bridge. This is not the original bridge, but this one was built in 1937. You can see all the fish below, and it is considered a major spawning area for the cutthroat trout. Up until 1973, you could fish off the bridge, but they stopped that due to the decline in the fish. There is a campground and an RV campground here also. I look down and there is a bush of pussy willows I think, they look like cotton.

Russ found a ranger who was very knowledgeable and informative about the park and its rules and regulations. He did purchase a fishing permit for $15.00 which is good for 3 days, but he will only fish one day. I'm really glad Russ decided to fish. I know he felt a little guilty because I didn't want to fish, but I really wanted him to; I know he was looking forward to it and I didn't mind one bit. I wanted to take a break and just sit in the shade and read for a while. We drove around the lake until Russ found a place he thought would be a good spot. The native fish in the lake are the cutthroat trout, the mountain white fish and the Arctic grayling. The trout is a beautiful fish related to the salmon, but the cutthroat is especially pretty because of its markings. They have larger black spots, clustered by the tail, and are gray, gold, or copper hues. But the real difference is the bright red, pink, or orange marking beneath the jaw, that gives him his name. He is a prized game fish, with fly fishing the most popular angling method. At Yellowstone, they can run from 6 to 26 inches as adults, with 6 to 10 inches in high elevations and the largest fish are found in this area. The numbers of waters where native fish are found have been substantially reduced, mostly because of the non-native fish including brook, lake, brown and rainbow trout, but also from over fishing. When you catch the cutthroat trout there is a "catch and release" unharmed policy at Yellowstone, in order to keep their population growing. But any of the other fish you can keep or destroy it, you may not throw it back alive; if you should decide to keep it the hotel will cook it up for you though, or should I say, them. How about that!

Today is a very hot day, so we decided to go ahead and eat and of course, visit the gift shop and claim this a day of R&R, which in our language means a *nap*.

When we got up, I convinced Russ it wouldn't bother me at all if he would go ahead and fish. I could do my nails, write in my log book, do my crossword puzzles, and read. I am finishing Dr. Oz's book *You on a Diet*. Please don't laugh. Anyway, I won my case; Russ got all his gear together and fished from the walled bank of the historical Yellowstone River. If you don't have your own gear with you, you can rent it and even a boat from the marina if you like.

There is no one else here, so we pulled the car over in the shade and I figured I'd do my nails and then walk down to him and get some pictures. After quite some time, I went in search of the big guy and he wasn't where I left him. He had wandered down a good ways. Boy, was he in his element now, pole in hand moving slowly along the bank. He saw me coming with the camera rolling and with the rod in his right hand and the other empty, he lifted his arms straight out to the side and shrugged his shoulders with a great big smile on his face. I was giggling inside at my sweetheart and then he raised his fingers like 2, I'm assuming he must have caught two fish. The closer I got to him the more excited he was, I knew he must have a grand and impressive story to tell me and I could hardly wait to get to him. This turned out to be my most favorite picture of him, and my most favorite shared experience with him, because it colored a picture of his very true heart. Sure enough, he started talking a mile a minute about the beautiful cutthroats he caught, when he noticed a man and his young son were standing a few feet away and they were watching him. So my sweet and considerate man went up to them and asked the Dad if it would be okay for the boy to take the rod. The Dad said, "Sure," so Russ asked the boy if he'd like to feel what it is like to pull in a fish. The boy was quite eager to do that, so Russ showed him how to hold and cast the rod and let him pull in the next fish. The Dad was very grateful and the little guy was so excited, happy—not to mention proud of himself. Russ said other people were there then and they weren't having any luck, but when the young'un cast his line, *boom!* He got one right away, so they threw the fish back, cast the line again, and he had number 2 just like that! Russ said that really made his day and I'm thinking I'll bet it made that nameless child's day as well. I think that little man will remember that experience the rest of his life. And Russ spoke of it the rest of the day and my heart was full of pride for his generous act.

We figure it is time to get ready for our sunset critter hunting drive, that we love so much in the evenings. This will be our last night here, the only place we stayed a whole four days. On the way up the mountain, we pass a large number of reddish-brown lodgepole pines, all kind of crowded into one space, with snow in front and toward the edge of the road. I understand they are that color here because they are bedazzled by the sun, but as we maneuver up the road into the shade, they become victims of a fire—black, dark, and dreary. Speaking of fire, Yellowstone had a huge fire in 1988. They hadn't had much rain at all that year and a record low snow pack, priming the park for its most intense and massive forest fire in its history. It was on all the news and in the newspapers as thousands of firefighters were sent there. Tourist areas were evacuated and thick black smoke dominated the skies. Almost every development in the park and around it were threatened. Yellowstone's scenic wonders and legendary landscapes were becoming transformed into a fiery wasteland.

In the end, close to 800,000 of the park's 2,221,800 acres burned that summer causing an estimated property damage of over $3 million, $120 million to contain the fire, 9,000 firefighters, 117 aircraft, and 100 fire engines were brought in from all over the country to help fight.

Here we are thirty years after the fact, and the fires' beneficial aspects are much better known now. Now, it is understood that such fires are necessary, because they renew the grasslands and improve wildlife habitat, believe it or not. The rain and snow break the remaining ash down into vital nutrients. The fire causes the pine cones to burst open and release seeds, and as a result, the forests begin their natural renewal process. We learned this in Sequoia National

Park as well, about the tall Redwoods. And this didn't keep tourists away either, as Yellowstone still remains one of the most popular attractions in the world.

Well, fires are not always an effective occurrence, but we can see in this case they are useful. But I don't feel like this chapter is complete until I address other occurrences, those that are rather sad and tragic. We all know if we go out in the wilderness, there are things that can happen or seem to attract more dangerous situations than the norm. And that is why they have rules and rangers to protect us and information to teach us to take caution.

Over 300 people have died in this park, widely ranging from death by scalding hot springs, bison or bear, poisonous plants, avalanche falls and some from fires. During the 140-year history of Yellowstone, 7 people have been killed by bears. The year 1986 was the year the photographer I wrote about was killed. However, more people have died in the park from falling, drowning, burns from falling into the thermal pools, and suicide than have been killed by bears.

Of course, we have no control over natural disasters like earthquakes. The very first earthquake recorded was June 25, 1874. On November 14, 1897, an earthquake caused dishes to fall to the floor, and people were even thrown out of their beds. Three years later, another quake caused considerable damage to Grand Central Hotel at Casper, when a 2 to 4-inch crack extended from the first to the third story. Then there's the quake that happened in 1959, at a 7.1 magnitude. That quake triggered a landslide in which 28 people were killed; this quake being considered the most destructive. In 1975 a 6.1-magnitude quake struck with minimal damage, and in 1985, 3,000 minor earthquakes were detected, which has been referred to as an "earthquake swarm." There are many more, some lasting for several days, but it is comforting to know seismic activity is recorded regularly.

It is just so important that people heed the warning signs and watch their children. If there are retaining walls, do not climb over them, do not venture off alone on hikes or at night or off the trails, especially where the earth's crust is thin. I just can't express that enough. I never once felt afraid because I knew we were doing everything according to rules while we were there. I shrink to think of the time we ventured to see the fall at night. (We shouldn't have done that.) This information was researched from National Park Service information and Utah Education.

And lastly, I thought it would be fun to list some facts about this electrifying park: (1) There are 5 entrances. (2) There are about 10,000 features in the park. (3) 10 percent of Yellowstone is covered by water. (4) 80 percent is forest. (5) Elevation is between 700 and 8,500 feet. (6) Yellowstone is the world's first national park. (7) It consists of 2.2 million acres. (8) It contains about 200 erupting geysers. (9) The bighorn sheep male weighs in at 275 pounds; the female 75 to 150 pounds. (10) Bison weigh 2,000 pounds and can run 30 miles/hour. (11) 90 percent of Yellowstone is barely touched. (12) Yellowstone is divided into 5 countries—Geyser, Lake, Canyon, Roosevelt, and Mammoth. (13) The highest temperature ever recorded was 98 in 1936; the lowest 66 below 0 in 1933. (14) Yellowstone Lake sits at an elevation of 7,733 feet above sea level, making it the highest elevated lake in North America (and is centered over the Yellowstone caldera). (15) Pushed upward by a churning sea of magma, the land in Yellowstone has been rising at the rate of around one inch per year. (16) During the summer months, 25,000 people visit Old Faithful. (17) 96 percent of Yellowstone is in Wyoming, 3 percent in Montana, and 1 percent in Idaho. (18) The only place in the US that has more earthquakes than Yellowstone is California. (19) Upper Geyser Basin, the home of Old Faithful, contains the densest concentration of geysers in the world, with 140 geysers in a single square mile or 25 percent of the world's geysers. (20) On average in the summer, the water temperature of Yellowstone Lake is 41 degrees. The average survival time in water that cold is 30 minutes.

Now back to our movie and where the sky line is. It is painted a most surreal pink, and the trees are silhouetted in front of it. As the sun quickly sinks on this peaceful night, it is on fire with a now hot-pink color and I can't help but think of something I read, so beautiful and appropriate, but I don't know the author…"No human hands could paint a picture so beautiful!"

I know at the end of most movies or books, it says, "The End," but no, no, no, we are far from the end! First, it is a new day, we still have a while before checkout, so we will play a game of cards and dilly-dally around until we have to leave. Then we will pack up our own Old Faithful, Mona, stop in the little store at Fishing village and get an egg biscuit, ice and of course, post cards. Then we plan to go back to Colorado and see our son and family, see Rocky Mountain National Park and who knows what other great adventures we may happen upon.

Of course, we had to look for our greeting brothers, Billy Bob and Bubba Bison, and say our farewells, but it looks like they split before us! So we pointed Mona toward Cody, which isn't very far at all. But before we could pull out, some guy approached us and said "About a half a mile up the road there are some big-horn sheep." See! That is what I'm talking about! When people see exciting things in the Parks, they love to Pass it on.

Naturally, the scenery is as dreamy as always, never to disappoint. But the mountains, as phenomenal as they are, are a different color. They are brown and leveled-like, but I couldn't stop running the camcorder to capture their rich beauty. There are buffalo (tetonka) along the side of the road, enjoying the very green grass, some munching, some strolling, and some are even rolling in the sand. I bet that heavy coat is itchy this time of year. You wouldn't think something that huge could roll around in the sand like that. He sure is churning up a huge cloud of dust! Then, we come across some guy parked at the side of the road very close to a bison lying on the ground, attempting to take a picture. I think the bison didn't like that idea very much. He got up on his feet and his head was down, like in a charge position. I thought sure we were going to witness a bad situation any minute. Then this kook gets back in his car, drives over to another bison, and does the same thing all over again. Highly *not* recommended!

This is the part where the scenery is perfect for any movie, especially ours. Snow adorns the woods and with the contrast of the dark trees, that tells you we are high in elevation again. Picture perfect—my most favorite snow scene being the place we are passing right now, with a beautiful pond in front of the snow-laden mountain. The middle of the pond still stinging with ice and snow, just begging visitors to take a picture of it. And then, without warning, as usual, we came upon a long, thin waterfall, probably more snow run-off than waterfall, but more eye candy just the same, keeping the ride unpredictable with each turn. Then I yell out in wonder, "Look what we found way up here in the mountains!," and here sit two small cannons, yes, I said cannons! On the mountainside, pointed at the mountain to the left of us. I asked Russ, "What the heck are those sitting there for?" and he said, "For avalanche prevention." Well, that made sense to me.

Of course, I had to research that too, and there really is such a thing as avalanche control to reduce the hazard to human life, activity and property. They use many methods, I didn't see cannons in my research, but I did see special guns, different kinds of gates, explosives, etc., so maybe this is one way.

Oh! Yippee! We have found the big horn sheep up on the mountain just kind of hanging out. I'm excited, they are so huge. This big guy looks like he is taking a nap. Then we spied another one, laying by a long thin fallen tree and yet a third up behind him, with his back half turned to us. Oh, there is another one and he is laying down, but he is looking right at us with his neck stretched to get a better look, I guess. This was one of the animals I really wanted to see, especially close enough to get good pictures of them.

This is just so much fun. We found another pretty waterfall ahead, okay, snow run-off. Now back to having another roller-coaster, hair-raising ride with these challenging curves. To our left, it looks like someone attempted to build a stairway up the steep curve, but it was crumbling at the top and kind of disappeared. After many more curves, *woohoo*, and many more waterfalls, yup, snow run-off, we decided to use the next pullover, which is right on a sharp curve, but it is a designated pullover. Russ's door is near the road, but he parked the car so close to the edge, that if I open my door, I might as well kiss him goodbye as I slip down a rocky ridged edge. I will stay put, but the scenery is so remarkable. Russ really has to keep his eyes on the road so it is a treat for him to be able to pause and just gawk for a little while. He said, "Why don't you get out and get a few shots?" "What, are you out of your mind? I am right on the edge and I am not stepping out of this car!" End of conversation. I think my stomach is doing some flip-flops right now from that whole idea. Oh yeah, it's a very impressive view, but on the other hand, it is also a very long way down, especially with that beautiful river running alongside of us. We are looking at the East Arm River and it looks like it is pretty angry running that fast and rough too.

We are approaching the bottom of this scenic mountain that spewed out such mind-blowing adventures. We get out to stretch and this mountain isn't done with us yet, only to relinquish yet another of its stunning gifts. Flitting around us is the tiniest and most vibrant bird. *Wow*, he is bright, bright yellow with a bright-red head and black wings and tail. There are small yellow markings within the black on his neck. We're thinking he must have a nest close by because he darts in and out of theses stick-like branches that are in a pile. When Russ zoomed in with the camera, he could see a little bug in its bright yellow beak. Well, now he is trying to hide from us, then he comes back out and serenades us and allowed us to be close to him for a very long time. He is called a Western Tanager. What a spectacular creation he is!

Officially, we are exiting Yellowstone National Park, forever a thrilling highlight in our memories. But the gift of scenery is still with us, as we pass several deer, I'm sure they are trying to wave good-bye. We come across a corral of horses on our left and the North Fork Shoshone River following us on the right with delicate bright-yellow flowers lining each side of the road. Such a prefect farewell for this exhilarating park.

But before we pull off, some other people pull in and we Pass it on to them about the big horn sheep. They were excited; they had a couple teens in the car. I know we probably would have rode right passed them, had that nice gentleman not told us to be on the lookout.

CHAPTER 14

Oh, Honey, Let's Stop Here
Ew, Honey, Let's Stop There!

The scenery changes again, and the mountains are becoming oddly shaped, although they are beautiful in colors of oranges. We could swear we are back at Arches but the colors aren't as bright. The shapes are just as weird though, like Russ, (meaning weird), who has burst out in a loud rendition of "America." He stops about 4 miles later to announce the shapes of the rocks. "That looks like a huge foot," and it truly does, big toe and all. "That looks like the arch at Arches," all of them in front of that beautiful blue sky. He sure can keep me laughing, this guy of mine.

It seems like we are approaching something different…Oh, it is a memorial for fire fighters. I'm calling to Russ, "Oh, honey, let's stop here!" Yippee! We have found another wonderful sight to explore. It is called The Firefighter Memorial plain and simple and is located at the trailhead of the Blackwater Fire Memorial Trail. It is a long stone wall of orange-ish stone, almost brick-like but bigger. Also there is a walkway, like a sidewalk, but of darker burnt-orange right in front of the wall and then a walkway of stone. Embedded in the wall is a large plaque with a heading that says "Shoshone National Forest Blackwater Fire / August 20–24 1937." It is comfortable here, yet powerful, at the same time. We decided to take a little sight-seeing trip around it. There is a path toward the back, where there is a large quiet pond, with a white path surrounding it and benches. It is beautifully circled with sage, a purplish color, and very green grass. A perfectly peaceful place to escape with your thoughts and prayers. A rugged little winding path continues on for hikers and bicyclists, but not being prepared for hiking or running into a grizzly bear (after all this is grizzly country), and big ole rattlesnakes that love this area as well; this spot suddenly becomes a little more frightening.

And speaking of frightening, a lightning strike caused this fire those many years ago, consuming much more than 1,254 acres, causing 15 firefighters to die and 38 more injured, as a sudden gale force wind whipped the fire into a roaring inferno. More firefighters were killed in this fire than any other US National Forest in the 103 year span between the "Great Fire of 1910" in Washington state and the "Yarnell Hill Fire of 2013" in Arizona. I'm glad we listened to our spontaneous bones and stopped to take time and learn more about this beautifully dedicated place.

At last, we are in Cody, Wyoming. We found a Wally World and got some lures, water, hand sanitizer, etc. Got gas too, and now the price is $4.09, but what are we going to do? We can't get stuck along the way.

The scenery continues on, very much like Arches with all kinds of different shapes and colors and delicate yellow flowers covering the green mountainsides. One of the more outstanding shapes being a rock that looks like one of those stone heads on Easter Island. Others look like small castles and strange squares. One rock looks like a monster with a big tooth, back to back like bookends with another monster just like it on the opposite side. There are big deep caves, towers, and a flock of penguins in the field. Now this is weird, as we are driving down the 4-lane road next to the Shoshone River, and it is getting wider as we go, the white stripe dividing the lanes is no longer in a straight line, but it is really zigzagging! *Woohoo*, somebody was having a high time. *Ha!*

Mostly, we are enjoying the sights of the Shoshone River, because the smell of it is not so good, more like sulfur. How fun, we have come upon the Wild Bill Cody Dam and Reservoir and Visitor Center. And here I am again, squealing, "Ew, honey, let's stop there!" These are the most fun of all, the sights we didn't plan or weren't aware they were ahead. We thought we'd go on in for a visit and look around.

This damn dam (ha, couldn't resist after seeing Chevy Chase's movie), is called a concrete arch-gravity dam, and is named after the Wild West figure William "Buffalo Bill" Cody, who founded the town of Cody. The dam is 70 feet wide at the base, 200 feet wide at the crest, and 325 feet high. At the time it was built, between 1905 and 1910, it was the tallest dam in the world. The crest was raised 25 feet more in 1985, to increase the reservoirs capacity. We were able to walk out toward a railing, where we could see the river straining up against its big walls and piles of logs backed up against its barriers, too. The Visitors Center was small, but we picked up a couple of post cards and a damn magnet, teehee. We also bumped into some bikers that we had seen on the road earlier and had a nice little chat with them.

As we leave the town, there is a bronze statue of a bucking bronco with rider and hat on and lasso in his hand. I'll bet that is Wild Bill. Then comes a building with "CODY WYOMING RODEO… CAPITAL OF THE WORLD," written on it and then under that, in even bigger letters "STAMPEDE PARK." I can't get the signage on the next building, but it is beautiful with the mountains teaming high behind it, the American flag to the side of it and several tee pees next to that. We are traveling south down Route 120 and the next town on the map we will visit is Thermopolis; maybe Clark Kent lives there. No, just kidding, I know he lives in Metropolis. Here it turns into byway 20. This is just a captivating drive all the way, with the beautiful purple flowers all over the place. Well, no wonders, byway 20 has recently been designated an official scenic byway. It snakes about 34 miles through the foot hills of the Owl Creek Mountains. Thermopolis is one of those stunning little towns whose elevation is higher than its population. It also claims to have the largest hot springs in the world. Suddenly, there is a tunnel ahead, carved right into Rattlesnake Mountain and I have to scream my usual "*Woohoo*" as I do every tunnel and every bridge. I know, how immature. Well, no sooner do we get through this tunnel and we can see another just a few yards ahead, and now, oh my gosh here comes a third! I saw no signs or warnings, so we didn't see that coming. What a pleasant surprise! *So*, of course, I researched it out and found that these tunnels, cumulative in length, are one-mile long, the first tunnel being the longest. As we erupt from the last and smallest tunnel we find ourselves in a place called, Colter's Hell, which is a semi-active geyser basin. Again, to the left, a mountain with large letters engraved in white across the top "World's Largest Mineral Hot Springs." Even a herd of Buffalo are here to greet us and I find myself once again saying, "Oh, honey, let's stop here!" It is called Hot Springs State Park and it is very nice, so we decided to check it out. The park is actually built all around the hot springs, which pours out millions of gallons of mineral water every 24 hours at a constant temperature of 135 degrees F. Some of the water is cooled and piped into bathhouses for public use. It is free to go in and take a dip in the pool if you like, unless you rent towels, then there is a small charge. The park is beautifully landscaped and is quite an interesting layout.

From another stream, the water flows over an enchanting Rainbow Terrace, which is very colorful and spills down into the Big Horn River. We are walking down a wooden boardwalk with no sides to it and the water underneath flows down the sides and looks like a solid waterfall. The colors are very soothing soft colors of beiges, white and sandy brown. There are many different formations in the water and one especially large one off to the sides, that looks like a boulder or mound of minerals these same colors with a fence around it. It looks to be about 30 feet high to me. Across from there is a garden of red and yellow flowers.

I'm glad we stopped and visited the park, but we are starting to get tired. We have had so many exciting and unexpected sights to see today. We are near Riverton so we will stop here for the night, and in the morning, we will start toward Troy's house in Colorado.

Well, here we are, looking at another beautiful new sun-shiny day. Russ had checked us out of the motel and pulled Mona around to the front. While he was gathering the luggage on one of these nice big rolling luggage racks, I went on ahead with our "infront seat stuff". You know, our atlas, maps, camera, water, notebook and all. It was our morning routine. I was probably in my head, too. Trying to imagine what awesome things we would see today and what new adventures we would experience. When I began to realize, Russ was taking a really long time. I turned to see where he was, no sign of him. Then I looked out the rear-view mirror. Oh, heck! He was running down the hill behind me, chasing the nice big rolling luggage cart with our luggage on it!!! Thank goodness, he got hold of it before it crashed, or he got hurt. Here he comes huffing and puffing up the hill, cart in hand. Poor baby, I felt so sorry, but at the same time, I couldn't help it, I was gut-splitting laughing. The hazards of travel, right? That's my man. We will stop to eat breakfast at Trail Head Family Diner. Ummm-Yumm! We can't wait to see our son Troy and family in Colorado. But he is almost two hours away from Denver. A lot of sights can be seen in two hours. As we are driving, we see a lot of prong-horned antelope, herds of sheep and even antelope mixed in with cows and their babies. Not to mention the electrifying scenery. It is unreal to drive down roads that are cut right through the mountains, the dips and curves of the ranges and the way the clouds dip down to caress the tippy tops of each. The odd formations jutting out of rock every once in a while stand out so gracefully. The peaceful river that follows alongside us is like, a friend tagging along, all quiet and serene. And the overwhelming bluest of blue skies.

It looks like they have a train set up like our Marta in Atlanta. I also noticed the walls along the expressway are all either painted on or there are etchings of ducks or some type of neat design. It makes for an interesting drive. The bridges are different too, almost all of them are unique in some way. The one we are approaching has an arch over it and I think it is called Speer Blvd./Little Raven Street Overpass.

To our right, we can see what looks like an abandoned mine. It is beginning to sprinkle a little and then, here we are again, entering another tunnel. Only this entrance is a rugged and jagged black hole, just waiting to swallow us up as we round the curve and fall in. *Woohoo!* It is very dark, but we can see the white light at the end, and as we near the exit, we can see yet another jagged tunnel, which is small because you can see the beginning and end of it all in one. And, oh man, as we exit the second tunnel we are about to round another curve and there sits yet a third short tunnel which is also small, not jagged but nice, neat and structured. What a fun adventure, I think this state must love tunnels, certainly no boredom here.

We have been driving a good while now. After passing a lot of sheep, horses and a few poised and beautiful reddish-brown llamas, we wanted to get some gas and lunch. We approach a detour with a gas station in the middle of it. They were asking $3.83/gallon. Hmmm, he must have been hurting because of the detour. Finally, a McDonalds is up the road, we had lunch, stretched a little and then crossed the Colorado state line at 3:30 p.m. The scenery is making color changes back to the whites, creams and the pretty tangerine and orange colors. The little river is widening and there are campers and trailers parked at its edges. Both the Colorado and Eagle Rivers are running fast and full. Some of the mountains are sharply tilted with their beautiful colors and those close to us seem a little smaller. A huge mountain has a tiny round window at the tippy top, kind of like those at Arches. We are in Denver and passing the football stadium, (the Sports Authority at Mile High) which makes me happy, because that is a sign we are getting close. Through the Johnson Tunnel once again and loving it. It took a couple hours, but we are finally entering Eagle where we got a motel and called everyone to let them know we had arrived; that was around 7:00 p.m. We had a late, late dinner around 10:30 from Taco Bell. No wonders we are gaining weight!

Well, it is a new day with new excitement in the air. Interesting, we found a set of keys in one of the drawers in the motel room, not ours, so we will take them to the desk. We can't wait to see the Grand-young'uns and take them to breakfast, uh, brunch, well, maybe lunch! But when we called their mother, she said Syd was working and Skyler had to be back at 4 for a family reunion on her side. We dropped the keys off at the desk and they said they knew they were there, that they belonged to a pilot who occupied the room before us, but they didn't need to disturb us to pick them up. Apparently, the pilot realized he had left them and had called. That was considerate of them. We got to visit a few minutes with Syd and then took Skyler to eat and, of course, we wanted to do the Grandparent thing at Wally-World, if you know what I mean. Such fun! Syd was home when we took Skyler back, so it was nice to get to visit with him a little while too. Hard to believe he is working! Boy are we getting old. No, we aren't, they are!

Troy and Karen were at her daughter's soft ball game and then had to attend a wedding. So we took a little drive to Sylvan Lake State Park, which is surrounded by the White River Forest. The lake itself is 42 acres and a peaceful drive ensued with a most inspiring vista. Colorado is another beautiful state with dynamic beauty unfolding in every single curve in the road

When Troy and Karen got home, we went and visited for a little while, saw the work he did on the kitchen, the vegetable garden and of course, Maggie's flower garden, and before we knew it, the day had to come to an end.

We all met for breakfast at my favorite diner in Eagle, and while we were there, Dick Cheney's entourage went by. It took a very long time, but isn't that interesting? You never know when something new and different is going to happen and that certainly wasn't expected. We decided we would go back to the motel and do some laundry (which I never do on Sunday,) but we were going to visit Karen's sister and family for dinner. Oh and what a wonderful dinner it was! Her son did the steaks on the grill and they were out of this world. Right where I have felt like I have been (out of this world), these past few weeks. And he is only a teenager. I must have done something wrong. My teens didn't do that.

Afterward, we went back to Troy's and visited for a little while. So nice to see our son and his family and it's always hard to leave. But, in the morning, we will make our way to Rocky Mountain National Park. Yippee!

After loading up the car, we met our son and family for one last meal at the diner, slowly trying to let go of them. We gassed up Mona, they took a picture of us together for a change with our look-alike Yellowstone shirts on and with sweet goodbyes we headed for the scenic route. First, we had to drive across Route 70 which heads west, on past Vail, until we do a complete sharp left north onto Route 40, which is the true scenic route. This road will take us straight into the park. We arrive at a town called Granby and about 3 miles further is Lake Granby. Grand Lake is Colorado's largest and deepest natural lake. One thing you can be sure of is it is huge, blue, and dazzling. Russ would really like to fish here but the water was very rough. So we drove a little further up the Grand Lake and it seemed a little calmer, but not much. So we wandered on up to the Marina where Russ had a little chat with some local fisherman over a cup of coffee, but then decided to continue on our way.

We are smack in the middle of Indian Peaks Wilderness, which straddles the continental divide. Most of the peaks we can see here are named after Indian tribes, such as the Arapaho, Apache, and Navajo. Altogether there are seven peaks, each over 13,000 feet, each one within 100 feet (in height) of each other. As if they were all in competition with one another, kind of like my boys when they were trying to outgrow each other.

Amazingly, we have driven right through lunch and wound up at the Kawuneeche Visitor Center. Naturally, you know the post cards and magnets are calling me. Rocky Mountain National Park has five different Visitor Centers. As we drive on, we stop to take a picture of the big sign announcing our official arrival to Rocky Mountain National Park. The nation's 10th national park, making it only one out of over 380 parks in the National Park System. We wanted to stop off and see Irene Lake, but all the passages were closed. There are elk everywhere nonchalantly grazing, while some are laying in the fields in large groups. Some of the gentlemen buck are off in a close field, very well dressed with huge racks, just like men at our parties, when the men sometimes end up in the living room having their male conversations, while the women are in the kitchen. And Mrs. Moose is busy munching with her adorable baby behind her, but not socializing with the elk. Moose are very reclusive animals though, especially with humans. The elk didn't seem bothered at all by the humans watching and filming them for forever pictures. There are 3,000 elk that reside in the park. All this makes us feel very close to nature and Russ is especially loving it.

In the distance is the great Rocky Mountain chain, the world's longest mountain barrier, rolling from Mexico to Alaska for 2,700 miles. Actually, Rocky Mountain Park could be called the "top of the world for everybody."

As we drive up the mountain, it begins to sprinkle enough to turn on our wipers, well, at least it isn't snow. After the shower, we pulled over to explore a little. The mountains in the distance are covered in snow. There is an instructional sign here with names and pictures of the Never Summer Mountain range. I got a kick out of the name and I believe it too. There is a picture of the range on the sign, only they don't have snow on them like ours do. As we are kind of just strolling along, coming to greet us is a big ole porcupine. I didn't know they got so big. Oh dear, Russ and I kind of back off saying "nice kitty." He didn't seem too worried about us, but we weren't feeling too stupid at the moment either. Well, maybe a little stupid, I got a picture of him! He is not pretty, poor thing. This place is just full of fun critters. As we walk a little further next to a pile of big logs is a turkey prowling around. And then, as we get to the car a little gray bird was right next to it. My getting closer to him didn't seem to bother him at all either. He sure is a bold little character. I bet if I had a handful of seed he'd take it right out of my hand. He is gray and fluffy with a long beak. The tip of his wings are coal black and the under tail is pure white. I had to know more about this little guy, so I researched it under the National Park Services, and found out he is called Clark's nutcracker. Named by Clark and Lewis. I also found out that he loves to eat pine seeds, which are richer in calories than chocolate. They form long-term relationships with their mates and their eggs are pale green. They are related to the jay and crow family.

We continue driving and Russ is singing at the "top" of his lungs as we get closer to the "top" of the mountain. Whichever one of these "tops" is the scariest, I'm not sure. The snow drifts beside us are 3 and 4 feet high as we go and the scenery around us is so picturesque.

We see another pull-over so we take advantage of it. The signs say we are at Cache La Poudre River and the Ute Trail below. The Cache La Poudre River originates in the Rocky Mountains and flows across the plains to merge with the South Platte River and extends for 45 miles. Then we return to our van and the graceful curves and unpredictable roads. The rocks on the side of this mountain are huge and look loose; piled on top of each other, and seem like they might tumble down at the slightest sneeze. The next turn, brings us to a wall about 3 feet high made of these rocks. There is snow on all the mountainside around us melting and making little waterfalls that are tumbling over the little rock wall. So pretty and soothing and some of the snow is forming little streams, too. And while we are talking about snow, there is a little reminder or maybe I should say warning about pink snow. Do not eat "pink" snow. The color is caused by thriving communities of algae. This snow may look like and even taste like watermelon, but does not set well with the digestive tract.

Then all of a sudden "elk"! Wow! And they are all buck, with racks ranging from small to extra-large. These mountains are full of surprises and unpredictable as always. Which rings double in my ears, as we roll on the very edges while passing picture book brooks, foaming white on top. But, as usual, I continue to whine about the curves, the speed, and edges until we come to some refreshing bright white flowers; bushy on their stems and then, some black-eyed susans. And finally, some lavender flowers on a long stem, called mountain blue violets that all seem to calm me and put me back in my comfort zone.

Rocky Mountain National Park encompasses 265,761 acres of land in Colorado's front range. The peak is split by the Continental Divide, which gives the eastern and western portions of the park different characters. The park contains 359 miles of trails, 150 lakes and 450 miles of streams. Three million visitors come here each year. There are 72 named peaks higher than 12,000 feet, the highest of these is called Longs Peak which rises to 14,259 feet. It is visible from almost any point. But as intriguing as Longs Peak is, not all leave it safe or even alive. Between 1915, when Rocky Mountain became a national park, and 2010, 344 park visitors have died as a result of accidents such as car crashes, heart attacks, and various other reasons. Sixty of the fatalities were climbers on Longs Peak, others were as follows: 4 by hypothermia, 3 by lightning, 3 by exhaustion and exposure, and 2 by suicide. I only bring up these facts to bring people to some very threatening realizations of extreme dangers.

We have been driving on Route 34 for a while now, and it is called Trail Ridge Road. It is the highest paved through-road in

North America and a landmark achievement for its day. They call it a byway. Colorado has 25 byways, 10 are designated as America's Byways, meaning they are nationally recognized for their outstanding scenic and historic attributes. In fact, only one other state has as many nationally designated byways as Colorado and that is Oregon. They have 10. And just think, all of this is only 65 miles northwest of Denver!

Now we are on a dirt road and there is a tiny critter in front of us, on the very edge of the road (right where I don't want to be). It looks like he is going to make a run for it. Yup, there he goes, he scrambles in front of us, and when he gets to the other side, he stands up on his hind legs and just nonchalantly looks at us as if to say, "Humpfh, no big deal." I bet you thought I was going to say "He stands up and waves at us." He doesn't know how lucky he is! Mona is a fierce, green, mean machine!

We are at the summit of this mountain and the view is exhilarating. Wow, what a sight. We are actually equal to all the mountains at 12,183 feet, which makes all the other mountaintops stand at our eye level. We are truly riding on the edge again and there are snow markers all along the outer edges of the road. It looks like we are driving in the clouds and we could reach out the windows and touch them. There are plots of pure white snow to our left and on the edges of the inside of the road. The clouds are becoming dark and gray and I'm praying it doesn't snow before we get to the bottom of this thing. There is a pullover ahead, so we park and pull out the camcorder to record these beauties and take a moment to just catch our breath. This is the tundra, above the tree line, where the average temperature of the warmest month is about 49 degrees F. Interestingly, the temperature drops about 3.5 degrees F. for every 1,000 feet you travel up. Most of the time the tundra is a frigid, forbidding, and windswept land.

There are elk herds all over the top of this amazing mountain, with patches of snow to add to the drama. I can't believe what I am seeing right now. Two elk are fighting and standing up on their hind legs. Wow, what a sight. Most people wouldn't see that in a lifetime. Then the ride becomes even more cliff hanging and it even got hairy for Russ. Hahahaha. Now he knows how I feel most of the time. It is quite the descent, as we curl through split edges of mountains and big boulders of rock in piles. Big signs say *CAUTION!* No kidding.

Just a little more than half way around Rocky Mountain National Park, still on the scenic route of 34, we come to a town called Estes Park. This was just another thing we came upon, not planned, which we seemed to do more often than not. We just kind of let things fall into place "spontaneously," as we were "driving" and we were always happily surprised. We are told that this is where the Rocky Mountains Park headquarters is located. It is beautiful here and I am glad this is where we will end our day. The directional signs are amazing. We found a motel and Russ got himself a fishing license in hopes of fishing here. We also found a place to eat called "Hunter's Hop." I had pork chops and Russ had 1/2 rack of barbecue ribs. Talk about delicious food. Spontaneous can really be a wonderful thing! It is around 8:00 p.m. now and as we drive to the motel, 2 elk stroll in front of our car. It's getting to be a common thing these days to see a critter be near or in front of us at any given moment. "See those elk in front of us, honey." "Ho hum, yeah, I guess they're on their way home again." We are really going to miss all this when we get back to Georgia.

So we are camped in for the night, but at about 3:00 a.m., I am awakened to the most pleasant sound of rain. How nice… zzzzzzzzzzzzzzzzz.

At 5:45 a.m., we are both rudely awakened by the sound of a roaring motor cycle outside our room. Okay, that's fine, but at 6:00 a.m., it was still running. Uh-oh, for a minute there, I thought Russ was going to shove him off the side of the mountain with Mona. Then they started hammering and doing construction. I think they are adding on to this motel. So I get up and shower and the big guy has gone back to sleep, hammering and all. Ohhhh my.

After breakfast, we thought we'd ride around Estes Park and sight-see a little. We headed back up our scenic Route 34. No critters yet, but the flowers are so brilliant in color. A ranger had told us the big horn sheep usually cross the street between 12:30 and 2:00 every day, so we thought we'd hang around a while. Unfortunately, no luck today, so we moved on seeing only one elk. Russ is keeping his eye out for a place to fish, driving on 36 toward Bear Lake. The River seemed to be moving too fast and turbulent. So we took a shuttle bus over to Bear Lake, which is about 10 miles long and at a lofty 9,475 feet in elevation, with a beautiful scenic trailhead all the way around it, which ascends even higher. We are, once again, right next to the Continental Divide. We stopped at Sprague Lake and it is about 13 acres and a very shallow lake and then Glacier Basin, which is a very nice campground with a motel as well.

This day went fast, but a beautiful scenic experience it was. We will go back and have dinner at Hunter's Hop again, if you find a great place why not? We rode around a few more minutes after that since it is our critter time, but only saw a couple of beautiful elk and a mule deer.

While we were traveling around the lakes today, I received a call. Definitely not good reception, but I could tell it was a male speaking, so I told him, "I can't hear you, but if you can hear me, I will call you back as soon as I can get good reception." As soon as we got to the motel, I called him back and come to find out it was my friend's son. He said my friend had passed this morning and wanted to let me know. "*What!*" She died of cancer of the brain. "Well, how can that be? We were in touch all the time on e-mail, Christmas cards, etc. She did not tell me she was having any trouble." I felt awful, she kept it a secret. I could have seen her and been praying for her all that time. And now, here we are in the Rockies and there is no way I can get back there right now. I talked to Mark a little while and filled him in on our history and let him know how much I loved her. We were friends in high school and she was my maid of honor. Such a long friend ship and such a loss. Once again, God has brought me back to the reality of life.

Now it is Wednesday, and we slept in and didn't even check out of our room until about noon. We had a relaxing morning (after all our hard work, right?) Russ took me to town and we got some shirts and of course, post cards and a hat for him. All of a sudden, it became very windy and we could see a big dark cloud off in the distance, over one of the mountains. It's so unpredictable in the mountains how quick weather can change. This little town is really something. It is adorably quaint and very accommodating to tourists. It has a huge assortment of little stores, benches, parking, and restrooms are made available all over the place, which is great for seniors, but also for people with little ones. There are flowers everywhere: hanging pots, flower boxes, and along the sidewalks and even climbing on walls. So vibrant are the colors of purples, reds, oranges, yellow, hot pink. All are just breath-taking. We wandered across the street and we found a rapid little river running through the city that looked like it would accommodate river rafting. We sat on a bench for a bit and became hypnotized by the sounds and the pretty and bubbly turbulence.

Well, today is going to be another fishing day for my honey. He got a fishing license for only $5.00 and it is good anywhere in the state of Colorado. I'm thinking that is the only cheap thing in Colorado! So I brought all kinds of things for me to do, while he was busy fishing. Like nail polish, my book, a puzzle book, and my journal and some pens and pencils. I will be a happy little camper. It will be just a simple relaxing day *out* of the car for a bit.

There is a pretty and brave little bird walking around by us. He is a pretty good size, with a pure black head and neck, a black body except for his underside which is pure white. His wings are black too with a white flash going across the top of them, and a black tail and black leggings. Russ said he is a magpie. I sure didn't know they were so pretty, especially when he gets in the sunlight. Next to the road, we come to a brook like no other. It is wide and running fast over huge rocks, topped with very white foam and the sound of it is so pleasing and relaxing. You can tell they have had a lot of snow this year because the rivers are so full, and all the snow melt and bubbling creeks. That is a good thing for Colorado.

We have come to a big river, where men are donned in their waders and hats busily casting, stopping, tying knots, watching and waiting for that monster fish of a life time. Looking up at the lush mountains surrounding us, there are still snow patches and monstrous rocks jutting out and up into the striking sky. We look back to the water with tall dark, dark-green trees, lining the river banks and think no matter where you look, there is dramatic scenery.

We drive on, looking for a place for Russ to fish. The green fields are full of elk perking their heads up to see what we're going to do. Russ finally found a spot he thought he'd like to fish, so I stuck around a while to take a few pictures of him, thinking just maybe he'd catch one while I was there. But no, so I found me a picnic table in the shade and just scanned the area, which was really very busy. Lake Estes sits in the middle of everything, like a center piece. There is a wide sidewalk going all the way around the lake for a complete five-mile loop. A little bit up the way, on the lake, is a Marina where you can rent any kind of boat imaginable and people are getting different kinds of bikes, too. There is a little motor boat and a person kayaking on the lake. And right now on a sidewalk next to me comes a woman and a child on a double bike with a canopy, how cute. I learned later that these are called a "pedal cart." I wonder what they will think of next? Then came a couple on a bicycle built for two. There are people picnicking and many are eating at several of the picnic tables scattered around the area. There are a few children playing along the shore. Even though this weather was sent from heaven, it is sunny, but cool with a light breeze and the water looks like it is as cold as ice. Brrrr. This is the best little mountain getaway yet, not to mention a spiritual experience too, simply because of the natural and unforgettable surroundings. There are endless discoveries and activities for the young and old alike. Just sitting on this bench, both the day and the place is winning my heart! Estes offers backpacking, bicycling, hiking, rafting, camping, lodges, horseback riding, even paddle boating; you name it, it all spells stress relief. As I started to take my nail polish off, I noticed two young men cutting the grass around the walk. They took their shirts off (ooo yeah) and I noticed they're arms were real brown and tan (of course I did; no, it wasn't like that), but they're chests and back were as white as Lily Flour. Really. I remembered we had a great big bottle of tanning lotion in the car, so I asked them if they'd like some. One young man said, "For real?" So I went to the parking lot right behind us and handed it to them. (No, I didn't offer to put it on them!) I'm mom! Anyway, after they left, something in the grass caught the corner of my eye. It was a cute little ground squirrel, I guess he heard all the commotion and he got nosey. Got a cute picture of him standing up on his hind legs.

My history information of the park tells me that in September of 2013, there was a big flood at Estes that flooded the whole city and destroyed so much with mudslides and water. It was quite a disaster for them to repair and recover from.

Well, here comes Russ strolling up the sidewalk toward me. He didn't catch anything so we decided to move on. We drove out of town up Route 36 and toward Sprague Lake which is a shallow, 13-acre lake. We thought we were going up Route 36, but no, we were way off. We grabbed our trusty map and discovered we were on Route 7. But, oh well so what, we've played everything else by ear and we are really enjoying the scenery. We found a pretty wide and clean, fast running river. Russ said if he could hit next to some of those big rocks there are little holes where trout like to sit. It was a pretty good hike off the road.

He got a strike right away, but it was small. I'd guess about 8 inches. I was following him with the camera, but not too close because he was climbing all over these huge rocks. No way was I going to try and do that, but I did go down pretty far. All the time keeping my eye out for that one lonely black bear that might be looking for lunch. The river is loud and foaming white and the leaves on the trees are rustling and dancing. I know good and well Russ is not going to hear me if I do wind up doing battle with anything. They say there are only 20 to 30 black bears in this park. But they sure didn't say where. We keep looking to see one, but not this far away from the car!

I am standing here surrounded by tall wild grass, swaying in the breeze and pretty bright-red wild strawberries growing by my feet. Oh, he got one, another small one, he no sooner throws that one back and gets another. They're all the same size, don't they have any mommies and daddies? I am nervous standing here so far away from him. I am getting good shots of his mini catches though, thanks to zoom lenses. I raise the camera way up and over and the sky is the color of a deep turquoise blue, with a huge oblong and pointy rock standing on its very edge. Wow, another balancing rock! And then as I scroll over my shoulder, I notice one lonely tree standing in the middle of the mountain. Well, Russ is turning and moving out, I guess he decided enough of that. All in all, he caught four trout and had a wonderful and interesting day, as I did.

We walked on a little further and came to a structure. Oh, wait a minute. Here sits another one of nature's most beautiful birds. This one is all black except for a bright-yellow beak and some red and white scratches of color on the edges and bottom of its wings. He is called a red-wing black bird. Now, isn't that original. We don't seem to frighten him at all.

But back to this structure. It is a small church and the sign says St. Malo Center. The church itself is known as "The Chapel on the Rock." It is built solidly on granite at the bottom of Mount Meeker, a 13,916-foot peak in Rocky Mountain National Park. It was built in 1935 and its walls are formed with square rocks. There is a cross on the top of a tower and its roof divides into several peaks. There are vibrant purple and lavender irises all around, next to a log fence. Several yards from there, is a huge all-white statue of Jesus on an enormous rock or boulder and He is holding up His right hand, as if to bless us. The same flood I spoke of in Estes, struck here as well. The mudslide made a quarter-mile wide path through the little valley where the church sits. It took boulders and hurled them down Mt. Meeker, along with mud, water, and trees that snapped in pieces like pencils. It was a heavy forest and everything in it went, except the chapel. The slide *did not touch it!* When all that massive debris reached the chapel, it simply parted like the Red Sea and went around it! The townspeople said the power of the water was horrific. But none of the water or the mud touched the interior of the little chapel, either. Afterward, there was thick mud laying several yards in the front of the church in the valley, with broken trees and branches laying in piles, like pick-up-sticks. A miracle? Come to your own conclusion. I know one thing; a strong foundation is everything!

There is gentle blinking lightning off in the distance and I think the sun is trying to tell us it is time to move on. It is getting late, so we decided to go back to town and eat. We found an Italian restaurant for tonight and then back to the motel to reminisce this awesome day and every single detail of our adventures.

Today we are going to Arvada, Colorado, to visit our daughter-in-law's grandfather. When my son lived in Marietta, his wife's grandparents would come to visit every year and each time they would visit us Russ would make this awesome delicious meat loaf. He made it just for them upon request, each time. Since the grandmother has passed, we wanted to visit our friend while we were so close.

As we sat at breakfast earlier this next morning, a gentleman started talking to us about the loss of his wife. He was traveling with his son. This has no bearing on my story, except I wanted to point out what a smile can do. That's all we did, we gave him a "good mornin', accompanied by a big smile and he in turn poured his grieving heart out to us. Perfect strangers.

So anyway, we gave Charles a call (the grandfather we were planning to visit) and he was thrilled we were on our way. While driving to his place, we decided our next stop would be Pikes Peak. It was a beautiful drive down to Arvada, we visited with Charles about 2 hours or so. After leaving Arvada, we saw a sign advertising Garden of the Gods and it got our curiosity all aroused. It was an "Ew…honey, let's stop there!" It was probably about 100 miles or so, and the next thing you know, just like all the other adventures on this trip, we found ourselves pulling in to the site of huge and oddly formed orange-red rocks. We are just off Route 25 going south, near "Colorado Springs" exit 146.

Research claims "Garden of the Gods" was created millions of years ago, when the sandstone rocks came roaring up from thousands of feet deep in the earth. Then sculpted over the following millennia by glaciers, rivers, wind, and rain. The park has grown to 1,334 acres and is considered a National Natural Landmark. Before we are even barely close to the entrance of the park, a mule deer starts walking next to us. We were going slow anyway, so we just waited until he decided where he was going. He was just meandering, walked in front of Mona and on over to the other side of the road and into the woods. A huge thin stone slab greets us with the words written Garden of the Gods and underneath Colorado Springs. As we enter the park, which is free by the way, we are immediately aware of an enormous red rock. It is teetering on a platform of shale rock that is smaller than the rock itself. It is said, the rock had fallen millions of years ago during a geographical upheaval along a natural fault line. This red rock is made of sandstone and is named Balanced Rock. It weighs in at a whopping 700 tons. To the left of this natural entry way is another huge rock, as big as a yacht and it is named Steamboat Rock.

There is a beautifully paved wide path throughout the park, on which you can bike, walk, or ride a horse. Many of the rocks are tilted vertically and faulted into "fins." Reminding us of the many fins we saw at Arches. Many of the different monoliths have names. Three tall fins stand huddled together called The Three Graces, a group of both thick and thin large and tall are called Sentinel Spies and then there are Kissing Camels, Siamese Twins, Llamas Heads, and Cathedral Valley, to name a few. I think someone has an entertaining imagination. The park is laced with one-seed juniper trees, maybe a thousand years old, that twist and turn with their roots shooting down into the red sand. Many of these breath-taking surprises are big round and flat rocks, in a giant balancing act. One on top of the other, like someone was trying to see how high they could pile them before they fell. It is not a huge park, but a nice walk that lends to peace and tranquility. As we pass a large group of mountainous gray rock, here sits a beautifully marked bird. He is all black, except his chest and under his wings, which is pure white. Even his bill is pure black. He has a very long tail and he is called a black-billed magpie. Related to the jay and the crow, he is a raucous and rowdy bird. He sounds mad.

Garden of the Gods and the Colorado Springs vicinity has much to offer. Things like helicopter and hot air balloon rides, river rafting, kayaking, horseback riding, hiking, skiing in winter, a flea market all year round, campgrounds, zip lining, trail running, a cave to visit, a zoo, museums, festivals in summer, and restaurants galore. There is a restaurant placed right on site, so that you can see the grounds while eating. You can even be married here if you so desire. On the grounds, is a nature center and trading post. You must have a permit to climb in established areas and have good equipment. There have been several fatalitics over the years because the climber was not wearing safety equipment or the equipment was faulty.

Well, believe it or not, you can actually see Pikes Peak from here. How interesting since that is our next destination. We'll be right there! Oh…honey.

CHAPTER 15

A Nail-Biting, Hair-Raising 19-Mile Ride

Between driving and spending time in God's Garden, we pretty much took up the whole day, so we decided to look for a motel, and devote tomorrow to the peak. We drove around a bit, found a motel, and unloaded Mona. After we got all situated, we realized we had a small balcony. How nice. When we walked out on it, we discovered we had a perfect overview of the Garden of the Gods! How about that! See, being spontaneous is so much fun and adventurous. But I have to admit, had we looked closer at the map and planned the trip down Route 25, we probably would have stopped at several of the following, which we really didn't realize were there until we got to the motel. When you travel south toward Pikes Peak on Route 25, the very first attraction is the United States Air Force Academy (exit 156B). The academy is considered one of the most beautiful university campuses of the service academies. We didn't realize it was open for visitors to tour the grounds and visit the Cadet Chapel, with its A-frame architecture, heavenly stained glass and elegant pipe organ. It seems Colorado enjoys this type of architecture. It reminds me of the way the airport is built as well. They also show a film about cadet life and a history of our service men and women.

The next exit was The Flying W Ranch (exit 147), an old western town where they serve barbeque beef and chicken and have western stage shows after every meal. After Garden of the Gods, is the Fine arts Center at exit 141 (Colorado Ave. or Route 24), just loaded with attractions on the way to Pikes Peak. First, is the ProRodeo Hall of Fame and Museum of the American Cowboy. Displays of cowboy gear/clothing, memorabilia, Western art and sculpture, and a nice little water garden is also found here. Next, is the Ghost Town Museum. This splits off onto Manitou Ave. in historic Manitou Springs. We are now at the foot of Pikes Peak. Miramont Castle and Museum and Cave of the Winds are just off to the right, but we are moving straight ahead to Pikes Peak, also known as America's Mountain, because the scenic views inspired Katherine Lee Bates, a teacher from Massachusetts, to write "America the Beautiful" in 1894.

Pikes Peak is a 14,110-foot dynamic mountain. It's not a national park though, so we couldn't use our passes and had to pay $10.00 each, which of course, was well worth it. There are 4 ways to get to the top: hike (most people that hike use Barr Trail), ride a bike, drive, or take Pikes Peak Cog Railway. Of course, we chose to drive and they do ask you if you have good brakes when you get your ticket. And *that* my friend, ought to tell you something right there! And it is suggested that if you leave your vehicle for an extended period, you should leave a plainly visible note on the windshield saying where you are going and when you will return! How far can you go? Oh, my! I wonder if I should view these things as red flags?

The road starts off great and looks very safe with nice paving and guard rails. We notice there is a covering over the mountain that makes me think of a hair net. I assume this is to protect us from falling rock. This is Pikes Peak Highway and will be a roller coaster 19-mile drive, which more than half a million people achieve every year. Supposedly, it should take about two hours to the top not including of course, if you should stop here and there for pictures and sightseeing. And not only should you have good brakes, you should have plenty of gas as well. I'm so excited for another adventure. The camera is ready and I have to admit, I am a little tense after all those warnings!

Just a little history for you, because it is so interesting. Pikes Peak was named after Lt. Zebulon Montgomery Pike, who arrived at the peak in November of 1806. Pike was an early explorer (later General Pike); however, he and his men were scarcely dressed to take on the fearsome snow and bad weather, in order to reach the summit. In the early 1800s, Pike's Peak served as a beacon for wagons racing to the west in search of gold. In 1873 the US Army Signal Corps built a weather station on the summit, manned year round until 1889 by a lone enlisted man, who is replaced periodically after a short tour of duty.

The sun is just a-shinin' and everything is going smoothly. We are simply enjoying the ride and the mountain. If you cut the mountain into thirds, the first part is where you might see deer, elk, porcupine, or the occasional mountain lion or black bear. And of course, a wide variety of birds. We reach mile marker 1 on a big curve and this is the beginning of the montane zone, which means we are around 8,000 feet up already. And you can tell, because it is getting a little cooler. Mile marker 2 is a camera point, which we always take advantage of. It is interesting to look down on the roads you just traveled a few minutes ago. At 3 miles, we pass picnic areas, and at 4, we are able to pull over again to take pictures. Here we take pictures of a huge thick square rock sitting atop another larger square rock, that gives the appearance of a huge pillow sitting on a huge mattress. Only in my mind, I'm sure. It is named Valentine Rock. Well, there you go, get it? Pillow, mattress, Valentine...I got a great shot of it though.

This is steep and rough terrain and yet so dramatic and captivating. The curves are sharper and I'm wondering what has happened to the guard rails. Oh boy, I think we are in for a ride for sure. I know one thing, I don't think I could do this in fog or snow, or rain, for that matter. Although they are good at keeping the roads clear; can't move the fog out of the way! Mile marker 6 is the Crystal Creek Reservoir. It is a very peaceful and serene area. You can fish or go non-motor boating here, too. This reservoir is one of three that are part of the North Slope. We will pass the other two, North and South Catamount reservoirs at mm 7.

Okay, where did our paved roads go? And now we no longer have guard rails either, but we are driving on pretty brown packed dirt. Well, there are two humongous boulders on the edge, if we aim right, I'm sure they would keep us from going over. The scenery in the distance is incredible and I guess a fair trade for any fear I feel right now. There is snow on the peaks and the sky is so endless and blue, with great big white fluffy clouds.

Looks like road ends and we will go off

I am seriously looking for the end of the road here, because it appears we are going to drive right off the end around this next curve. We are really climbing and the curves are increasingly sharper. Mona is even more determined to continue this movie. And I am pushing a hole in the floor where there should be a brake. Russ is very quiet as I cringe and continue to push like I am in labor. "Oooh, Russ, go slow," I say through clenched teeth and notice he is gripping the steering wheel very tight, making his knuckles white. Oh, now this curve coming up has a guard rail and I give a sigh of relief as I convince myself it's going to be okay. Don't forget a half million people do this every year, right!

We are passing mile marker 8, on to 9, and this is the part of the drive (the second third of the mountain), where you will see chipmunks, snowshoe hares, pine squirrels, woodpeckers, and other birds. It is called the Sub Alpine Zone and we are about at the halfway mark to the summit. There is another picnic area here called Halfway Picnic Grounds, so we pulled over and took a picture of the hairpin turn we just drove up. Looking up and out is another view there just are no words for, which will really put me at a handicap here; that is if I want to continue to write. We see a lot of snow on the mountains, which happens as you climb higher, but that also means it is getting cooler.

Mile markers 10, 11, and 12 are just one curve after the next and every single one makes you feel like there is no road at the end. It feels like you will drive right off the mountain, so it certainly is not a boring ride. Guard rails are few and far between, like, would they really keep you from going over anyway? But the road is paved here. Some of the curves are complete you-ees and some are complete circles. But both of us are like zombies and neither one of us are taking our eyes off the road. The road directional signs almost make you want to laugh, because they are complete you-ee arrows with 10 mph under them. I really don't think you can even do 10; it is almost impossible! Between mile markers 12 and 13, we have reached the Alpine Zone, the last third of the mountain, and we come upon the Glen Cove Inn. To get to mm 14, you go in a circle almost to the reverse direction to mile marker 13, only with a huge gap in between. Whew! After a few more sharp curves, we reach another pull out, called Elk Park and we are now at the tree line. Though the typical summer day may mean warm weather at the base of the mountain, its likely 30 degrees cooler on the summit. Glad we have our sweaters in the car. Thunderstorms are another issue. They can pop up at any time in the front range of the Rockies. If that happens, it is always safer to stay in the vehicle.

In some places, the snow is right to the edge of the road. And on the right side, it has been plowed to heights of four to five feet high; then two feet and then five again. After a few more curves, we come to a great big curve that appears we are just going to sail right off into those big clouds ahead. The next curve there is another vehicle coming toward us, and I swear that car looks like it is coming in on air, like a plane skidding in. I'm just glad he is staying in his own lane. That turn had a guard rail at its very roundest part on the outer edge.

This is very steep, the air is crisp, it feels dangerous and now the speed limit is 5 then 10 then 15 and 5 again. Some of the few overlooks are overgrown by trees, but the overlook while driving is phenomenal. That is, for the couple of seconds you are brave enough to take your eyes off the road. As we round the edges (no pun intended), between mile markers 15 and 16, I'm wondering how much more of this can we take? At mm 16, I see a sign that says Devil's Playground! Well, no wonder this part is scary. We are at 13,000 feet now and nearing the summit.

Well, no pavement, no guard rails and just plain dirt with no line separations for a road, when out of nowhere, several vintage cars come towards us flying flags and waving their arms. Somewhere around 16 different cars; mostly Nash Metropolitans, an old convertible and who knows what else. I heard they have races up here every year called Pikes Peak International Hill Climb. I am ready to be at the top, when we see warning signs of flagmen ahead. Right then, a marmot runs in front of the car. He looks like a very large rat to me, except his tail is a little fluffier. But no, I think maybe it is more like a very large squirrel.

We have come upon our foretold flagman, and the back hoe, I kid you not, it is right on the very edge of the curve ahead! I hope they pay him well! *Scary!* I can't even imagine. Just sitting here and waiting on this ledge is scary enough and to that Russ replies "Yeah, Buddy!" Finally, as we move on, we approach mile marker 19, which is taped all around with duct tape???? We pull up and Russ hops out, ready with his camera and heads to the edge. And me, I am trying to get my wobbly legs to move. "Move legs!" All I want to do is find the rest room. After I became steady, I found the gift shop and as I walked into the bathroom there was a lady in there who was in charge of the care of the restroom, I guess. She said, "Are you all right?" I said, "Fine, how are you?" And she said, "Well, I was just wondering because you look kind of pale." And I'm thinking, oh, great, all I need to do is pass out in the bathroom. I can just see it, squatting forward and either landing on my head or doing a summersault right out the door! And on top of that, Russ is out there on a big photo shoot, completely oblivious that I haven't returned yet! I got out of there as quick as I could and I know that lady put some kind of voo-doo curse on me, 'cause by the time I found Russ, I had a splitting headache and I think my eyes were trying to cross. I really didn't feel very well. That is the moment I learned about altitude sickness, also known as mountain sickness. You're just not getting enough air. Symptoms are headache, which gets worse, loss of appetite, trouble sleeping, nausea, weak and tired, and dizziness. Neither your fitness level nor being male or female plays a role. It can be dangerous and it can affect your lungs and brain. When this happens, you can become confused, can't walk straight, feel faint, have blue coloring to the lips and fingernails. If you hear a sound like a paper bag crumpling when you breathe call 911. It can be deadly. So the best thing to do to keep all this from happening, as soon as you start feeling weird or have a headache, is to *go down* the mountain.

We knew we needed to get down, but I'm glad Russ had taken so many neat pictures of the cog railway that had just dropped off a train full of excited passengers, oozing out of the bright-red train. I found this to be a very interesting rail, because I had never heard of a cog railroad before. I just had to research it. The rails are raised to allow clearance for the spur gears which guide the locomotive. Located in the middle of the track are what they call a "cog rack." The track is designed specifically for the unique cog engines. The cogs engage into the rack through a system of gears. It's like teeth on the wheel that lock into similar teeth on the track. The cog rack railroad can climb grades up to 48 percent, depending on the type of rack system it has. Most can go no faster than 15 mph, or they run the risk of dislodgement from the rail. The top speed at Pikes Peak is about 9 mph. They use a double cog track. It takes about 3 hours to reach the summit on an 8.9 miles of track. I have to say, my opinion of course, that ride looks almost as scary as driving up, they are right on the edge the whole time. They are open year round now, so you can experience the train all four seasons.

Russ got so many phenomenal shots of the mountains special offerings. Unforgiving landscape for as far as you can see, no wonder "America the Beautiful" was created here. Colorado has 53 moun-tains 14,000 feet and higher. They fondly refer to them as the fourteeners. And my last fact for you is, these roads will be completely paved in the year 2011.

At the top of the peak, the partial pressure of oxygen is only about 60 percent of what it would be at sea level, so a faster rate of respiration is required by those not regularly at high altitudes. It is said that you can see 4 different states from up here.

Pikes peak Are you kidding me!

There is a great big sign that says, "Summit Pikes Peak—14,110 ft.—Pike National Forest." We made it! So down we go and of course, we are now back to our friendly flagman. The backhoe is now in the very center of the very narrow dirt road, which leaves very little room on either side of him. The flagman puts his hand out for us to stop. We had to wait a pretty good while this time. Soon we are motioned to go around the backhoe on the outer edge of this very narrow curve. *Is he kidding?* I said, "Russ, don't you dare! No way are we doing that," and we didn't either. As we sit there staring back at them, both of our heads nodding back and forth simultaneously, refusing to acknowledge any connection with "drive around stupid!" Waving hands frantically, the flagman finally got the message and moved that backhoe in so we could pass. We did a lot of stupid things on this trip, but I don't have it written on my forehead yet!

Anyway, our descent was uneventful as we navigated our way around the challenging curves. For some reason, the pictures were easier to take as we twisted around and down the peak, we could see them better in the down position somehow. On one of the trails, there is a sign that reads "Big Foot Crossing…due to sightings in the area of a creature resembling Big Foot this sign has been posted for your safety." Love it! My son Tracey would love it, too. I think he really believes there is a real Big Foot! Do you think that sign is for real?

My phone rang and it was Troy wondering where we were wandering. We were still about 10 miles from the exit and he wanted us to meet him and his family in Royal Gorge. He had a few acres in the vicinity, so he wanted us to come see it first. He said he was waiting for us in Royal Gorge at Wal-Mart, well, I felt bad because 10 miles away coming down a spiraling mountain, can take a lot longer than ten minutes. Plus, the time it will take to go from the exit to the Wal-Mart.

Nice that it wasn't too far, but once we caught up to him, we followed him to an RV Park so he could get some propane gas for his grill and some water. Talk about a bumpy road and hilly ride…no, I don't think one could even call it a road; it's more like a wide dirt path. Troy had a little camper there and they brought hot dogs and brats with them. We had a great visit just being together and sharing our latest adventures and thrilling ride, taking pictures and just kidding around. And of course, feeding our faces on the wonderful dogs and brats he cooked on his little grill.

As the sun began to set, it looked like it was going to rain, so we decided to pack it in. We made plans to meet with the kids at Royal Gorge Bridge and Park in the morning. It was a truly spooky ride on the way out of his land, because it was pitch-black. I don't know how Russ ever did it, but he managed to get us out of there.

Oh, boy, this is going to be so much fun tomorrow. This will be one of our spontaneous side trips. Yippee, can't wait!

CHAPTER 16

Spontaneous and Done

Today is June 28th, Saturday, and we are away from home for two whole months. I'd like to say here, that we stopped and got gas and it was $3.89/gal. Remember, this is 2008, and I do realize we are in a tourist area; however, it is nowhere near that much now.

Troy and family met us at Royal George near the train station, next to a sort of beach and the kids were making sand castles. So "Grampy" (Russ) got his rod out of the car and Troy and he fished for a short while. Russ caught a brown trout.

Then we hit the gift shops and of course, I got post cards and magnets! Just behind the Visitor Center there is a huge "water clock", also known in Greek as a depsydra. Water transfers from bucket to bucket and gives you the exact time you start your journey to the bridge. The original clock was destroyed by a fire 30 years ago, and this one was lucky to survive the fire of 2013. It is the only water clock in Colorado and one of three that exists in the world. Very interesting.

Oh, boy, we see a carousel and every one of us hopped on. Russ taking pictures the whole time, all of us laughing waving, and having fun. And me feeling like a kid again. So fun, haven't done that in a long time.

It cost $42.00 to enter the park. The gondola and children's rides are included in the ticket. Once we arrived at the entrance of the bridge, it completely took my breath away! Oh, my goodness, the immensity of the bridge, the height and the rushing water is stunning; but the wind! The intensity of the wind makes me feel like it is going to blow me away…far away! One thousand feet above the mad Arkansas River and almost ¼ mile long from mountain edge to mountain edge. It sure does look like more than a quarter mile long to me. Many people are driving across and many taking a little ride over provided by the park. There are flags about every fourth cable, flapping fiercely and the wind is furious and howling around 40 to 50 mph. I hesitated for a while, when I felt my daughter-in-law at one side of me. She took my hand and my son took the other. So hand in hand and feeling the security of the world now, off we go. I can feel the bridge vibrating under my feet as I intensely march onward, very carefully and aware of all sounds and people around me. But I apparently wasn't aware of where my husband was, because I heard Troy and Karen snickering. I realized they were getting a kick out of Russ, who was on the edge of the bridge filming the river and seemed to be in his own little world. He was backing up, not even aware the bridge was not his alone, and traffic was just sitting there waiting for him to move. The kids tried yelling at him, but with all the noise of the wind and commotion of the tourists, he couldn't hear a thing. Soon, we all landed safely on the other side (not too soon for me)!

Royal Gorge is North America's highest suspension bridge. It was originally built in 1929 with no serious injuries or death. It cost $350,000 to build, but today that cost would probably exceed twenty million. It is 1,260 feet in length, 18 feet wide and the towers are 150 feet high. 2,100 strands of #9 galvanized wires are in the cables. The cables weigh 300 tons alone. There is 1,000 tons of steel on the floor of the bridge. The bridge will support in excess of 2 million pounds.

As we near the end of the bridge, we can see two people on a giant swing. Actually this is a ride they call, the Royal Rush Skycoaster. Oh, my! Only for the young! This ride, 1,200 feet over the Arkansas River, is a free fall sweep at 50 mph! It is rated the scariest of rides by Skycoaster, Inc. Depending on the weather, of course. It is available to you from March 12 to September 30 at an extra cost. Did you even know such a ride existed in Colorado? Breathtaking even to watch for a minute, listening to their screams from below.

We have ended our trek across this masterpiece of a bridge and an amazing sight appears of the Sangre de Christo Mountains. The scenery is definitely worth the walk, to be encompassed in such a profusion of color. Beige and orange and pink-tinted rugged peaks, staring back at us in its rustic splendor. They are splashed with colors of green trees and blue skies and as a backdrop, misty mountains in the distance. The tiny river below, looks like a small snake, winding through the walls of the canyon. The blue sky feels like we are actually walking in on it from high above. Thrilling! Even the smell of the fresh mountain air and people's voices and shouts of glee, mingled in with the breath of the high winds.

We come to a small replica of the railway and the smallest in our crowd squeals with delight, as the girls help our little passenger aboard. He (Anthony) is having a great time waving and posing for the camera. There is a little stand close by selling funnel cakes and such. Oh my goodness, we absolutely had to stop and get a funnel cake. Russ just loves them. He used to get them in Pennsylvania when he was a kid. Next, we spy a few ponies just waiting for our little one to come take a ride. Troy lifts him on board and he and the girls lead him around the ring for a little while, on a little pony named, Rocky. He is one happy little cowpokes! Now wait a minute, I'm having trouble deciding who is the happiest here; Troy or Anthony 'cause Troy is sporting as big a smile as the little guy!

Our map they gave us when we entered the park, shows us there is a little petting zoo not far away, so we hopped on a tram nearby and found goats, sheep, llamas, and burros. There are a few tiny kids we are allowed to pet, they are just adorable. Just passed that, is a Wildlife Park, where there are buffalo or bison (tetonka), elk, and reindeer in a huge gated area. Some of the bison are just laying around like a large pet and the elk are wandering aimlessly about. Sad to see them behind fences though. But the size of their racks are out of this world. You'd think they'd have a big and forever endless headache. But they impressed us.

Every now and then, we hear screams coming from the Skycoaster. Can't help but look up and smile. (Hmmm, glad it's not me!) And then when you look down, you see the angry Arkansas

River, all white and foamy on the top and train tracks winding close to the sides of the canyon.

The bison and elk are molting from the hotter weather and they look like someone having a bad hair day. They are huge and hot, I'm sure. Well, now it seems we need to cross back over the bridge, this time via the tram, for another ride called the Incline Railway. This is the world's steepest incline railway, featuring a 45-degree angled and closed in structure, which you stand up in as it descends over 1,500 feet to the canyon floor. That means a third of a mile from the rim of the canyon to the edge of the Arkansas River. Pure granite walls are on each side of you as you descend, but as I watched it (for some time) and checked it out (very carefully), I decided it didn't go too fast and thought I could probably handle it. And besides, we wanted to get down to the bottom of the walls by the River and see what we could see. There are 30 passenger cars in all, painted a bright red. The cage closes around you and there is a bar to hold on to, as you watch the rushing river come closer and closer toward you.

I notice they have bird feeders hanging everywhere for the hummingbirds and they are just full of the most beautifully fluorescent multicolored birds. It is a joy to stand and watch them flit in and out and all around. I never realized before now, they make this tiny cheep as they whiz passed you. They are such amazing little creatures.

From the ledge of the canyon, as we wait in a short line for our turn, we can watch the Aerial Gondolas going over to the other side of the canyon. It is considered the world's highest aerial gondola and the world's longest single-span aerial tram. It glides more than 1,100 feet above the Arkansas River, with the most scenic 360-degree view of the whole entire area. Each gondola holds up to 8 people, with a total of 6 cars going back and forth at one time. This ride is handicap assessable. This is one of the structures that was destroyed by a huge fire in 2013, after we were there. It has since been replaced of course, along with 20 other structures.

They also have a zip line which is 1,200 feet up as well. I think someone doesn't have enough to do, so they sit around and think of how many different ways they can scare you half to death. The zip line has bucket-like seats (no hands)! This ride is extra cost.

There is certainly no problem waiting for our turn, because there is so much to watch and see from this point of the cliffs. The birds, the skycoaster, and helicopters that are flying frequently over us. At last, it is our turn and I wasn't even nervous. It looks to be a very tame ride.

Well, that was a fun new adventure and we are at the bottom of the canyon now. Everything is so loud with the rushing river in front of us. We are facing canyon walls, separated by the powerful Arkansas River, white with froth and fury. Suddenly, we see kayaks, three in all, one of them upside down. Oh my gosh, we can't tell if its occupant is upside down inside it or if he has freed himself and coming around the bend. They are rushing passed so fast, the other two men seem to be frantically looking for their friend. All at once, he appears from nowhere and is clinging to one of the huge jagged rocks on the edge of the bank. His buddies get hold of him and his kayak and off they go out of sight. That would simply terrify me. But all is well that ends well.

We can see smoke in the far distance and we notice more helicopters are busily flying over with enormous buckets of water. Something else we have never witnessed. Now we are curious about that. We will have to keep an eye out.

The train and tracks are easier to see down here and how it wraps itself around the gorge. It is called the Royal Gorge Railroad, Colorado's oldest scenic railroad. Not only can you ride the train through the stunning scenery of the Gorge, but you can also dine, as you watch the treasures unfold in front of you. There is a whole assortment of entertainment on the ride, even if you have children aboard.

There are just a few more things I'd like to mention. There is a play land for children with ropes, nets, bridges, slides, and a cute little carousel that has horses to climb on and a three-story play land. Also an attached maze. Included, is a splash pad with water features; seasonal, of course. This is all sitting on a beautiful grass lawn, to jump and run and roll on, with tunnels to climb through. A child's little dream land. It includes a picnic area, too. And I don't want to forget to tell you there are Kennels available for your pet. All you could possibly ask for.

There are 2 or 3 restaurants in the park; we visited the Cliff Side Patio. For history buffs, there is a Plaza Theater and history expo, which includes history of the bridge and the men who envisioned and built it. Colorado history, history of the Royal Gorge Rail Road War and many, many more fun facts, drama and scenery surrounding the park, all are part of the presentation. And for a surprise, there is a magician here in peak season.

To finalize this chapter, I just can't quit until I tell you about the dangers of parks, as I always do. Just be careful of cliffs! Yes, we become comfortable in our surroundings and forget to be cautious. I only write about these things to caution you and make you aware of your surroundings. Can't stress enough: *be careful!*

Some friends of mine just recently went out west and did a similar vacation as ours. But when they got to Royale Gorge, it was closed. They were shocked by this and asked around in their travels and found there was a death in the park. It is unfortunate and heartbreaking to even write about this, but with a little research, I came up with a very distressing story.

A 28 year old conductor fell off the train and was run over while it was backing up. She met her husband there on this very same train in 2008, which is the year we were there. She fell in love with him and the train and went to conductor schooling. So sad for her family.

In addition, there were 4 rafting deaths in 2014. In July of 2015, a woman fell 400 feet to her death from an observation deck over the canyon. In the same year, a woman fell to her death after a marriage proposal. She was just proposed to, started jumping up and down, and lost her balance and fell off the cliff. In 2012, three separate incidents occurred, two in March and one in May, where people jumped to their death off the bridge. It is said the average number of suicides in the previous 12 years is about one a year.

In June 2013, most of the parks' structures on both sides of the gorge were devastated by a man-made fire. The fire jumped from the south to the north side of the gorge, just west of the bridge and burned 3,218 acres, of which 2,156 acres was park property. The bridge itself sustained minimal damage; however, 48 of the parks' 52 buildings were destroyed. I am glad to report that no people or animals were injured or killed by the fire. It took a little more than a year for repairs.

So there you have it. We ended our day with dinner with the kids, at a Chinese buffet and that put an end to our visit with our son and family. It is always sad to leave them.

It is Sunday and this will be a driving day, pointing dear Mona's nose south on Route 25 toward New Mexico, so we can return home through the southern states this time. We entered New Mexico around 5:00 p.m. It seems like their mountains are small in comparison to where we have been and most of them have flat tops. We managed to get as far as Tucumcari, New Mexico, where we rounded the Tucumcari Mountain, just west of Texas. It's been a long driving day, so we got a motel for the night.

After breakfast, which we got at the motel, we fed Mona and ventured on toward Texas, where we arrived at 11:49, but we lost an hour due to time changes. It's a beautiful bright day with a temperature of 68 degrees. Turning over to Route 40, we got to Oklahoma, ate lunch, and for the life of me, I don't know why, but we decided to go to the Oklahoma City National Memorial and Museum. Oklahoma City is almost in the center of the state. By now it is 5:30 p.m., so we are too late to make it to the museum, which is a chronological self-guided, interactive tour, through the story of the bombing. But we were able to visit and tour the outdoor memorial, since it was still open to the public.

It all started when Timothy McVeigh parked a Ryder rental truck, filled with explosives in front of the Alfred P. Murrah Building. One hundred and sixty-eight people were killed here that day, including nineteen children, and it destroyed the north face of the building

It is incredibly peaceful here. We certainly didn't expect to see such a serene, beautiful and unique memorial. It was easy to see that intensive and intricate planning went into this dramatic achievement. This memorial stands to honor the victims, survivors, rescuers, and all who were affected by the Oklahoma City bombing on April

19, 1995. It encompasses the ground in which the Murrah Building once stood.

Placed here is a large long pool of water, called the Reflecting Pool, where NW 5th Street once was. Here, at shallow depth, there is gently flowing water over polished black granite, with soothing sounds. At the foot of the pool on both ends, stand twin bronze gates. They are called, "the gates of time." The eastern gate is engraved with large numbers "9:01," which represents the time of innocent life before the attack, and on the western gate "9:03," the first moment of recovery and lives changed forever. And "9:02" was the actual time of attack. The outside of each gate bears this inscription: "We come here to remember, Those who were killed, those who survived and those changed forever. May all who leave here know the impact of violence. May this memorial offer comfort, strength, peace, hope and serenity."

On one side of the reflecting pool, there is a striking field of green grass that is called the "field of empty chairs." One hundred sixty-eight chairs to be exact, one for each life lost. They stand there in place of tombstones, eerie and silent. They are in perfect rows, the smaller chairs representing the nineteen children killed in the attack. Three unborn children died along with their mothers that fatal day.

The chairs sit evenly in 9 rows, representing each floor of the building on which the person worked, or was located when the bomb went off. The chairs are also grouped according to the blast pattern, with the most chairs nearest the most heavily damaged portion of the building. The western most column of 5 chairs represent people not in the building. Each bronze and stone chair sits on a glass square base, and each base is etched with the victims' name. The chairs represent the empty chairs at the dinner table of the victims' families. The base of each chair is translucent and illuminates like a beacon. The whole field is lined with granite salvaged from the Murrah Plaza.

There is a huge wall, which is the only remaining original portion of the Murrah Building; the north and east walls, called the Survivors Wall. It includes several panels of granite, salvaged from the building itself and is inscribed with the names of more than 600 survivors from the building and surrounding areas, many of whom were injured in the blast.

At the north end of the memorial stands a more than 100 year-old American elm, now called the Survivor Tree. It has become an emblem of the memorial. Workers recovered evidence hanging in its branches and embedded in its bark. The force of the blast ripped most if its branches off, glass and debris were embedded in its trunk and fire from the cars parked beneath it blackened the rest. But almost a year later, it began to bloom again and now thrives. It is surely a witness to the violent tragedy. The inscription around the inside of the deck wall around the Survivor Tree reads "The Spirit of this city and this nation will not be defeated; our deeply rooted faith sustains us." There is a black walkway leading to the tree.

Around the tree, there is a groove of redbuds (Oklahoma's state tree), and many other trees planted on the lawn around the tree. This is named the Rescuers Orchard. Like the people who rushed in to help, this army of trees represent the many rescuers who came to the aide of the survivors, they protect the Survivor Tree. The non-native trees represent the rescuers who came from outside Oklahoma to help.

On the opposite side of he chairs and pool, is a large and deep inline, like stairs where you can look down upon this awesome, extraordinary and beautifully planned place, that is like no other.

Across the street from the Murrah Building, two churches sit as testimony to this disaster. Both of them were heavily damaged by this horrible blast. One church sits across from the 9:01 gate and one across from the 9:03 gate. One church called, The Heartland Chapel and one, And Jesus Wept. I'm thinking how appropriate! At the last church mentioned, a sculpture was erected of Jesus with His back to the destruction and His Hand over His Face. His Head is bent in despair. In front of Jesus is a wall with 168 gaps in it, representing the voids left by each life lost.

And in case you don't remember, Timothy McVeigh, the American terrorist, was convicted and executed on June 11, 2001, by lethal injection. This was the deadliest act of terrorism within the United States prior to 9-11 and remains the most significant act of domestic terrorism in US history. And that is all I am going to say about him.

We are both feeling quite somber now, as the day is almost ended. We are still on Route 40 east. We decided to take a different way home than the way we came, so we got onto the Indian Nation Turnpike, which takes an abrupt turn to the south; the toll was $1.75. It is now up to $5.50, but I guess that is if you drive the full 105.7 miles, but we did drive about 80 percent of it, got off at Antlers, and continued east again toward Arkansas. This is the longest toll-way in the state. The only dining option along the entire turnpike is McDonald's. Law enforcement along this turnpike is provided by Oklahoma Highway Patrol XC, a special troop assigned to the turnpike. When we exited, Russ asked the toll lady where the money for the tolls went, to Oklahoma or the Indians and she said "to Oklahoma." Of course, I had to research that and found out a good bit of interesting information. First of all, Oklahoma has 10 turnpikes, more than 6,000 miles of pavement, which makes the state second in the nation for miles of toll roads. The state does not make a penny on their toll roads. Apparently, bondholders are profiting off the tolls and from what I read, not everyone is happy about that.

We are crossing many bridges over little dried-up creeks. New Mexico seemed very dry as well. We will call it a night, and we will be doing a lot of driving tomorrow.

It is Tuesday, July 1st, and we have driven a good while. In fact, it is 3:30 p.m. already. We found a place called Buddy's Ranch and stopped to eat there simply because all the grandkids call me Buddy. Of course, I had to buy a shirt, 'cause it had my name on it! We found a pamphlet at the restaurant about a place called, Crater of Diamonds State Park in Murfreesboro, Arkansas. We got all excited and had visions of what we needed to do or buy. This park is a 37½ acres plowed field of wide open spaces. The world's eighth largest in surface area. They say a unique geological occurrence brings diamonds to the surface in their natural matrix. It is said to be a world famous site and the only diamond area in North America open to the public. So of course, we are hyped up, especially since they say an average of 600 diamonds are found here each year! And there are other precious stones found there as well, such as amethyst, agate, jasper, quartz, calcite, and barite. We were raring to go, so we found a Dollar General to purchase a couple cheap shirts, and gloves. So we get all our gear and get ready to get some shovels and buckets and go out to the field, which is wide open dirt and sun and hotter than Hades. We stand there a minute and look over the situation, then we look at each other, read each other's minds and said "Heck no, it must be 98 degrees out here!" We turned around and watched people walking to their cars that looked like they were regulars here, because they had buckets on their shoulders and all kinds of gear. We hopped into our air-conditioned Mona and went back to the hotel. And that was that!

The grass here in Arkansas is so strikingly green. Well, we have no cell service here. Today we will continue south and hit the corner of Texas through Texarkana, back into Arkansas where we see sheep, buffalo with calves, donkeys, and brown long-necked birds. Then we drove down to Shreveport, Louisiana, went east on Route 20 and stopped for the night in a town called Ruston which is halfway through the northern part of Louisiana. That was fun, hitting all those states in one day. My goodness, we are seeing a lot of armadillo, all roadkill though. Russ said there are quite a few chicken and cattle farmers here. We are on the most beautiful road. These back roads always give up breath-taking surprises.

Today, we will continue east on Route 20 into Mississippi and over the drastically, still overflowing Mississippi River. We stopped and took pictures of the beautiful bridges. The main bridge is The Vicksburg Bridge and the one parallel to it is the Old Vicksburg Bridge. I understand that the bridge is struck by barges repeatedly. Suddenly, I realized I didn't have a magnet from Louisiana! Don't you know, my sweet hubby turned back around and drove back over the bridge and we went to about five different gas stations before I found one. He is an amazing guy for sure!

We continued across the state of Mississippi on Interstate 20 and decided we would probably stop in Birmingham, Alabama, but once we arrived in Birmingham my dispatcher husband said, "Oh, what the heck, our drivers make it from here to Marietta in three hours"; so we might as well go for it. And we did! Plus, it sure made a whole lot more sense to put the air conditioner on at home in the night hours, instead of the hot day hours. Indeed, the house was very hot, but the air conditioner took care of it in no time. We got home about 11:30 p.m. It was a very long day.

It is July 3rd and it is so good to be home. We went to the bank, took care of errands, turned in our left over travelers checks, and went to the post office, which of course, had a very long line. I had to laugh, because Russ had to carry a big ole plastic crate chock full of mail. Then, we went to my sister's house and took her out to dinner. After all, she kept an eye on our house and watered our plants all that time. And she made us some welcome-home cupcakes, too. Tomorrow is the 4th and we will celebrate with friends and family. What a wonderful life we have. God is so good!

CHAPTER 17

Food, Gas, Potties, and Lodging

Well, how else should I put it! We went to many great restaurants on this trip, and I can honestly say there wasn't one we didn't enjoy. There were only two negative incidents. The first, was at the lodge in Washington called the Paradise Inn. By the time we got there and got registered, the diner was closed. We were at the top of Mount Rainier with nowhere else to go, and they wouldn't even offer us a sandwich. You may recall the incident, but we had all kinds of snacks in our car and resorted to those. And the second, was when we ate at Buddy's, and I found a piece of cellophane in my coleslaw. I assumed it was part of the packaging. I tried not to complain, but we did mention it and we got a free dessert. Otherwise, we enjoyed all our meals. I think my favorite was the time we were on our way to Alaska and we were lodged by Princess at the Cook Hotel. We had no idea where to go, so we started walking block by block and found a hole in the wall called, The Brewery House. By this time, we were desperate and tired and could walk no more. This is where we had the best meal ever. I usually don't choose pork chops, but I wasn't familiar with many other offers on the menu. They were better than any I ever had. Pike's Landing in Alaska was fun! We wound up being there on Mother's Day, for which they had a huge buffet. It cost a hefty price of $44.00 but was worth every single penny of it. I have to mention a place we stopped at in Rocky Mountain National Park, near Estes Park called, Hunter's Hop. Russ had barbecue ribs and I got hooked on those pork chops. Their food was absolutely delish, amid the most awesome scenery. In fact, we went back and ate there again on the second night. We chose Denny's a lot, several treats at Dairy Queen and lots of coffee at Mickey D's!

What I mean by gas…uh huh, is the food we fed Mona! Gas was cheap in some places and not so cheap in others. Of course, it stands to reason that the times it wasn't so cheap were mostly near the national parks. In Colorado, gas was only $3.56, in Fairbanks, Alaska $3.94; but when we got to Yosemite in California, it soared to $5.10. Shell stations were generally always the highest, but I gotta tell ya my most favorite station was when we stopped in Oregon. Gas was $4.09 as we traveled toward Crater Lake and this was the place where they "require" the attendant to pump the gas for you. You remember…I had such a good time laughing like a fool at Russ, as he wrestled with the attendant over the hose. I have to chuckle even now.

Potties provoked the same wonder and overwhelming smell of gases as Yellowstone. I have to say Shell gas stations out west (specifically Oregon) are the worst, if you must go (potty, that is). The two and only times we stopped at Shell's; all they had were porta-potties. One in particular was on a hillside and so were the potties. I was so sure I was going to find myself in a mess rolling down that hill, quickest stop we made to date. At Arches, after our hike, we stood in a long line so we could use a hole. made to look like a potty, because there was some kind of old brick lining the hole in the ground. Good thing I still had some balance and tissue in my purse! Some potties were little tiny brick outhouses, some had no tissue, some had tissue you could hardly get off the roll, because it was so thin it would tear in tiny increments, which took a while until you could get enough. And if there is no tissue at all…"Ah hem…ma'am, ummm, in the next stall…would you mind passing some tissue under the partition?" Oh, how embarrassing. But if you are all alone and there is no tissue, well, maybe…just maybe, you can dodge to the one next to you while your pants are wrapped around your knees, and pray no one comes in right at that moment.

Sometimes they furnished the paper seat cover, but I learned there is definitely a technique to getting those out of the containers.

And then once you do, you have to try and figure out where that little piece goes that hangs down. In the front or the back? And do they always have to tear in half? Of course, once you figure all that out, technique comes in when you try to sit on it before it falls into the commode…like it knows right when to dive in. Some places even have soap and some don't. Thank goodness, Mona always carried our hand sanitizer for us.

And those paper towel dispensers! Usually empty, or you stand there and wave at it and nothing wants to come down. Oh, and the hand dryers. They go from none, causing you to wipe your hands on your own clothing, to broken dryers; and then there are these new dryers that practically blow the skin right off your hands and you can see every vessel, as the skin slides in another direction. Oh, they also have a new kind that you slowly put both hands in like you are dipping them in for a manicure. Wait, did I just come up with a new invention? Some potties had an attendant waiting to service you and some needed attendance so you could get service.

We stayed at all kinds of motels. Most with air-conditioning; and some with none. Some had the essential bathroom and a vanity and some had no vanity at all. In some, the vanity and bathroom were divided. Most lodges didn't have the essentials like hair dryers, exhaust fans in the bathroom, bags for dirty clothes, and some of the lodges had very poor lighting and no telephones or cell phone access. One of the lodges, I remember, had such a small bathroom with such a small mirror over the sink, I could hardly get my arms up to fix my hair. Nope, no TVs either. Better check on air-conditioning if you go in the summer months, because most don't have that either (out west I mean). Most of the lodges, I noticed, are fairly old, remodeled nicely, but old, and have wooden creaky floors. Their lobbies are gorgeous and huge, with fireplaces and piano entertainment and beautiful relaxing chairs, flowers and huge picture windows, big tables to play cards or board games. Or you can just sit around and socialize. But the lodges do cost so much more, you would expect more in the guestroom department. Some of the lodges serve expensive breakfasts in nice big dining rooms. I am definitely not trying to put down lodges, but if one is not expecting it, it sure can be a culture shock. Like me, for instance. I had never had that privilege before.

Some shower spouts are only for very short people. My husband had to stoop way down to wash his hair and upper torso. Some showers are really tricky, intended for rocket scientists only. It's hard to figure out how to even turn them on. That's always fun when you're standing there cold in your birthday suit. Some actually charge extra for a bathtub, if you are the type that likes to soak. Most motels give sample size shampoos, hair conditioners, hand lotions, makeup remover, bags for dirty clothing, local TV programming with movie channels, Wi-Fi, shower caps, ironing boards and irons, little pads to write on and pens, even lots of info on local restaurants and entertainment and info about the town you are in, and places to see in the area, maps, and postcards. Some have luggage racks to lay your luggage on and racks to carry it in and out. Some have rocking chairs on their outdoor pretty porches. Some have elevators; some don't and some have separate rooms that supposedly have never been smoked in or had pets in. And some have lighting over the beds, you can turn your own on to read while your partner sleeps and some don't. Some offer enough plugs that you can charge your cameras and cells, and yes you got it…some don't. Hubby can't even plug in his razor to shave.

When it is particularly late and very dark and you stop, only to wake up and realize you are next to a truck stop! Watch out for that, we did it a couple of times…very noisy. Some motels give senior discounts, and nowadays; some have Bibles and most don't. And many will try to meet your needs if Bibles are not handy at the time, simply for the asking.

But all in all, it was a most excellent adventure. Most people are good, friendly, and helpful. And most of all…*home* is always sweet home.

CHAPTER 18
The Final Chapter

The talk of our big trip was in the air. Just before time to pack and making arrangements for our trip to Alaska, Russ told me his wrist was hurting. I thought maybe he twisted it or he had carpal tunnel. Hmmm, so I asked him if he would like to make an appointment with our doctor before the trip. The words that came out of his mouth next, I believe, came directly from God. He said, "No, I think I will wait until we get back and then I will go." Of course, I reminded him we would be gone at least two weeks, was he sure he wanted to be uncomfortable that long. He said no, he'd wait. Little did we know we would be gone over two months!

At any rate, he never complained once of his wrist while we were gone, but then he rarely complained of his physical status ever, and what an amazing trip it was! But he did keep his promise to me and saw a doctor as soon as we got home, and within two weeks, we had an appointment. We saw our primary physician who took an x-ray and could not see anything abnormal, but she quickly referred him to a neurologist, which I thought was unusual. A few weeks later, we saw the neurologist who ordered several tests that I knew could not be good. And they weren't. We had to wait through Labor day week for delayed results because of the holiday.

I knew the doctor, since I worked at the hospital, and it was with a heavy heart he had to deliver the results to us. Russ was diagnosed with ALS, commonly known as Lou Gehrig's disease. Anything the doctor said to us after that seemed to come out of his mouth in slow motion. We both sat there gaping at the doctor, tears streaming down my cheeks, and Russ just sat there speechless; the last words I heard were, "I am so terribly sorry." I don't even remember getting up and leaving his office.

It is not my goal to sit here and write about this horrible, debilitating and fatal disease. But I will say the next three years of our lives would be changed indeed. Russ said he already knew. He had looked his symptoms up on the computer. He was always much smarter than me on the computer.

The next two hardest things in our lives would be to tell our children and then simply deal with the disease. Which we did. I watched Russ progress from walking alone to falling, then a walker, a wheelchair, a motorized chair, and then to being bed bound. Next, he was unable to speak, he had a feeding tube, a tracheotomy, a Foley catheter, and had to be suctioned every few minutes, while on a ventilator.

From day one, I cannot ever once remember him complain. I was his primary care taker throughout his illness, except for a young woman from a service that the VA reimbursed a couple days a week. Which gave me the opportunity to grocery shop or see a doctor or whatever, those couple hours she was there. We had many visitors, the kids were always there, friends and pastor visited frequently. Many told me what an inspiration he was to them. One dear friend told me it was because of Russ he went back to the Lord and church. No sweeter thing could have been said to me at that moment.

Russ died a few days before Christmas with all his loved ones surrounding him, and I hope you will believe me when I tell you he died with a smile on his face. He is buried at the National Veterans Cemetery in Canton, Georgia.

Now I can fit the pieces in the puzzle. I can understand why on some of those nights on our vacation he looked so tired, so worn and sometimes very old. It was not my imagination at all.

And this is why I believe when Russ said, "No, I think I will wait until we get back and then I will go," to see the doctor, those words were from God. Because if he had gone to the doctor before we left and got that diagnosis, we would have never taken our trip. We would have never experienced God's beauty, His perfect creation.

I think if we had gone on our trip after that diagnosis, there would have been a cloud over us the whole time. We surely would not have experienced it quite the same.

It meant the world to us to have seen such beautiful portraits by His Hands as we fought ALS. And we both believed God was right there with us through this fight, too.

The stone on his grave reads *He held out His Hand and I took It*

CHAPTER 19

The List

Clothes

- Pants, shirts, blouses, skirts, dresses, work-out clothes, formal wear:

These are the fun things to pick out!

Travel tip: Some people have found that rolling your clothes, rather than folding them saves wrinkling—also if you put tissue paper in-between each article, it will save from wrinkling as well.

- Suits—male and female—They do have one or two formal nights on the cruise. Women wear anything from church clothes to long gowns and men wear anything from a regular suit to a tuxedo. (If it's not a wedding, no tux for my hubby, but he looked so gorgeous in his suit)
- Ties and belts
- Shoes, dress shoes, sandals, hiking boots, tennis
- Bathing suit!
- Underwear—in winter be sure to include long johns (or thermal underwear, which ever you prefer to call them). We were really glad to have them, especially when we went on the glacier! Brrr.
- Bras and special bras—you know—the ones you wear under those special dresses, sweaters, turtle necks, and strapless gowns.

- Slips—Sometimes a formal length for your gowns. (Can you buy them anymore?)
- Camisole—I bet some of you younger gals don't even know what that is. Well, it's an undergarment resembling the top part of a full slip and you wear it under thin clothing, they're pretty. Sometimes they are trimmed with lace or ribbon. We wore them all the time in the '50s and '60s. Maybe today they are referred to as camies or maybe a shell.
- Nighties/PJs—Take warm ones in winter unless you have an "Armstrong heater" (my man) like I do. Ha ha ha.
- Bathrobe—Some motels where we were and on the ship offered a bathrobe already hanging in the closet for you to use. Free, but you don't take it, of course.
- Slippers—This is where I made the mistake of taking cuddly, bootie-type slippers. Not a good idea. I don't know about you, but I have a thing about stepping on those motel room floors. Every time I had to make a potty call in the middle of the night, I had to put the booties on. It would have been so much easier to be able to just step into some of the slide-on slippers. I confess, I did get some slide-ons in our travels.
- Stockings, knee-highs or special occasion stockings—If you wear them, take more than one pair in case of a run. I know, most don't wear them at all anymore because they have such nice tans.
- Socks and TEDs—Socks are self-explanatory, but TEDs are the elastic stockings to help prevent blood clots and varicosities (great support). I did use these on days we hiked, a secret I learned from working in the hospital. Even the nurses use them because they are standing on their feet all day.
- Regular gloves and winter gloves—"Back in the day," I'd sometimes take regular gloves to wear when I put stockings on, so my rough fingers didn't cause a run. As far as winter gloves go, simply stick them in your coat pocket, so you'll always know where they are.

- Neck scarves—for dress (they seem to be the thing lately) and for winter.
- Hats—my husband wears ball caps a lot and now that we are seniors and see a dermatologist regularly, we have a hat to protect us from the sun. It must cover your ears. A ball cap is not enough. Also, don't forget to put sun tan lotion on the back of your ears.

Cosmetics

- Lotions—facial and hand creams
- Face creams and cleansers
- Base
- Concealer
- Liquid and/or compact powder
- Eyebrow pencil
- Pencil sharpener—I forgot mine, because it wasn't on my original list. I have a little cheap one that sharpens both the thin and wide pencils (eye brow pencils, that is). Russ wound up sharpening mine with his knife.
- Eyeliners—All the colors you use (like black, gray, blue, etc.)
- Eye shadow—All the colors you use (green, brown, blue, etc.)
- Mascara and mascara remover—You might even want to take waterproof mascara
- Blush—All the shades you use (pink, red, peach, etc.)
- Lip liner—Your favorite shades
- Lipstick and gloss—again, your favorite colors

Hint: Have all sizes of plastic zip-lock bags available and put all liquids in them, also remember to tighten all lids. And don't forget airport requirements on sizes.

Other Needs

- Lip balm
- Talc—if you use it
- Razors—Yours and your husbands'—I did take mine in my suitcase that we checked in. Just be sure it's not in your *take on*! My husband had an electric one.
- Q-tips and cotton balls
- Brushes, combs, hair pick
- Deodorant
- Cologne and/or perfume
- Shampoo, conditioner, body wash, body sponge
- Gel, hair spray, mousse
- Shaving cream—if your honey uses it. My husband finally settled for the electric razor.
- Tooth brush, floss, toothpaste, mouth wash, etc.—Denture powder, cup if needed.
- Makeup mirror—I did carry a small flip sided one with magnifier on one side.
- Hair dryer—Most motels have them in the room for your use, but some of the lodges do not.
- Curling iron, hair straightener, etc.
- Shower cap—some motels have them for you if you even use one
- Nail polish, nail polish remover, file, cuticle cream—I take better care of my nails on vacation than any time—what fun.
- Jewelry—do not put that in the suitcase—keep it in your purse.
- Lint roller—needed that for my black pants.

Medicines

- Your everyday required medicine—Of course, being seniors, we have our daily medicines, not that seniors are the only people that take them.

- If you are traveling with children be sure to take Tylenol, Ibuprofen, cold med, etc.
- Medicines for headaches, Tums, Imodium, Ibuprofen, aspirin. You know what they say about heart attacks. Take an aspirin stat. And be sure to take all your special medications, for instance, if you are a diabetic, allergy medicines, asthma, etc.
- Eye drops/nose drops
- First aid kit—you can put your own together, which I had intended to do, but when we were in Wal-Mart, they had the neatest little first aid kit all put together for about $10.00. It is made by Johnson & Johnson and includes an instant burn cooling patch, Neosporin, a glow stick, band aids (several sizes), a survival wrap to prevent heat loss, tape, gloves, band aids for knuckles and finger tips, tweezers, eye pad, 2x2 all-purpose dressings, a tongue blade (I think that's in there to help immobilize a broken or sprained finger), several cleansing wipes, Motrin, Tylenol, Imodium (which I did use), an instant cold pack, itch relief, an emergency light, a little first aid guide booklet, plus, all that is in a nice little plastic container, small enough to slide under my seat, our designated place, so we could grab it quick without searching for it in an emergency.
- Doctors' orders—If you require lab work—as needed. Our doctors really worked with us on this. I am on blood thinners so I had to have lab work done every 2-3 weeks. And that was an adventure all by itself.

Miscellaneous

- Your address book—There are two books that travel everywhere I go. My address book and my Bible.
- Kleenex
- Plastic bags—for your dirty clothes. Some motels have those for you too. Some don't.

- Presents—if you are traveling to a special occasion such as a wedding, graduation, etc.
- Pictures, tapes, CDs—sometimes I like to update the family or friends we haven't seen in a long time.
- Cards—playing cards, gift cards, greeting cards. We actually did play cards on about three different occasions.
- Wipes and diapers—for those traveling with little ones. Actually, those are handy to have for everyone. The wipes that is!
- Feminine products
- Passports—we got ours through the post office
- Tickets—plane, ship, a ball game, etc.
- Sunglasses and reading glasses
- Camera, film, digital camera, camcorder, batteries, memory cards, etc.—definitely don't forget disposable cameras (always keep one in my purse for those "just in case" events), they are twice as expensive in gift shops.
- Cell phones and chargers.
- Books, magazines, puzzle books—There are those moments when your spouse might be asleep. And I did get a lot of reading done!
- Laptop—I don't own one, but I saw a lot of people with them. Some motels have computers available to the public. We had to enter our HGTV contest every night after all!
- Pens and notebook
- Pillows—for the car or use in motels. Most motels offer really nice fluffy pillows now and usually 3 apiece.
- Blankets—we always keep a couple nice-sized throws in the car. You never know when you'll need one, for instance, if you should get stranded. Of course, when the kids were small, we carried more.
- Maps, brochures, directions (well, did you know you won't find a gas station around that carries maps anymore?). Your GPS has replaced them! I could hardly believe it. But we had them and an atlas. AAA will really help you.

- Magnifying glass to read the map, this was one of my most favorite items. The one I bought had a light on it as well. It was an item I never thought of, but found by accident in Wal-Mart.
- Snacks—that's an easy one.
- Games, color books, crayons (be careful not to leave in a hot car, I learned that the hard way when our kids were small, what a mess!), reading material, and there are a variety of car games. You can buy an assortment in the stores now. Play letter games (like the alphabet on signs), list states from license plates, sing, play CDs, and just be creative. Most motels have swimming pools, even inside warm pools, small gyms and outside playgrounds. What fun.
- Most cruise lines accommodate passengers with disabilities. All Princess staterooms are wheelchair accessible. If you use a wheelchair, please be sure to call the cruise line in advance and notify them of your specific needs. Lifts may be limited; batteries to your chair must be a dry-cell type. Bring your own wheelchair as availability may be limited. Some ships have areas that are not wheelchair accessible. You will probably need someone to accompany you.

The Car

We took our car to our mechanic for a general (long trip) check-up. He checked the oil, the brakes (we knew we'd be traveling over some very steep mountains), water and tires. In his opinion, he felt the car would be safe. We have always had to carry power steering fluid with us, because there is a little leak and as long as we keep putting the fluid in everything is okay.

Now let me tell you about our old minivan. Like I said in the beginning, she has her own little problems. Over time, she has become like a person. We call her "Mona"! She truly comes by that name honestly, because every time the steering fluid gets low, she begins to make a moaning-groaning sound. Fill her up and she's a happy little camper. Mona is a good ole gal, but she is possessed…

in a sweet way. The reason I believe that, is because she does such strange things. Such as when I used to go to work (I used to work first shift at the hospital) and it was usually dark when I left the house. One morning, I was on my way to work and the overhead lights began to click off and on, sporadically. It did that for a long time and I began to chuckle—until I got to a corner where I had to stop at a long red light and cars were pulled up next to me. The lights were still blinking on-off-on-off. I was afraid to look at the person in the car next to me. He probably thought I was doing something stupid. Well, they continued to do that all the way into the parking deck. I parked and ran around the car opening and shutting all the doors and lifted the rear gate, thinking maybe that might make them stop. There wasn't anything I could do, I just figured by the time I got off work the battery would be dead, but it wasn't, to my surprise *and* happiness. She only did that one other time (in the daytime, thank goodness) and then she never did it again. A few months later, the locks on the doors started clicking up and down, up and down in an off-beat rhythm, almost as though she was trying to click me a happy little tune. They'd go and stop, go and stop. Now, that was kind of spooky after a while. She did that several times and still does that every once in a while. But now the locks don't lock automatically after I start the engine. Sometimes they do, other times you can be in that silly car for half an hour and all of a sudden—*click!* She still does that to this very day like a child seeking attention! Mona has her own personality, that's for sure.

Now back to our list. I'm sure though, if you have a baby, you will have to add much more, such as strollers, bottles, diapers, toys, baby food, and the list is endless. And I did see a lot of people with little ones along the way, tackling that job just fine.

Of course, if you head south, take a beach blanket, beach toys, maybe a big ball, a Frisbee, a kite and beach towels. If you take a camper, stock it, cook meals ahead, make reservations. Most RV parks looked filled, so you will probably have to consider reservations. And if you are taking your boat, make sure lights work after hitched and check the tires on the trailer.

We figured we'd be gone a while—at first, maybe a month, then it turned into two months, and then, however long we wanted. Being gone that long (as if the list wasn't long enough already), we discovered there are still a few things we'd better add to it.

Things to Add for a Longer Trip

- A cooler—we kept water, slim fast drink and diet coke. If you break down, you'll be prepared with water and blankets.
- Flashlight—actually, we always keep a flashlight in the car and make sure your spare is in good shape, too.
- Fishing gear—Russ carried a little portable rod the boys gave him. Also lots of lures/spinners.
- Plan to hunt? You know what you need. Bear spray?
- Binoculars
- Bug spray—after that woman told me about the huge mosquitoes, I figured we'd better take some. Even though we were traveling early in the year, we did have one occasion to use it.
- Rain gear
- Hiking boots—I never wore hiking boots before, but it was fun and very interesting, and I felt cool strutting around in them (like I knew what I was doing).
- Toilet paper—Thank goodness we had that!
- Rainex—our son told us about that. We put it on the windshields before we left. Glad we did too, it really works. Thanks, Trent!
- Detergent—most motels have little laundromats, for which you will need many quarters.
- GPS—Now, this is going into foreign territory for us. We are just learning how to use our cell phones! Yup, I think we are the last people in the world to get cell phones and my daughter still wonders why I don't answer right away. Well, heck, I don't know where I leave it half the time, and what's this about listening to a message she left? But hon-

estly, I really didn't even know what a GPS was until one day at lunch, I was in the break room talking about our trip (what else?), when one of the techs mentioned it to me. She had hers in her purse and got it out of her locker and showed it to me. She explained how helpful it had been to her and I just thought that was amazing. Sounded like it came out of a James Bond movie to me. I couldn't wait to get home and tell Russ about it, and he got right on the computer and started searching. It really was neat shopping for one; we did use it quite a bit. It was extremely accurate and it felt like there was yet another person in the car, we couldn't help but talk back to her. We were warned never to leave it in the car. Great advice.

- Suitcases—since we had to have two suitcases each, for our trip to Alaska, we needed to buy two more. That was another excursion, because Russ is stuck in the old fashion mode of the hard shell type suitcase, which is almost impossible to find. None of the department stores carry them anymore, I know, because we went to every one we could think of. Then we found a luggage store in our mall, which somehow we walked right passed when we were there. We found what we wanted and they ordered two for us. Boy, the price on those has sure gone up since we got our older ones.
- Cords—we bought a cord to charge our cell phones in the car if we had to.
- Stamps—regular and post card stamps. I knew I would be sending a lot of post cards. My Bible study group said "keep us informed"; my exercise class said "let us know where you are," and my friends from work said "keep in touch with us." And I did. Not to mention all the kids, grandchildren, family and other friends.
- Careful with the credit cards.
- Music—I was so proud of myself to think of this one! Mona is old so I still have a tape deck. Took lots of, Jeff

Foxworthy, Oldie Goldies, and Disney's Jungle Book and Lion King.

- It was so much fun running around and shopping for all these things, probably because I had such a good time spending money.
- Big things like backpacks.
- Compass and scopes, camp stoves, matches, or a lighter.
- Maybe golf clubs

The House

The last time we went to visit Russ's sister in Florida, our house was broken into. That was really a frightening experience. It was weird too, because we walked in the house and after putting the luggage down, I went in the kitchen and the back door was wide open. We had locked it (French doors), but someone had kicked it in. I called 911 and Russ ran for the gun. So we will never leave the house unprotected again. Here is one more last thing you need to consider before leaving.

- Outside sensor lights—I've always wanted them; my son came and helped Russ put them up. Shame on us for not having them before now. Thanks again, Trent.
- Timer lights for inside the house.
- Security cameras—now this is quite an ordeal—comparing prices and the installing. Trent to the rescue. It would have cost a whole lot of money to have the wires strung through the walls professionally, but the cameras are up and wires are strung all over my house. I could just picture coming home and finding a thief hung up in all the wires, only too ready to surrender. Can't you just see it?
- Window locks and/or alarms
- Dead bolts, chain locks
- Ask someone to check your house regularly, water plants, mow the lawn, and pick up your newspaper. Gathering newspapers in your yard is a sure sign no one is home.

- Arrange for your pets' care if you have an animal. If you plan to take your pet on the cruise, call the cruise lines in advance. Regulations vary.
- Stop the mail or have someone pick it up for you. This was an interesting turn of events. When we went to the post office, the post master told us the mail could only be held for a month. Then he asked us if we were going to be out of the states, and Russ said we were going to do an Alaskan tour up into Vancouver, Canada, but we'd only be there a few minutes. But the post master said, "Oh, since you are going out of the country, we can hold your mail indefinitely." He stamped our request and we were done. Just like that!
- Bills—Russ took care of most everything on line and there were banks we could deal with across the nation.
- Travelers' checks, cash—however you decide to do it, divide them between you, so if your purse or wallet is stolen, you may lose, but not all. And traveler's checks are safe, because the numbers on them are recorded. But not all places accept them; most do, but not all.
- All in all we had a ball shopping for everything, I believe it was as much fun preparing, shopping, and anticipating it all, as it was when the day finally arrived to pack the car and move on up the road. *Home at last.*

About the Author

Ginnie is a widow for 7 years, a mother, grandmother, and great-grand-mother. She raised five children, raised two grand-children and now has custody of a great-grandchild who is three years old. She was a licensed practical nurse for ten years and retired in 2008 as a unit secretary. After her retirement, she and her late husband, Russ, took their last vacation together. She felt inspired to write about that experience in order to share the beauty of God's world and His great love. She resides in Georgia with her great-grandson, Layson, and is presently working on another book.